ARTHUR WALLIS: RADICAL CHRISTIAN

'A fitting tribute to this great man of God would be that those of us who remain catch something of his spirit and pledge ourselves to see the outpouring of the Holy Spirit, not only in Britain but worldwide.'

Peter and Linda Lyne

'He caught a glimpse of the heart of God in revival, and it spoilt him for all the earth.'

Alan Scotland

'I cannot ever think of my beloved friend without thinking of revival and intercession.'

Joy Dawson

'His example will encourage us to pray that others of like calibre will be raised up to follow in the steps that he has taken.'

Roger Forster

'Arthur Wallis truly modelled for us what it means to find out what God is doing in your generation and wholeheartedly give yourself to it.'

Larry Tomczak

'Words are inadequate to say how much I owe to his godly influence on my life.'

Barney Coombs

'"Even now," he said on that July afternoon two months before passing, "I'm not thinking about retiring or dying. I'm still looking for revival."'

Joe Tosini

'Arthur gave me a deep sense of the understanding of teamwork, and taught me to approve and uphold other leaders whom God has chosen.'

Ian Andrews

'Arthur enriched my life . . . (he was) a judicious leader and a loyal and fair friend.'

Ern Baxter

'. . . a great encourager and a great visionary.'

Bob Dunnett

'He would take you back to what the word of God says and apply it with love, care and affection to your life.'

Don Double

'May younger generations emulate his spiritual passion and personal integrity.'

David Tomlinson

'Right up to the day he died we were eagerly anticipating the future, believing the best was yet to come. His death does not rob me of that expectation. Arthur's most fruitful years still lie ahead.'

Eileen Wallis

Arthur Wallis: Radical Christian

JONATHAN WALLIS

KINGSWAY PUBLICATIONS
EASTBOURNE

Biblical quotations are from the Revised Version; the
Revised Standard Version copyrighted 1946, 1952, © 1971,
1973 by the Division of Education and Ministry of the
National Council of the Churches of Christ in the USA; and
the New International Version © 1973, 1978, 1984 by the
International Bible Society.

Front cover photo by Carmen Moll
25 Oxford Street, Southampton
Back cover photo by Graham Newby

British Library Cataloguing in Publication Data

Wallis, Jonathan
   Arthur Wallis.
   1. Great Britain. Christianity. Wallis, Arthur
   I. Title
   259.092

   ISBN 0–86065–852–X

Printed in Great Britain for
KINGSWAY PUBLICATIONS LTD
1 St Anne's Road, Eastbourne, E Sussex BN21 3UN by
BPCC Hazell Books, Aylesbury, Bucks.
Typeset by J&L Composition Ltd, Filey, N Yorkshire

Contents

Introduction

Writing my father's biography has been an enjoyable and stimulating project for me. I have thought of many questions I wish I'd asked him, learned many things about him I did not know, and come to appreciate all that he did and stood for in a far deeper way than I ever did when he was alive. He will always have a very special place of love, honour and respect in my heart, and writing his biography has only served to reinforce this for me.

When asked which of his books he would most like to be remembered for, his immediate answer was *The Radical Christian*, hence the title of this biography. He was a man who could never compromise over what he believed to be God's will, a radical Christian utterly dedicated to seeing the purposes of God fulfilled in his generation. He had a vision for revival which God burned into his heart as a young man. Although experience and maturity widened and developed his understanding, his passion and commitment to that vision never weakened.

My main aim in writing his biography has been to paint a picture of the man behind the public ministry. What sort of a man was Arthur Wallis? He never fitted the description of genius or superstar, he had no exceptional gift or talent, but he was completely and utterly committed to God and to his purposes.

He was not a brilliant academic and never went to Bible college, but he was a diligent student of the word of God. Although a leading charismatic, he looked for character rather than charisma. He never shied away from criticism, and was always far more concerned to be approved by God rather than men. He was never afraid to confront his brothers, but always strove to maintain the unity of the Spirit.

He did not seem motivated by personal ambition and was always glad to promote the interests of others. Put a tennis racquet in his hand, however, and he displayed the competitive determination (although not the ability) of Bjorn Borg! In common with the great saints of Hebrews chapter 11, his vision was for far greater things than he ever saw in his lifetime. He possessed a hope that constantly motivated him to overcome obstacles and set-backs and to press on towards the high calling of God. One of his favourite expressions was 'The best is yet to come'.

He would have wanted this book to point on rather than look back, to convey a vision rather than glorify a man, and to inspire others to pursue that vision for themselves. I trust that it will have this effect on all who read it, and that many hundreds of God's people will take up the mantle and rise to the challenge of the days in which we live.

In writing my father's life-story I have deliberately concentrated on his background and early years and have picked out the incidents and experiences which I felt were of most interest and significance. I have not avoided dealing with mistakes he made. The man who never made a mistake never made anything, and he would always face up to such things honestly and openly before God. I trust that I have adopted this same spirit.

Anyone who is radical in his pursuit of God will be no stranger to controversy, and he was no exception. He realised very early in his ministry that, when it comes to revival and the moving of God's Spirit, criticism and suspicion 'go with the territory'. In his first book, *In the*

Day of Thy Power, he wrote, 'If we find a revival that is not spoken against, we had better look again to ensure that it is a revival.'

I have endeavoured to deal with the periods of controversy in his life as openly and as fairly as possible. I have not attempted to give a dispassionate birds-eye view of each situation, but rather to show things from his perspective, faults and all. I have excluded some issues, particularly those of a personal nature, which may have been relevant at the time, but which did not directly involve my father. When reading chapters like 'The Pitcher Is Broken' and 'Division' it should be borne in mind, therefore, that my account is not intended to represent a complete and comprehensive coverage of all the issues and personalities involved.

My aim has been to let the facts of his life speak for themselves, to paint a picture of what he did and said and thought. I have tried to avoid including too much 'journalistic comment' and to write the book from a detached perspective. I refer therefore to my father as Arthur and myself as Jonathan. This may appear a little odd at times, but it did seem to be the most readable approach. I will have to rely on the reader to forget conveniently that 'Jonathan' is also the author!

I have made extensive use of quotes from my father's sermons and writings, and where I have included Scripture quotations I have used the version of the Bible that he used at the time (Revised Version in the early days, then Revised Standard version, and latterly the New International Version).

I have received much encouragement from many of his friends and colleagues, and could not have written this book without their help. I would like to thank everyone who has given me their time: Peter Wallis, Leith Samuel, Oscar Penhearow, Jack Hardwidge, David Lillie, Bill Patton, Graham Perrins, Campbell McAlpine, Blyth Harper, Bryn Jones, Mike Stevens, Peter Lyne, Hugh Thompson, David Mansell, John Noble, Barney Coombes, Gerald Coates, Tony Morton and Joe Tosini. Of course the one person who has given more time and help than anybody has been my mother and I am especially grateful to her. My thanks also to Fiona Hulbert who has patiently examined the script and made valiant attempts to eliminate as much 'evangelical jargon' as possible! Last, but certainly not least, I would like to thank Sylvia and Fiona who have had to manage for long periods without a husband and father as I have closeted myself in the study with my word-processor.

1

I'll See You in the Morning

'I'm very sorry Arthur, I'm very sorry Peter. I'm afraid I have some very bad news for you.'

Arthur stared at her in shocked amazement. A strange feeling of numbness and disbelief swept over him. A confusion of thoughts raced across his mind like leaves blown by a storm, and yet somehow he remained strangely detached, unable to react.

It was almost as if he were looking down into that living-room in Bristol from some high vantage point. He saw himself standing there, frozen, his brother beside him with an arm on his shoulder. He saw the lady standing there, conscious she was not their mother, yet reaching out to them with a mother's compassion.

There was an unreality in those moments, as if time had suddenly stood still, and yet he knew deep down that it was only too real. The sickening truth of it seemed to fill his stomach, and a cold sweat broke out on his forehead. In just a few seconds the dreams of months and years were shattered; his youthful ideas faded into insignificance; his ambitions suddenly felt hollow and meaningless.

There were tears in her eyes, her voice was full of love, her words were gently spoken, and yet for him those words carried the devastating power of a hurricane. They resounded in his mind again as he struggled with his thoughts and emotions.

11

'I'm very sorry Arthur, I'm very sorry Peter. I'm afraid I have some very bad news for you. Your dear father went to be with the Lord during the night.'

☆   ☆   ☆

It was 22nd July 1940. Arthur, who was seventeen years old, had just left school. A day or two previously his father, Captain Reginald Wallis, had undergone an operation. The surgeon, Professor Rendle Short, was also a good friend of the family. It was at his Bristol home that Arthur and his elder brother Peter were staying, to be close at hand while their father was in hospital.

The brothers were at that time living with their parents at Claverham in Somerset. Their mother was also staying in Bristol, but with other friends, and so she was not with them when they were told of their father's death.

Captain Wallis had been severely wounded in France during the First World War while serving as an officer with the London Regiment. After his convalescence he remained in the army for several years before resigning his commission in 1921 to take up a full-time post as General Secretary to the Dublin Young Men's Christian Association (YMCA) where he became affectionately known as 'The Captain'.

Arthur and Peter were born in Dublin and spent their early childhood there, but in 1933 the Captain resigned from the YMCA and started working as an itinerant evangelist, and the family moved to England. In 1939 the Captain was taken seriously ill while conducting a successful series of campaigns in Australia and New Zealand. He was forced to cut short his trip and return home.

His illness was diagnosed as a duodenal ulcer, and in early 1940 he underwent surgery. It was not successful and within a few months the problem recurred.

Professor Short was consulted and decided that further surgery was inevitable. Despite his skill as a surgeon, Captain Wallis died a day or two after the operation.

☆   ☆   ☆

Alone in his room, Arthur collapsed onto his knees, buried his head into the bedcovers, and sobbed uncontrollably. Waves of grief and despair welled up inside him, and all he could say through his tears was, 'God, why did you do it?'

The bottom had dropped out of his world, or so it seemed. His mind could not take it in. Why should God take his father in his prime, aged only forty-nine? Why would God cut short a life which he was using so powerfully in his service? Why would God deprive him of the father he loved so dearly at a time when he needed him so badly?

Why? Why? Why? In his bewilderment his questions seemed to spill out to God in a jumbled torrent.

He took from his Bible a letter which his father had written to him eight months earlier, on Arthur's seventeenth birthday. He had been at boarding school, and his father in Scotland. It was a simple note, hastily scribbled in the back of a car, and yet every word seemed so precious to him as he read it again:

15/11/1939 En Route, Scotland

My Own Dear Boy,
    You are 17 tomorrow—hardly believable! Many happy returns and may HIS blessing which maketh rich be ever your portion. I am on the road so cannot send you a present with this. I will give a combined Birthday and Christmas gift of your own choice later on. Am on my way to see Dr McAlpine in the hope that he can get me well. May be up here a month or so.
    Trust you are enjoying the term at school and doing well. Very pleased with your half-term report! Excuse haste and scrawl. Writing this in car.

God bless you, my son
Your own

Dad
PS Will send you a little tuck from Scotland!

As he read these words, he thought about his dad, a large and handsome man, over six feet tall, fair and well built. He had always been a larger than life character to Arthur. He loved everything about him—his wonderful sense of humour, his never-ending supply of funny stories, his whole-hearted devotion to God.

He was a man who threw himself into everything he did with complete and utter commitment. He had given his life to serving God with single-minded dedication and there was something manly and direct about his approach. Insincerity and humbug would wither before his vigorous attack. The word 'compromise' was not found in his vocabulary, and he had no time for what he saw as half-hearted or wishy-washy Christianity. His countenance seemed to radiate a deep sense of joy and peace. He was always such fun to be with, so full of the joy of living.

Arthur's thoughts went back to the night before, when he had last seen him in his hospital bed, following the operation. Even in his pain and weakness the joy of the Lord had shone from his face. He had been full of hope and encouragement for Arthur, Peter and their mother.

He remembered his father's parting words to him that night, 'I'll see you in the morning.' The thought that he would not see his dear dad again in this life was too much to bear, and the tears rolled down his cheeks.

Only the deep sound of his sobs broke the silence of the room as he poured out his heart and his emotions before God. It was a silence of God's presence, a silence in which he knew sorrow but not despair. In the stillness of those moments, he began to experience a very real sense of peace. God's love seemed to wrap itself around him like a blanket. There was a deep ache in his heart as he faced up to the loss of his earthly father, but an even deeper security in the love of his heavenly Father.

He thought again of his dad's last words to him, 'I'll see you in the morning.' A ray of hope arose in his heart. He would not see him again in this life, but he would see him again, 'in the morning'!

Still the question remained in his mind, 'Why, Lord?' He remembered how he had prayed at the time of his dad's first operation a few months previously. The surgeon had not held out a great deal of hope and Arthur had expressed his feelings to God in no uncertain terms. 'You must heal him, Lord,' he had insisted, with all the fervour of an uncompromising teenager. He had then proceeded to give the Lord a number of very good reasons why healing was imperative.

Much to his relief, his father did recover. He had thanked God and felt encouraged to believe that his dad was going to be restored to full health. At the same time he realised that his attitude had been very demanding, and apologised to God for the way in which he had prayed.

When a few months later the illness recurred, and a second operation became necessary, his prayer had been very different. Again he earnestly begged the Lord to heal his beloved dad, but there was a new sense of faith and trust in his praying. He was able to commit his loved one into God's hands with a peace that the responsibility for the outcome was not his but God's.

With the operation being conducted this time by Professor Short, a fine Christian as well as a very skilled surgeon, Arthur was confident that God would bring his dad through to full health. It seemed strange to him now that God had appeared to answer his prayer when his attitude had been wrong, and not when his attitude had been right.

It was a mystery. He could not understand it, yet in his spirit he knew that God had answered his prayer. It was not the answer he expected. It was certainly not the answer he wanted. But he knew God had heard.

By praying, 'Not my will but yours be done,' he had committed his father to the Lord, handing over all responsibility for the outcome. The Lord had chosen to take him up on that commitment.

In his infinite wisdom and love, God had a different plan from any that Arthur would have chosen for himself. He couldn't fully take it in, but as he knelt there before God, a broken weeping teenager, something of this plan and purpose for his life was beginning to unfold.

It was as though his father's mantle had fallen onto his shoulders. He knew in those moments that he was to give his life in service to God as his father had done. It was as if God simply said to him, 'Arthur, I want you.'

'But I could never take my father's place, Lord,' he whispered. 'I could never do the things he's done. I haven't got his gift or ability. I'm far too shy and self-conscious to be a preacher.'

God did not seem too interested in his excuses. Again he said, 'Arthur, I want you.'

In those moments of darkness, grief and brokenness, a flame was being kindled in Arthur's heart; a new commitment and determination was rising within him. He knew that God meant business with Arthur Wallis, a seventeen-year-old boy fresh from school, untrained, shy, self-conscious and not especially gifted.

'God, if you can do anything with my life,' he resolved, 'then I'm at your disposal.'

2

A Valuable Inheritance

The death of a loved one is not just a time of great sorrow and mourning. It is also a time of deep appreciation when you realise, probably as never before, just how much that person meant to you during his or her life.

It was like this for Arthur. How would he ever fill the gap in his life left by the loss of his father? He often thought of things he would like to have said to him, questions he wished he'd asked, deep thoughts he wished he'd shared but never had. He suddenly felt so weak and vulnerable without his father's strength and wisdom to draw upon.

The weeks and months that followed were a time of reflection, when memories which had seemed incidental would fill his mind. Childhood experiences began to assume a new importance to him. He would remember things they had done as a family, places where they had lived, visits to friends, times of great joy they'd spent together, feelings of loneliness when they'd been apart.

He knew he could not change the past. He could no longer say the things left unsaid or do the things he now wished he'd done. He couldn't go back and relive past joys, and yet he found real comfort in their memory. It was all part of a healing process in his emotions. God was taking him back over his life, helping him to realise that his heavenly Father had been with him at every point.

17

How good it was to be part of a close, loving family. His father, a warm-hearted and generous man, always showed him and his brother Peter real love and affection. The Captain did not spare the rod when it came to discipline, but always remained a sensitive and caring dad. His overriding desire was to see Peter and Arthur grow up to be fully committed to God themselves. He also brought a great sense of fun into the family and taught them something of the joy and appreciation of life.

Arthur's mother, Mary, was an affectionate and vivacious lady, the daughter of a French Jerseyman. At times she could be over-protective and possessive, but she was immensely fond and proud of her two sons. Always very smart and particular in her dress, she had been brought up very properly and sent to a Swiss finishing school. She was an excellent cook and a lively hostess, but would also be very sensitive to anything which might be considered by others as out of place or improper.

Arthur could remember occasions when his father's robust sense of humour had been a bit much for her. The Captain could call on a great fund of jokes and funny stories, and didn't need much of an excuse to start telling one. Mary, on the other hand, would often be afraid that his choice of story might cause offence, particularly if there were ladies present.

'Oh Reg, no, no, not that one!' she would protest. 'No, not here, not here!'

This provocation would provide him with just the encouragement he needed, having started, to finish!

It seemed to Arthur that his mother was always on the go. She possessed great resources of energy, and a tenacity that would see something she had started through to the bitter end. At other times she could be irrationally nervous about the silliest of things.

He could never understand the inexplicable fear she had shown when his father took proud possession of their first car, a baby Austin 7. In her era, it was rare for a woman to drive, and she did not understand the techniques of controlling a car. When it came to a steep hill she was very afraid that if they stopped, the car would start rolling back down the hill out of control. On one occasion she even insisted on getting out and walking up the hill while Reginald and the boys went up in the car! The male members of the family thought this was a great joke, but she was not amused!

Peter was just thirteen months older than Arthur and they were the greatest of friends. Like most brothers they had their moments of squabbling and argument, but throughout their childhood they always did things together and were often mistaken for twins. Arthur could see much of his father's outgoing and warm-hearted personality in his brother, whereas he was far more shy and reserved.

He could remember times when, as a small child, his deep-seated self-consciousness had led him to mis-behave. Often this was simply a cover up for his own insecurities. One such episode resulted from his acute sense of what was—and more importantly what was not—suitable clothing for a boy. To have a mother who is a keen needlewoman is not an obvious advantage to a small boy. When Mary proudly produced a pair of neatly tailored blue velvet shorts for Arthur to wear, it proved a positive liability! No self-respecting six-year-old would be seen dead in a pair of shorts like that!

He tried every form of protest he could muster, but to no avail. Those shorts had taken hours to produce, and his mother was in no mood to see her efforts wasted. Besides, she was convinced they suited him admirably, and could not understand what all the fuss was about!

Having failed to get his way by straightforward protest, it was clear to young Arthur that he would have to resort to somewhat more underhand methods. While playing in the garden one day, the solution to his problem became apparent. He spotted a rather rusty nail sticking out of a fence post at the edge of the garden.

'That post would be an interesting place to sit,' he thought to himself.

He climbed up onto the post, being very careful to ensure that the nail embedded itself into the shorts but not into him. Having got himself precisely positioned, it just remained to jump quickly down. The plan worked perfectly! The nail ripped a nice big hole in the back of his shorts rendering them beyond repair, but leaving him otherwise unharmed. The only remaining problem was coping with his mother's fury.

Of course she immediately saw through this little 'accident' and marched him in to see his father. He knew he was in for a thoroughly painful session! The Captain's instrument of discipline was his army officer's baton, a solid length of wood covered in leather. Having endured a thorough beating, Arthur felt genuinely repentant. But in the cool light of day this temporary affliction seemed a small price to pay for the relief of never having to wear those blue velvet shorts again!

For all of Arthur's early years the family lived in Dublin where his father was Secretary of the YMCA. They had a number of close friends who seemed to be very much part of their family, and Arthur had the privilege of looking back on a very happy childhood.

His first memories were of Harold's Cross, a suburb on the southern edge of the city, where the family were living in rented accommodation. A few doors away from their house lived Gerald and Annie Brady, an Irish couple who were unable to have children of their own. They became a real uncle and aunt to the brothers, who used to run in and out of their house as if it was their own.

It was here that Arthur could remember his first school, a small kindergarten run by a couple of ladies. About twenty children attended, and they all sat at a big round table to learn reading and writing. After a year there he moved on to a somewhat larger Protestant school at Grosvenor Place in Dublin.

The Captain had by this time made up his mind that

his sons would get a better education in England. He made arrangements for Peter and Arthur to start at Winterdyne, a Christian preparatory school for boys situated in Southport, Lancashire. Most of the hundred or so pupils were day-boys, but there was a small contingent of about twenty boarders, a number of whom came from Ireland.

'You're big boys, now,' the Captain said, as he gave his sons a really good pep-talk to prepare them for this big step.

At the ages of eight and seven respectively, Peter and Arthur were young to be separated from their parents for a term at a time, but their father was convinced that the discipline of boarding school life would do them good. He sought to instil in them as much confidence as he could before they left to face the rigours of school on their own.

Mary, on the other hand, was not at all happy about parting with her little darlings! After all, they were still so very young, and it took the Captain's full powers of persuasion to convince her that it really was in their best interests. Somewhat unwillingly she came to terms with the idea, but she was not looking forward to being separated from them for so long.

How would they cope without her? How would she cope without them? What if they hurt themselves? What if they became really homesick? What if they were bullied by older boys? The questions all flooded through her mind as the time of the boys' departure approached.

Arthur could still picture quite vividly the autumn day in 1929 when his parents had sent him and Peter off to boarding school for the first time. They were to catch the mailboat from Kingston (subsequently renamed Dun Loaghaire) to Holyhead. From there they would take the train to Liverpool and then on to Southport. The brothers were to travel with a teacher and several other boys from the school.

Kingston was about ten miles drive from their home, on the southern side of Dublin Bay. Arthur was filled

with a mixture of trepidation and excitement as they
drove up to the impressive harbour built of grey granite.
There were three steamboats in regular service, the
Munster, the Linster and the Connaught. They were
fast vessels, only carrying mail and passengers, and
Arthur was looking forward to the crossing which lasted
under three hours.

They met the rest of the party on the quayside, and
the time came to say goodbye. It was an emotional
moment for Mary and she took Peter into her arms, and
kissed and hugged him. When it came to Arthur,
however, it was a different story. He was a big boy now,
and big boys weren't seen kissing and hugging their
mothers in such a public place. It was just not the thing
to do in front of boys he would have to live with for the
next three months! Much to his mother's dismay and his
father's amusement, a discreet peck on the cheek was all
he would allow her.

His school terms as a boarder at Winterdyne were not
the happiest times of Arthur's childhood. He missed his
parents dreadfully, but he would suppress his emotions
and put on a brave face. Somehow when he and Peter
were with their father during their vacations, the problem never seemed so great. The Captain's joy and
enthusiasm soon banished any unhappiness they were
feeling about their school life.

'Stick it out lads,' he would say. 'It's all good for your
character.'

Their mother, of course, was far more sympathetic to
their feelings. During the school holidays she tried to
make up for their separation in every way she could.
How Arthur enjoyed her good home cooking compared
to the meals he received at school!

The food at Winterdyne was nothing to write home
about, except perhaps as the justification for an emotional appeal for some more 'tuck'! To make matters
worse the boys were not allowed to talk at meal times, so
there was little to take their minds off the uninspiring
fare. They were never offered second helpings except

on pancake day, when they could go and ask for more as often as they liked until the pancake mixture ran out.

The school had some very strict and somewhat petty rules, and Arthur would quite often get the cane. This was normally for some silly prank arising more from a sense of mischief than malice. There were forfeits for forgetfulness as well as for breaking rules, and he always seemed to be forgetting something. He would often lose his cap, or his pen, or some essential item of school equipment. Every Friday all the boys who had lost some of their belongings were lined up in front of the school to claim what was theirs. He seemed to feature in this lost property parade most weeks.

As he reflected on some of his childhood insecurities, he realised that he had never found it easy to express outwardly his emotions and true inner feelings. He was invariably too embarrassed to say what he was really thinking and would bottle up his fears and worries. When it came to expressing his love, he was equally reticent. Now that he no longer had the opportunity, he wished he'd been able to tell his dad more openly how much he really loved and appreciated him.

Like many youngsters brought up in a Christian home, Arthur committed his life to God at quite a young age. His father was a gifted preacher and one of his regular activities in Dublin was a Sunday evening after-church meeting known as 'the 8.30'. This weekly event took place in the Metropolitan Hall, a large venue in the centre of the city seating nearly two thousand. The hall was regularly filled to capacity and many hundreds of all ages committed their lives to Christ in response to the Captain's preaching. It was here that both Arthur and Peter, as young boys, stood up in response to a gospel appeal.

This outward act of commitment was an important stepping-stone in Arthur's spiritual development, but not a major milestone. He could not really tell whether it was at this or some earlier point when he actually became a Christian. From the earliest age he had been taught to pray and to bring his life to God, and over a period of years he responded to his parents' encouragement. Jesus was always part of his life and gradually became more real to him as he got older. This process neither started nor finished with his response at the Metropolitan Hall.

As Arthur looked back on his boyhood experiences, he could see that God had taken him through a variety of circumstances and events which shaped his character and deepened his spiritual life. In the midst of this process of development his father was always there fulfilling a central and vital role. Now he faced the reality that his dad was no longer available for him to lean on. This was not an easy thing to come to terms with. A solid foundation had been laid in his Christian life, but it was now down to him and God.

As Arthur thought about his father, many times of great joy and hilarity came to mind. Reginald Wallis loved to play practical jokes on the other members of his family. Quite often if they were out on a family walk he would suddenly vanish from sight only to spring out unexpectedly from behind some tree or bush.

This sense of fun did not take long to rub off onto Peter and Arthur and it probably accounted for a good few of the canings they received at Winterdyne School! Of course they used to take particular delight in playing practical jokes on their father at every opportunity. He would invariably respond with great surprise and mock alarm when they jumped out on him, even if he'd seen it coming.

After their period at Harold's Cross, the family moved out to the country village of Rathfarnham where they lived in the top flat of a large house called Ballyroan. This house was situated in extensive wooded grounds. It was reached by a mile-long drive from a road at the front, and had another long drive to the rear. Ballyroan provided a wonderful setting for two small boys, and Peter and Arthur spent many happy hours playing in the woods.

Arthur remembered with a smile one time when he and Peter did manage to fool their father. There was a little stream which ran through the woods at Ballyroan, and the brothers decided to build a bridge over it. They got a sturdy plank as a base, and built up earth and stones all around it. When they had finished, it looked as though it was made of earth alone and they called the Captain to come and survey their handiwork.

'I don't think this will survive under my weight,' he said, as he gingerly stood on the bridge.

When it didn't collapse he was greatly surprised and started jumping up and down on it in a vain attempt to fulfil his prophecy of destruction!

As one might expect, there were times when their boyish pranks went a little too far, even in their father's estimation. One day as Reginald was leaving Ballyroan slightly late for work, he started his car, only to find the wheels turning helplessly as the car remained stationary. Investigation of this phenomenon revealed that his sons had piled a load of spare gravel from the drive around each wheel. He was unamused, and they were summoned to shovel it away in double-quick time.

Another escapade which their father had viewed in a very dim light occurred when they were in their early teens. The family was staying in Edinburgh, where the Captain was taking some meetings. On looking through the telephone directory the boys were amused to discover that there were a lot of people in Edinburgh with the surname 'Smellie'.

When they thought no one would overhear, they got to the telephone and took it in turns to ring a selection of these people.

'Good morning,' they would say. 'Are you Smellie?'

'Yes,' would come the reply.

'Well, what are you going to do about it?' they would then say before slamming down the receiver.

They managed to play this trick on several unamused Smellies before their peals of laughter had given the game away.

When Arthur was eleven, the Captain resigned his position with the YMCA in Dublin and moved into full-time itinerant Christian ministry. This enabled them to move to England, where they lived initially in Southport, Lancashire. The brothers could now become day-boys for their last year or so at Winterdyne School. This gave Peter and Arthur the prospect of decent meals throughout the term as well as in the holidays!

Arthur finally left Winterdyne at the age of thirteen and became a boarder at Monkton Combe School, near Bath in Somerset. Peter, being a year older, was already there. Not long after this the family moved house from Lancashire down to Weymouth in Dorset. Although the boys remained as boarders, they were not too far away from their parents.

Monkton Combe was a Christian school with many denominations represented. A traditional English Public School, much of the day-to-day discipline was administered by those older boys who were appointed prefects. They wielded a great deal of power and could administer a beating to any boy caught misbehaving. Only serious matters would get referred to the masters.

The first-year boys became 'fags' which meant they were always at the beck and call of the prefects. On the shout of 'Fag!' any first-year within earshot would come running to see what errand the prefect required him to do. Although there was obvious potential for abuse, the prefects were chosen carefully and generally administered their discipline fairly. There was a really good feel about the school and Arthur looked back on his time there with great affection.

Sending the boys to Monkton was a lot more expensive than Winterdyne, and the Captain could not afford the fees for both of them. As the time approached for Arthur to go, the family prayed for God's provision. They felt sure it was the right school and that the financial need would be met. God wonderfully provided through some friends from Ireland who offered to pay Arthur's fees for the whole of the time he was there.

There was a very strong emphasis on sport at Monkton and Arthur, a natural competitor, threw himself into this side of school life with great enthusiasm. The main sports were rugby, hockey and cricket, and the school also had a very good rowing club and regularly participated in the Henley Regatta. Although he enjoyed most sports, Arthur was particularly good at cricket.

The school encouraged a number of different clubs covering a variety of activities and interests, and Arthur joined the drama club. Although basically shy and reserved, he somehow lost his self-consciousness when whole-heartedly throwing himself into a part. He enjoyed acting, even when as a smooth-faced youngster he was quite often required to play a female role.

Amid all this opportunity for exciting and enjoyable activity, there was one aspect of life that seemed less appealing to Arthur. His teachers actually expected him to study! He found it difficult to put his mind to academic work when there was so much else of interest to occupy his thoughts. He would so easily find his mind wandering from the subject in hand, and soon earned a reputation as a day-dreamer.

His parents were very concerned about the lack of application, and constantly tackled him about it.

'It's up to you, Arthur,' his mother would say. 'You've got a choice. You either work hard and make something of your life, or you become a dustman. We don't mind, it's your life, although why we decided to send you to such a good school I can't imagine. You've got just as much ability as Peter, so why can't you work hard like him? You need to pull yourself together.'

Although it was now several years later, Arthur could still hear his mother's stinging provocation ringing in his ears. Her words had achieved the desired effect. He did want to make something of his life. What he really wanted to be, he decided, was a doctor. He certainly did not want to disappoint his parents, so during his final years at Monkton he disciplined himself to get down to his studies. For a student of average ability his academic results in the end proved very satisfactory.

In the midst of his sport, his drama, his studies and all the other youthful interests which filled his life, God was kindling a deep desire in Arthur's heart. It was a desire to see God's Spirit working in unusual power.

One Easter, just a couple of years before Captain Wallis died, Arthur accompanied his father to Wales. They stayed in the small Welsh mining town of Loughor in Glamorganshire where the Captain had been invited to speak at the Moriah Chapel. They went into the little schoolroom next to the chapel, where the great outpouring of the Spirit in the Welsh Revival had begun back in 1904. Their host, George Bassett, was himself a convert of the revival and a founder member of the chapel. He was a quiet man who never had a lot to say until you got onto this subject.

His face seemed to light up as he recounted some of the events of those days. He told them how the presence of the Lord seemed so real that it was almost tangible, not just in the chapels, but throughout the whole district. Hard-bitten sinners were convicted of their sin in the streets and cried to God in repentance. The reality of the gospel was on everyone's lips, and many hundreds and thousands were converted.

A strange feeling of awe and wonder filled Arthur's heart as he listened. It seemed almost too wonderful to be true. But these amazing stories created deep questions in his heart. They were questions for which he could find no answer. If God had done it then, why did he not do it again? Why were we so satisfied with the results of normal evangelism? Why were God's people not more concerned to pray that the Holy Spirit would again be poured out in this way?

A longing and desire to see God move in revival had been born in Arthur's heart. Now as he reflected on his childhood years he sensed that God was preparing him for something exciting in the future. He didn't know what that future might involve, but he was prepared to commit his life to God's purposes, whatever the cost.

He did not feel that he possessed the natural gifting and ability he saw in his father, but he also knew that the success of his father's ministry was really nothing to do with natural talents. It was a result of a life surrendered and devoted to God's purposes. That was the spirit that he wanted to emulate.

Arthur had seen that spirit demonstrated in his father's everyday family life as well as in the pulpit. It was a heritage that was his to take hold of. He had received a clear call from God. It was now down to him. He felt weak and unqualified, but his father's example gave him the vision and courage he needed.

Although he may not have been fully aware of it, Arthur had been left a valuable inheritance. It was not an inheritance of worldly title or possessions. In fact it was nothing that would carry any weight in human terms at all. Captain Wallis was not a wealthy man, but what he did leave his sons was an example of faith, character and godly values. Arthur, for one, was determined to emulate him.

Just a couple of years previously, while on his way out to Australia, the Captain had sent back to his sons a poem he had found. He no doubt meant it to express his heart for them during his long absence. His subsequent untimely death gave its quaint wording an added poignancy.

My Bequest

To you, O Son of mine, I cannot give
A vast estate of wide and fertile lands:
But I can keep for you, the whilst I live,
Unstained hands.

I have no blazoned scutcheon that insures
Your path to eminence and worldly fame;
Longer than empty heraldry endures
A blameless name.

I have no treasure chest of gold refined
No hoarded wealth of clinking glittering pelf;
I give to you my hand, and heart, and mind—
All of myself.

I can exert no mighty influence
To make a place for you in men's affairs
But lift to God in secret audience
Unceasing prayers.

I cannot, though I would, be always near
To guard your steps with the parental rod;
I trust your soul to him who holds you dear,
Your father's God.

Merrill C Tenney

At the foot of this poem, the Captain had simply
added an 'Amen!' and signed it 'Dad'.

3

Into Battle

It was the summer of 1939 when, due to ill-health, Captain Wallis returned earlier than expected from a successful evangelistic campaign in Australia and New Zealand. Though still not fully well, he was enjoying a few weeks' holiday on the Isle of Man with his family.

Over the years they had spent a number of holidays at Port St Mary, a seaside town on the southern coast of the island. Some friends from Dublin led an annual beach mission at the resort under the auspices of the Children's Special Service Mission (CSSM). There were a variety of activities, games and competitions for children but the focal point of the mission was a daily service on the beach.

The Wallis family knew many of the people who holidayed there, and so Reginald and Mary were able to spend time relaxing together and enjoying the company of some of their dearest Christian friends. There was much to occupy Peter and Arthur. Their days would be spent swimming, exploring the rocks, and helping run the organised CSSM activities such as beach-cricket, football, tide-fights and sand-castle competitions.

Arthur, who was sixteen, had just left Monkton Combe School, and was still uncertain about what the future held for him. The family were now living in a country house at Claverham in Somerset. He had obtained a job with a nursery firm which specialised in

31

growing tomatoes and was based near Claverham. He was due to start work there when they returned from holiday.

He only envisaged this as a temporary job, and really did not know what he was going to do after that. His father felt it would be good for him to gain some experience of the world of commerce and industry, but seemed quite happy for him to base himself at home for a while.

One of the workers at the beach mission was Leith Samuel, a young travelling evangelist in his early twenties. Just a year previously, while nearing completion of his training as an Anglican minister, Leith had 'crossed swords' with the Bishop. It was made clear to him that as an ordained minister he would be expected to teach doctrines such as infant baptism which he did not feel were scriptural. He could not submit to this with a clear conscience, and decided to withdraw from ordination.

Leith had first met Captain Wallis a number of years previously at his parents' home in Wallasey on Merseyside, and had got to know the rest of the family over several summers at Port St Mary. Being a few years older than Peter and Arthur, he was a friend they looked up to and respected.

One evening, Captain Wallis, Leith and a number of other friends were strolling along the cliff-tops. They were enjoying the fresh sea air and taking in the magnificent view of the sun setting across the bay. As they talked together the Captain singled out Leith and put his arm on his shoulder.

'Leith,' he said, 'I want you to see that my boys get my message. They won't take it from their old dad, they know him too well. They'll take it from you.'

Leith felt that this was not true. Peter and Arthur both adored 'their old dad' and took their spiritual lead from him in every way. Yet, although his tone was gentle and relaxed, Leith sensed that the Captain was discharging an important burden. There was a seriousness that came through in his voice. Both men were aware that the storm-clouds of war were brewing, and the future was tinged with uncertainty. Little did Leith imagine that less than a year later Captain Wallis would be with the Lord.

It was only after his death that Leith fully realised the significance of the charge that the Captain had given him. Peter and Arthur no longer had their father to turn to for spiritual counsel and guidance. Still teenagers, they were about to get caught up in the war effort with all the pressures and dangers that that would bring. They clearly needed him to fulfil their father's expectations. It was a responsibility he would take very seriously.

☆ ☆ ☆

As the train steamed its way out of Bristol Temple Meads station, Arthur wondered what his new job would be like. The world of commerce and industry was completely foreign to him, and he was about to enter it with some trepidation.

He was on his way to take up a post in the clerical department at Rubery Owen, a Midlands engineering firm. Mr Owen, the owner of the company, was a keen Christian and a good friend of Arthur's father. When the Captain had expressed a desire for Arthur to gain some experience in commerce, he gladly offered him this opportunity.

In many ways Arthur was not looking forward to this new challenge. With his father having died less than two months before, he was still emotionally tender. The pressure of meeting new people and adapting to a different environment was something that he could have done without. But he'd already left his previous job at the nursery, and did not have any other obvious openings. He resigned himself to going through with it.

It was September 1940, the Battle of Britain was at its

height, and in two months he would be eighteen. It was already twelve months since war was declared and he had decided to enlist. For the next year or so he would gain some experience in business, and he would then join the army.

His thoughts turned to the prospect of going to war. The thorny subject of whether or not a Christian should fight had been hotly debated in evangelical circles over the past year or two. His father was very much involved in this debate and aroused a fair deal of criticism for an article in *The Reaper* entitled 'Christians and fighting'.

The Captain maintained that it was primarily a matter of individual conscience.

> Now, though I am tackling the subject, let me say right away that I am not assuming the responsibility of answering these questions for you! Who am I to make dogmatic pronouncement on a subject about which true Christians – loving the Lord with equal devotion – hold diametrically opposite views? ... In a subject such as this, we fall back on Paul's words: 'Let every man be fully persuaded in his own mind.' ...
>
> If you ask me my personal attitude to war, I tell you quite plainly that as a Christian and one who has personally witnessed its ghastly brutalities, I hate it and renounce it with all the passion of my soul ... War is fiendish, ruthless, heart-breaking, inhuman, blood-thirsty! Its effect on the moral life of any belligerent nation is utterly devastating. It is monstrously infernal, and I loathe it with the most utter abhorrence.

Every Christian would no doubt share such sentiments, but in the Captain's view this still left an important question unanswered.

> Does such a hatred of war involve complete exemption from, and repudiation of, one's responsibilities as a national citizen if war does break out? Because you and I love peace and renounce war, does it follow that we must give our consent to all the implications of pacifism as we know it today?

For Captain Wallis the answer was clearly 'no'. His article went on to demonstrate from the Bible why to him it was not inconsistent for a Christian to take up arms. Having clearly stated his point of view, he concluded his article with a call for Christians not to be judgemental in their attitude to one another.

> If you feel it right to utterly renounce all national responsibility in the day of the country's crisis, then it is not for me to judge or criticise. I must respect your convictions, even though they do not bind me . . . If my sense of loyalty to king and country impels me, as a Christian, to do my part in the defence of home and loved ones and sacred possessions, then you must not judge me as being inconsistent.
>
> In the days of the Great War, some of my own personal friends were 'conscientious objectors', and for no other reason than honest loyalty to God and their consciences. Whether they were right or wrong is not for me to say. God is their judge as he is yours and mine. Knowing them to be genuine Christians as I did, I realised that there was not the slightest scintilla of cowardice in their attitude, and I admired them. It would have been much easier to do the popular thing.

Arthur realised that it was a matter to be decided between him and God. As a teenager with such a difficult decision to make, it was very natural that his decision should be strongly influenced by his father's viewpoint. Having decided to fight, he felt the important thing was not the rights or wrongs of the case, but whether as a young soldier he could maintain his integrity before God.

To a teenager, there was a naive excitement about going to war. He could imagine himself performing heroic acts and being commended for his fearless bravery. Yet he knew in his heart of hearts that the reality of death and destruction was unlikely to contain the glamour and exhilaration of his dreams.

'Birmingham New Street, this is Birmingham New Street.. . .'

His thoughts were rudely interrupted by the station

announcer, and he hurriedly gathered his belongings and made his way off the train. He was to be lodging with a Christian family in Birmingham, but Mr Owen had kindly invited him to spend the first night or two at his home in Sutton Coldfield. The chauffeur was meeting him at the station.

As he made his way through the ticket barrier and onto the busy station concourse, he spotted the man who was to meet him. His peaked cap and uniform distinguished him from the crowd as he waited by the station exit.

'Arthur Wallis?' he asked as Arthur approached him expectantly.

'Yes,' replied Arthur, 'that's me.'

'Welcome to Birmingham, sir,' said the chauffeur, taking Arthur's case. 'I hope you had a good trip.'

Arthur's belongings were loaded into the boot, and he climbed into the back of the luxurious car feeling very important! It was a ten-mile drive from the centre of Birmingham out to the Owens' home at Sutton Coldfield.

As they glided up the drive, Arthur caught his first glimpse of 'Newhall'. It was a picture-book setting, one of the oldest moated residences in England standing in the midst of spacious well-tended grounds. The interior was equally impressive, full of antique furniture and fittings, and beautifully decorated. As one would expect, a number of domestic staff were employed to help run the household.

Arthur was warmly welcomed by Mr and Mrs Owen, who very quickly put him at his ease. As he made his way up to bed that night he couldn't help but smile. It was an auspicious beginning for a junior clerk in an engineering factory!

'Good morning, sir, time to get up . . . . Time to wake up, sir . . . . Here we are, sir, a cup of tea.. . .'

Arthur stirred sleepily. It was seven o'clock and the butler had come to wake him. He propped himself up against the back of the four-poster bed, and rested the cup of tea on the bed covers.

'Now you are really awake, sir, aren't you?' asked the butler.

'Yes thank you,' replied Arthur sleepily.

'That's nice,' he thought to himself as the butler left, and promptly dozed back off to sleep.

With a rush of consciousness, he suddenly became aware of something wet and hot on his hand. To his horror he realised what had happened. His tea-cup had slipped and deposited its contents not just onto his hand but all over the bedclothes! As he looked down at the wet stain on the fine embroidered bed-spread he felt that his auspicious beginning had suddenly taken an embarrassing turn for the worse.

The butler was very gracious about it.

'Oh dear, sir, you have done it, sir, haven't you!' he remarked with a grin on his face, as he entered the room in response to Arthur's ring.

He immediately took charge of the situation and the tea-stained bedclothes were removed and laundered without Mr or Mrs Owen ever knowing what had happened.

☆   ☆   ☆

Clearly Christmas 1940 was not going to be an easy time for Mary Wallis and her two sons. The Captain's jovial presence would be sorely missed by them all, and the first such occasion is always the most difficult. When invited to spend the festive season at the home of the Weston family in Lewisham, South London, they gladly accepted. It was not a time that they wanted to spend on their own.

Peter was particularly keen on this idea. Earlier in the year he had spent a number of months working on a farm on the Isle of Wight. The farmer was a leading figure in the local Brethren assembly in Newport. John Weston regularly visited this church, and was the guest speaker on the day of Peter's baptism. On his most recent visit, he was accompanied by his sixteen-year-old daughter, Meg. Peter had been very taken with her.

John and Daisy Weston had a full house that Christmas. Apart from Meg, her brother and sister, and the Wallis family, there was an assortment of other relatives who were either staying there or who would turn up for some of the festivities. Fortunately it was quite a big house.

For Mary it was a difficult time, and she found it hard to enjoy the celebrations. It would not have been easy for her wherever they had chosen to spend Christmas. For Peter and Arthur on the other hand, to be in a large house with a crowd of other people was just the tonic they needed.

The house was well suited to party games; 'Murder in the dark' and 'Sardines' were a tradition with the Weston family. Arthur particularly enjoyed being the detective in 'Murder in the dark'; Peter seemed to best enjoy getting squashed into the broom-cupboard with Meg in 'Sardines'!

Arthur was enjoying his employment with Rubery Owen and Company, and felt he was gaining some useful office experience. Relationships in the office were not always easy for him. Many of the 'Brummies' he met were very friendly, but some seemed to resent this well-spoken upstart who was a friend of the boss. Learning to cope with the problems and petty jealousies that arise in an office environment was proving to be a valuable education.

Unfortunately for Arthur, he managed to contract a dose of the flu over the Christmas period, and ended up spending much of the holiday in bed. Meg had not really taken too much notice of him up to that point; she was far more interested in his brother. To her, although Arthur was dark and good looking, he seemed rather quiet and nervous; he had a habit of continually sniffing and she observed that he blushed very easily.

When he became unwell and was confined to his quarters, she rather took pity on him. She regularly brought him up a hot drink or a little food, and would sit on the end of his bed to chat for a while. On one such occasion they talked about his plans for the future.

'And what are you hoping to do when you come out of the army, Arthur?' she asked.

'I'm going to work for the Lord full time, and live by faith,' he replied without hesitation. Meg was surprised and fascinated. To her this was an unusual ambition.

'But how will you live?' she asked. 'Where will you get your money from?'

'The Lord will provide all I need,' said Arthur confidently.

It was clear to Meg that his mind was made up. Beneath that quiet and nervous exterior was a depth of resolve and a strength of character that she had not noticed before.

☆   ☆   ☆

'Arthur, upon confession of your faith in Jesus Christ as your Lord and Saviour, I baptise you in the name of the Father, and of the Son, and of the Holy Spirit.'

The voice of the Reverend Alan Redpath, pastor of Duke Street Baptist Church, Richmond, echoed in Arthur's ears as he was plunged beneath the waters of the baptistry.

It was the spring of 1942. After finishing his employment at Rubery Owen towards the end of the previous year, he enlisted in the army and joined the Royal Tank Regiment. Now he was in the middle of his initial training at the Royal Military Academy at Sandhurst.

Arthur had for some time been aware of his need to be baptised. As soon as his six months' training was completed he was to be sent to North Africa for his first spell of active service. He did not want to go to war without being obedient to God over this matter.

He was already corresponding regularly with Leith Samuel, who was proving very faithful in fulfilling Captain Wallis' expectations of him. Baptism was one of the matters they'd discussed together, and Leith had arranged for Alan Redpath, whom he knew quite well, to lay on a special baptismal service for Arthur.

He did not feel a dramatic sense of God's presence as he stepped up out of the water, just the quiet satisfaction and confidence that comes from obeying the Lord. It seemed as if God was simply confirming and reinforcing the call on his life.

He knew that when God said to him, 'Arthur, I want you,' he really meant it. A deep peace filled his heart. Whatever dangers he might face over the months ahead, he was safe in the hands of his heavenly Father. God had a purpose for his life, and he was going to live through the days of war to see that purpose fulfilled.

Abide with me; fast falls the eventide;
The darkness deepens; Lord, with me abide;
When other helpers fail, and comforts flee,
Help of the helpless, O abide with me.

It was 22nd January 1944. The voices of several hundred men echoed across the open deck of the troopship as it headed across the Mediterranean Sea towards Italy. Arthur and a number of other Christians had organised a time of hymn-singing and testimony for those on board. The response had been remarkable.

Arthur was acting as master of ceremonies, and introduced in turn each of the Christians who had agreed to take part. They comprised a variety of believers drawn from all ranks, and each man spoke clearly and confidently about his faith. It was thrilling to see scores of hardened soldiers listening spellbound as the joy and reality of a true faith in Jesus Christ were clearly proclaimed.

For many of these men it was their first chance to hear and respond to the good news of the gospel. They were en route to land behind enemy lines as part of a bold and somewhat risky strategy by the Allies. Arthur suspected, as he looked out on that sea of faces, that for many it would be not only their first opportunity but their last.

General Montgomery's 8th Army, and the mixed American and British 5th Army under General Clark had successfully landed on the 'foot' and 'shin' of Italy in the autumn of 1943. After taking the city of Naples in early October they consolidated their position in the south of the country. Meanwhile the Germans, under the command of Field Marshal Kesselring, strengthened their hold in the central and northern regions.

Several months passed without the Allies making any notable impression on the Germans' 'Gustav Line', which ran for 100 miles from the mouth of the Garigliano through Cassino and over the Apennines to the mouth of the Sangro. To by-pass that line and to undermine the German stronghold, some 50,000 men were to be landed at Anzio, behind the Gustav Line and only thirty-three miles south of Rome.

For Arthur, to be part of this force involved a complete change of direction. Until recently he had been serving in northern Africa in the Tank Corps. They were very short of officers for the Anzio mission, and requested volunteers to join the infantry. No one was very keen, and so a number of the more junior officers were selected whether they liked it or not. Arthur had been one of those chosen.

He was transferred to the Queens Royal Regiment, retaining his rank of Lieutenant. His confidence was not helped by the fact that he had never received any training as an infantry officer; it was a case of being well and truly thrown in at the deep end. In North Africa the battle was far-ranging and strategic, with the lines stretching over hundreds of miles of desert and little close contact with the enemy. Italy was going to be very different.

Although he had very little confidence in his abilities as an infantry officer, Arthur's confidence as a soldier of Christ was steadily growing. Before he enlisted he was determined to make his stand for Christ, and Leith Samuel encouraged him in this.

'On your first night in the barrack-room,' Leith said, 'be seen saying your prayers. You won't actually be able to concentrate on much praying. Just kneel down and count to ten for the glory of God!'

It had proved to be good advice. He had 'nailed his colours to the mast' from day one, and his fellow soldiers respected him for it. They also expected a high standard of conduct from him. On several occasions when some indiscretion escaped his lips the immediate comment was 'Fancy you saying that, Wallis.'

While in North Africa, through Arthur's witness, his batman became a Christian and they developed a close friendship. Sadly he was later killed in action and Arthur felt his loss deeply. With the opportunity now to testify to hundreds of men, all facing the possibility of death, he decided to tell the story of his friend.

The reality of death gives a great urgency to the gospel message, and Arthur was able to convey this in what he said. He told how his batman came to know Jesus in a real and personal way. He explained how he had experienced a deep peace with God through having his sins forgiven. For the Christian, death has truly lost its sting and Arthur could declare with confidence that his friend was now enjoying the presence of the Lord.

Within a matter of hours, they had landed at Anzio. The Germans were taken by surprise by this powerful invasion, enabling the British troops to establish the beachhead there with very little resistance. The days that followed, however, were to prove the most trau-matic of Arthur's wartime years.

Instead of capitalising on their advantage and driving

on over the Alban Hills to Rome, the force at Anzio
spent the next two weeks consolidating their position on
the beachhead. This gave the Germans time to develop a
powerful counter-offensive, and they managed to establish their forces and artillery in the hills around Anzio.
The British troops were hemmed in on the narrow
beachhead and came under heavy fire.

Arthur was sustained by an amazing sense of God's
peace during these difficult days. Around him were
continual death and destruction, but he knew deep
down that God had called him to a greater purpose. His
life's work had scarcely begun, and he was quietly
confident that it was not going to finish there on the
Anzio battlefield.

The regular letters he received from Leith were a
great source of encouragement to him. They were long
epistles, full of stimulating spiritual food as well as news
of what was going on back home. Arthur wrote back as
often as possible, telling as much as he could of his
experiences and sharing the things that God was
teaching him.

On one occasion the German bombardment was particularly heavy. Shells were falling all around their
position, each one creating a crater twenty feet across as
it exploded. Suddenly one landed right by Arthur's
trench and he braced himself for the worst. To
everyone's amazement it failed to explode. This incident
led some of the men in his battalion to believe that he led
some kind of charmed existence because he was a
Christian. What seemed like luck to his fellow soldiers,
Arthur knew was the protecting hand of God.

It was four months from the initial landing at Anzio
before the British forces managed to break out from the
beachhead. The 5th and 8th Armies had been continuing to attack the Gustav Line, and in a combined
attack on the night of 11th May 1944 they finally
succeeded in breaching the German defences at a
number of points.

This forced the Germans to diminish their strength at

Anzio in order to reinforce the main front. By 26th May the British managed to capture the high ground and achieve the desired breakthrough. The toll had been a heavy one. Out of an original battalion of over four hundred men, Arthur was one of only forty survivors. The others had all been killed or captured.

To be advancing at last was a great boost to their morale. They set out for Rome, consolidating their advantage and making steady progress day by day. When they were on the move, the men would march on foot whereas Arthur, as an officer, was given a motor-cycle to ride. This was a somewhat dubious advantage; he had to ride it so slowly that on a number of occasions he dozed off to sleep and nearly crashed the bike!

At one point during this northward journey, some of the men under his command found a goose wandering by the roadside. They managed to catch it, and enjoyed a great feast that evening. It had belonged to a poor peasant woman who was later seen weeping and bewailing her loss. The men thought this was a great joke, but Arthur's conscience was troubled by it. Although he'd had no part in the incident, he wondered whether, as the officer in charge, he should force his men to recompense her. However, not wishing to dampen their high spirits, he quickly put the incident from his mind.

The next day he was again slowly riding his motorbike as the convoy continued northwards. For some reason the vehicle in front strayed slightly onto the verge and there was an almighty explosion. Before he could even register what had happened, Arthur was hurled from his bike and found himself lying on his back in the middle of the track.

In a state of semi-conscious shock, not quite sure whether he was dead or alive, he was vaguely aware of the voices of men around him. He tried to open his eyes, but it felt as if a wet blanket was covering his face. To his horror he realised this was his own blood. In those initial traumatic moments he felt strangely detached from reality, and yet God's presence seemed very close.

He could only lie there helplessly amid a sea of chaos, and yet a supernatural peace and a calm filled his heart. It was as if God was saying to him, 'Don't worry, Arthur, I'm with you.'

Other injured men were also lying on the ground moaning, whereas everyone else was buzzing around like a swarm of angry bees. He gradually pieced together their disjointed comments and began to realise what had actually happened. The truck he was following had driven over a land mine, and he had been caught in the full blast of the explosion.

The pain of his wounds soon became more acute, and a feeling of nausea swept over him. His face, arms, hands and chest began to throb relentlessly as the anaesthetic of initial shock wore off. It was not cold, but he started to shiver uncontrollably. When the blood was wiped from his face he opened his eyes to find with great relief that he could still see. Having looked down at the rest of his body he quickly closed them again. He was not a pretty sight!

All the injured men, including Arthur, were placed on stretchers and transported south to the nearest hospital. Fortunately it had been a wooden rather than a metal mine, and so the damage caused by the shrapnel was not nearly as devastating as might otherwise have been the case. Arthur's wounds, although extensive, were essentially superficial. He'd lost his image as one who led a charmed life, but he knew that God's protecting hand had remained with him.

4
Love and Marriage

With a great sense of eager expectation, Arthur made his way up the drive to the front door of a large house in Harrow Weald, Middlesex. It was early January 1946, and he was just nearing the end of a month's leave from the army. This had been his first opportunity to return to England since he was posted to Italy nearly two years previously, and he was enthusiastically renewing contact with family and friends.

After his injury in 1944, Arthur was taken back to the base camp in Italy. He was out of action for several months. Following an initial spell in hospital he was removed to a hotel on the coast being used as a convalescent centre. It was an idyllic spot, on the cliff-top near Sorrento, and to recuperate there was a welcome relief from the battlefields of Anzio. By the time he had recovered, the war was virtually over. He had suffered extensive surface wounds, but the only lasting damage was cosmetic. He would bear the scars on his face, hands and chest for the rest of his life.

God provided a number of Christian friends during his convalescence, and Leith Samuel had continued faithfully to keep in touch with him by letter. Leith was by now married and he and his wife Mollie were staying at the home of her parents, Mr and Mrs Leys. Arthur had been invited to join them for a few days, and was looking forward to spending some time with Leith before returning to army life.

He was welcomed into the house by Mr and Mrs Leys and quickly made to feel at home. After an enjoyable meal he sat down with Leith to catch up on news. They talked late into the evening and Arthur began to share some of the things that God had been saying to him.

During his period of convalescence he'd plenty of time to think and pray about his future. His call to serve God full time was now even more clear in his thinking, but he was also beginning to entertain serious questions and doubts about his position as a soldier.

When he had first gone into the army he felt convinced that he was doing the right thing, but the harsh realities of war had forced him to think again. Could he really point his gun at a fellow human being when he was called to preach a message of love and forgiveness? The gospel of Jesus Christ invited men to repent and get right with God. How could he, as a minister of that gospel, send a man into eternity without giving him that opportunity?

This conflict increasingly disturbed Arthur. He spoke to fellow Christians about it, but could not satisfactorily resolve it. He had always been involved in the Officers' Christian Union, and greatly admired many Christian soldiers, including his own father, who had fought for their country. But at the back of his mind there was a nagging feeling that if he was going to follow through the word of God to 'love your enemies' he had to be more radical.

Although Leith viewed it as a matter of individual conscience, his thinking had developed along similar lines. He did not feel able to take up arms himself, even under the guise of serving his country. If he killed an unbeliever he was sending an unprepared man to hell; if he killed a believer he was depriving the church of a fellow brother. As Arthur wrestled with this issue he was quite grateful that he would soon be out of the army. In a sense the decision would be made for him.

The next day a couple of Mollie's close friends, Eileen Hemingway and Frances Heron, came over to visit. They had been at school with Mollie and were now nursing at the Middlesex hospital. Both had known Mr and Mrs Leys for a number of years and were regular visitors to their home. During their school-days Mollie had been instrumental in Eileen becoming a Christian.

Leith and Mollie prayed regularly for their friends, and often found themselves praying for Arthur Wallis and Eileen Hemingway one after the other. Somehow these two names got linked together in their minds, and they began to feel there must be something in it. Their prayers for Arthur and Eileen took on an element of creative match-making, and when they realised that Eileen's day off coincided with Arthur's visit they were intrigued to see if anything would transpire.

They all spent a very enjoyable day together. Eileen, a fair-haired girl, was quite shy and self-conscious and had very little to say for herself. Frances was dark-haired and more outgoing and talkative. They were both spiritually mature and keen to devote their lives to serving God; Frances in particular expressed a strong desire to serve God abroad. Arthur enjoyed the company of both girls.

After they departed, Leith was keen to find out what he thought about Eileen and decided to probe a little.

'What did you think of Mollie's two friends, Arthur?' he asked. 'Nice girls, aren't they?'

'Oh, yes,' replied Arthur. 'Frances seems a very nice girl.'

Leith smiled to himself. The best thing he and Mollie could do, he decided, was to keep praying and leave the match-making to God.

☆   ☆   ☆

In November 1946 Arthur was finally demobbed from the army and returned home to live with his mother. She had sold the house at Claverham soon after the Captain's death, and was now living in rented rooms on a farm at Down St Mary in Devon. Peter's romance with Meg Weston had blossomed and they were married in 1944 while Arthur was in Italy.

Mary Wallis had found the war years a lonely and worrying time. The fear of losing her two sons had been very real and she was relieved when they both survived relatively unscathed. It was a great joy to her to have Arthur at home at last.

Arthur gave much thought and prayer to the matter of further training when he came out of the army. He even considered the possibility of going to the Moody Bible Institute or Wheaton College in the USA. There were many friends of his father in the States, and he knew that some of them would be willing to help him through college. The more he prayed about this prospect however, the less peace he felt about it.

It was something he discussed at length with Leith, who felt that, although a Bible college education may be good for knocking spots off your character, it does not necessarily provide the sort of knowledge you are looking for. He could see that Arthur's heart's desire was to preach the word of God; the sort of theology and philosophy that he would be taught at college would not particularly help him to learn and understand the ways of God.

Arthur had already done a certain amount of academic study before he left the army. A variety of vocational training courses were available, and he enrolled for one on philosophy that was mainly attended by soldiers thinking of going into the Anglican ministry. He also started a correspondence course in New Testament Greek with London Bible College. A working knowledge of this subject would provide a basic foundation for his study of the Bible.

Arthur knew he needed a time of study and preparation for ministry, but decided against Bible college. He had begun to realise that God does not look on a man's academic qualifications but on his heart. None of the notable Old Testament prophets appear to have been called from the school of the prophets. In fact when Elisha was called to replace Elijah, he found 'the sons of the prophets' a bit of a pain in the neck! Similarly in the New Testament, the opponents of the Apostles were amazed to find that Peter, John and their colleagues were 'unschooled, ordinary men'.

It was clear from the Bible that God was just as happy to use shepherds and fishermen as scholars like Paul and Luke, and this reassured Arthur that he was making the right decision. It was something to be worked out between him and God. He would live with his mother, needing very little by way of financial support, and would discipline himself to complete his own programme of study.

Not long after Arthur's return from the army, his mother arranged for the two of them to travel up to Claverham to visit the Young family who owned a farm there. They had become close friends while Captain Wallis was still alive, and after his death Mary and her two sons had lived with them for a while. They had been a great source of help and support at that difficult time.

It was a dull December afternoon when Arthur and his mother arrived at Yatton station to be greeted by Mary Young, one of the daughters of the family. She had driven to the station in an old car to meet them and, to Arthur's surprise, brought Eileen Hemingway with her. He had not seen Eileen since they had met at Harrow Weald almost a year before.

Mr and Mrs Young had three children, Alan, Mary and Doreen, and Eileen was a close friend of Doreen's. They had met a few years previously while nursing together at the Queen Elizabeth Hospital in Birmingham. Doreen had invited Eileen to stay on the farm as soon as her midwifery exams were over, and it just so happened that Arthur's visit and hers coincided.

During the days that followed Arthur became increasingly attracted to this shy, unassuming nurse. There was calm strength about her that he began to appreciate.

When, at the end of a meal, she would quietly disappear into the kitchen to wash the dishes, he found himself gladly offering to wipe up!

He somehow felt keen to share his thoughts and feelings with Eileen and began to draw her out. He was surprised to learn that she too had been baptised by the Reverend Alan Redpath at Duke Street Baptist Church in Richmond. Sometimes he would confound her with theological questions, but he was impressed with her sincere desire to serve God. He learned that she was already booked in to commence studies at the Mount Hermon Bible College the following autumn so that she could gain more Bible knowledge and training.

On the last evening of their visit, everyone was seated round a roaring log fire in the sitting room of the farmhouse, and the conversation turned to plans for Christmas. Eileen, who was living with her parents in Southport and working in Liverpool, mentioned that she was planning to spend Christmas with her parents and brother at Chorleywood near London. She had arranged to meet Leith and Mollie Samuel in Chester and travel down to London with them.

Arthur immediately latched on to this. He too would be in the north of the country just before Christmas and needed to travel south to spend the festive season with Peter and Meg and the Weston family in Lewisham. If he could arrange a lift with Leith this would kill two birds with one stone; not only would he get to London, but it would be an opportunity to see Eileen again.

The next day Arthur and his mother returned to Devon, and Doreen and Eileen went to the station to see them off. They all shook hands and said their farewells, but Arthur found himself holding Eileen's hand rather longer than normal. His mother, not one to miss that sort of thing, remarked on it as soon as they were on board the train. She considered that Doreen would be a suitable companion for Arthur, and was somewhat surprised by this new development! He was in no mood to discuss his feelings and brushed aside her questions with very little comment.

Just before Christmas Arthur met up with Leith, Mollie and Eileen in Chester, and they all climbed into Leith's little Hillman Minx. This car, registration number ANN 101, had seen better days and was affectionately nicknamed 'Ann of Old Age'.

It was a cold, wintry day and the car did not have a heating system. Arthur and Eileen sat in the back with a rug wrapped around their legs. The combined effect of the small car and the need to stay warm kept them close together! They talked about books they were reading, and Eileen mentioned how much she enjoyed biographies. Arthur had just been challenged through a book called *Fraser of Lisuland* and he offered to lend it to her.

After their journey was well underway, Ann of Old Age decided that the whole thing was getting a bit much, and ground to a halt with a suspicious amount of steam emerging from under her bonnet. Fortunately they managed to find a nearby garage that could do the necessary repairs. By this time it was snowing quite heavily, and while they were waiting for the work on the car to be completed they found their way into a local park and began playing snowballs.

Arthur was pretty deadly when it came to snow-fights, and Eileen would only have to turn the other way for a moment to find a snowball unexpectedly hitting her on the back of the head. When he actually tried to stuff one down her neck, Leith was beginning to think he had gone a little over the top! The poor nurse was having difficulty defending herself against this concerted attack from a strong young army officer. But Eileen had begun to realise that Arthur really was interested in her, and so she was enjoying the attention.

When they got back into the car and recommenced the journey, they sat even closer to keep warm! They wrapped the rug round themselves again, and Arthur took hold of Eileen's hand underneath it, thinking this would not be noticed. Mollie was watching like a hawk however, and was well aware of what was brewing beneath the blanket.

They eventually arrived at Mollie's parents' house rather later than planned, and were more than ready for the meal that Mrs Leys had prepared for them. Just before Arthur left to travel on to Lewisham, he found himself alone with Eileen for a few minutes. It was an opportunity to be seized.

'Would it be all right if I wrote to you, Eileen?' he asked her tentatively.

'Yes, I'd love that,' she replied, and gave him her address.

☆   ☆   ☆

It was a fine, spring day in March 1947. Arthur and Eileen stood together on the deck of the Liverpool to Birkenhead ferry, the wind blowing through their hair. From the other side of the Mersey they planned to catch a bus out into the Wirral and to walk together in the country.

They had started to write to one another regularly over the past couple of months, but only met once after their eventful car journey. On that occasion Arthur had been speaking at a meeting in London and Leith and Mollie had taken Eileen along to hear him. She was more impressed with him than with the sermon he preached!

Arthur thought a lot about her over this period. He was definitely in love and, although he prayed much about her, it was difficult to be impartial. He tried to remain open to the possibility that God might have some other plan for his life, but his emotions told him that she was the girl for him. The more he prayed, the more right it seemed that he would one day marry Eileen.

He was obviously keen to see her again, and so he arranged to come up to Liverpool, where Eileen was nursing, and to stay with some friends. It was her day off, and this trip to the country was his first opportunity to spend a bit of time alone with her.

As they stood together, leaning over the deck-rail, the thoughts and emotions swirled around Arthur's mind rather like the turbulent water he could see in the wake of the ferry. All that he had been feeling over the previous few months surfaced in a burst of youthful impetuosity. He turned to Eileen and looked her straight in the eyes.

'Will you be my wife, Eileen?' he asked her, with a look of serious intensity written all over his face.

She was somewhat taken aback, but gave a simple reply, 'Yes.'

She too had been thinking and praying about their friendship. He was obviously interested in her, and she had fallen deeply in love with him. Although her intense desire and longing was to marry Arthur, she did not want to build up her hopes too quickly; they had, after all, spent very little time together. The fact that he had made up his mind so soon was a complete surprise, but her reply came without hesitation. In just a few seconds his proposal had dispelled the fear that her dreams of marriage might be ill-founded.

After such a dramatic start, their day together seemed to fly by. It was just as if they were floating on air, and they walked for several miles across the Wirral before their feet touched the ground! There was so much to share, and so much to learn about each other, and so little time in which to do it.

The next day, Arthur took Eileen back to have tea with the friends with whom he was staying. They took the tram from the centre of Liverpool, but got so engrossed in one another's company that they completely missed their stop. The route was a circular one, and before they knew it, they were back in the centre of the city, exactly where they had started! By the time they finally arrived for tea it was nearly suppertime.

There was a spring in Arthur's step as he boarded the train to return to Devon. He did not want to say goodbye to Eileen, and promised he would come and see her again before too long. He was on an emotional high, and the journey passed very quickly as he thought about everything they had done together. All in all, it had been a very successful weekend.

☆   ☆   ☆

In the back of Arthur's mind there were one or two nagging doubts. Outwardly he displayed the confidence and fervour of a man who was deeply in love; inwardly he was realising that he had acted rather hastily. Having prayed quite a bit about his relationship with Eileen, he was confident that they were right for each other. He just felt that he'd rather jumped the gun.

What would their friends and relatives think when they discovered that they had got engaged on their first day out together? Wouldn't they think him far too impetuous? Arthur began to feel somewhat insecure and self-conscious. He did not want to upset Eileen and made no mention of his doubts to her, but he did suggest that they kept their engagement quiet for a while.

Eileen couldn't understand why he didn't want to announce the good news. She was so excited that she wanted to tell all her friends about it. Was he really unsure about her after all? Was he going to change his mind?

A few weeks later Arthur travelled back up to Southport to meet Eileen's parents. Mr and Mrs Hemingway received him very well, and readily gave their approval to his request to marry their daughter. Eileen had become so 'religious' that they were beginning to think she would never find a suitable husband. They were delighted to be proved wrong.

One thing did concern them however. Arthur had no

regular job and was trusting God for his day-to-day needs. With the extra burden of a wife to support, how were they going to manage financially? George Hemingway was a branch manager for the Atlas Insurance Company and the concept of 'living by faith' was foreign to him. Eileen's mother, Mabel, was a God-fearing lady, but she too found it very hard to conceive of a trust in God that was relevant to such practical everyday things as food, clothes and housing.

Having made their point, however, they both accepted the situation gracefully. They could see that Arthur and Eileen were quite unshakable in their determination to 'live by faith', and were clearly very much in love. This would no doubt help them through any difficulties they might face as a result of their chosen lifestyle.

Arthur had saved up twenty pounds for a ring, and a few weeks later he went up to London to make the purchase from a diamond merchant recommended by Eileen's father. He was able to acquire a very fine ring with a sapphire and two diamonds for just the right amount.

On his next trip up to see Eileen, he took his purchase with him. As they travelled together on the train from Liverpool to Southport, he decided to surprise her.

'Close your eyes and hold out your hand, Eileen,' he said, with a twinkle in his eye. She obediently complied, and he promptly put the ring on the wrong hand!

Arthur was by now far more sure of himself. As he got to know Eileen more deeply, his love for her was growing even stronger. Perhaps he had acted rather impetuously by proposing to her quite so quickly, but his doubts were now far behind him.

Although it was now 1947, two years since the ending of hostilities, the effects of the war were still very apparent in the British economy. A massive amount of money and productive resources had gone into the war effort and the country was still subject to restrictions and rationing in a number of areas, particularly food and clothing. Getting the necessary supplies together for a large party was not easy, and so Mr and Mrs Hemingway decided simply to invite close family and friends to a hotel in London for an official engagement party.

Arthur and Eileen both accepted the need for a long engagement. Eileen was booked in to start at Bible college in the autumn of that year. It would not be practical to get married until the end of her two-year course.

Arthur was getting stuck into his own course of study. He had determined that during the period Eileen was at Bible college, he would undertake his own education programme, trusting the Holy Spirit to lead and guide him. Some of his Christian acquaintances could only see the potential dangers and pitfalls of this approach, but those he most respected, including Leith, encouraged him. He based himself in the heart of Devon, living with his mother, and saw this time rather like the Apostle Paul's period of preparation in Arabia.

One man who exerted a very significant influence on Arthur during these formative years was an elderly Brethren teacher by the name of G.H. Lang. He was a man who walked with God, ascetic and disciplined, and distinguished in appearance by a little nanny-goat beard.

When Arthur first heard Mr Lang preach some years previously, he was deeply impressed by the depth and originality of his teaching. The effect of his ministry not only stimulated Arthur's thinking, but created in him a deep hunger and thirst to know God. His emphasis on holiness, uncompromising commitment and discipleship were a great challenge and provocation to Arthur as a young man.

G.H. Lang was a truly independent and radical thinker; no man would be his master and he toed nobody's line. Whereas other teachers would skirt round difficult or controversial issues, he would face them head on and think them through in depth. His conclusions were not always popular. He exposed a number of Brethren 'sacred cows' and in doing so alienated many within the movement who were unable to see beyond the limitations of the traditional viewpoint.

To him the lordship of Jesus was very practical and down-to-earth in its application, and this brought a strong 'kingdom' emphasis into his teaching. His views on eschatology were quite unconventional. Most Brethren teachers believed that all believers would be caught up with Christ in 'the rapture' and would escape 'the great tribulation' talked of in the book of Revelation. Mr Lang did not hold to this view, but taught that only those Christians who were 'counted worthy' through aspiring to a holy life would be raptured. He did not believe in 'cheap grace' and was careful to emphasise the obligations as well as privileges of discipleship.

He was by now well into his seventies and still very active in the ministry. A prolific writer, he produced books and pamphlets on many issues and edited a magazine called *The Disciple*. Arthur was greatly attracted to this elderly saint and would visit his Wimborne home as frequently as he could. In many ways he became his disciple, and received a great deal of helpful and wise counsel.

'If you want to be used,' he said to Arthur, 'get to know the ways of God. Aim for God-knowledge rather than head-knowledge. This doesn't mean you can afford to be undisciplined or haphazard. Set yourself clear objectives and approach your studies in an orderly way. But never lose your primary objective, and that is to know God.'

This made a lot of sense to Arthur, and the goals he established for his period of study were set with this in mind. His first goal was to complete his correspondence course in New Testament Greek. A good working knowledge of this subject would be a great help to him in his future study.

Secondly he determined to get a good basic grasp of the books of the Bible. His aim was to understand the main theme of each book. What was God primarily saying through it? What were the lessons for us? He would read the book through, see what Bible commentators had to say about it, study the historical background, and then put together a summary of the book in note form.

His third goal was to make a detailed study of one book of the Bible. He chose the first epistle of John. He planned to spend time meditating on this book and going through it verse by verse, comparing relevant cross-references and producing detailed notes.

Finally he planned to do an in-depth study of a Bible theme. In choosing which area to cover he was very conscious of the advice Mr Lang had given him. His purpose was to get to know God and his ways and so for this part of his studies he concentrated on 'the one who would lead him into all truth'—the Holy Spirit.

Doors were already beginning to open for Arthur, and he quickly found himself preaching far more than studying and preparing. As his study programme began to slip, he realised that this was a new temptation. Preaching was his only visible means of support and it was not easy to refuse invitations although, living with his mother, his financial needs were minimal. He determined therefore that he would spend nine months of the year in study and prayer, and no more than three in preaching and travelling.

In the summer of 1947 Eileen finished her nursing job in Liverpool and came down to stay with Arthur and his mother in Devon for a holiday. Arthur had been away for a few days and they met up en route and travelled together to Exeter by train. From there it was necessary to catch a local train to Lapford, a little country station near the farm at Down St Mary where they were living.

Unfortunately, their train was late arriving at Exeter and they missed the last connection. However they

caught a train which took them part of the way to
Crediton, hoping to hitch-hike the rest of the way. They
were picked up by a coach-load of locals who were on
their way back from a day out. Obviously in a merry
mood after enjoying a few drinks, everyone was chatter-
ing away at great speed in broad Devonian accents. For
Eileen, a city-dweller, it was a bewildering introduction
to West Country life. She could not understand a word
they were saying!

Their holiday together consisted of simple pleasures:
long walks together through the narrow lanes, bird-
watching, picnics in the peaceful Devon countryside,
and an occasional trip to the seaside. Arthur was far
more adventurous than Eileen when it came to explor-
ation. He would love to get off the beaten track and
would always try to reach some spot that was unrea-
chable by means of the usual paths. Eileen was less
confident. Her initial reaction was invariably one of
caution.

'We'll get lost if we head that way, Arthur.'

'That field looks awfully boggy.'

'There's no way across that stream.'

'Isn't that a bull in the field?'

Arthur was not put off by her reticence. 'Come on,' he
would say, 'follow me and you'll be fine.'

They usually were fine. She would follow him as he
picked his way through hedges, scrambled up banks,
and negotiated obstacles. Once she had overcome her
initial fears, she enjoyed the sense of adventure. They
normally managed to reach their destination without
too many problems.

Occasionally, Arthur's pioneer spirit did land him in
deep water. On one walk they suddenly realised they
were sharing a field with a bull who was beginning to
take a lively interest in them. They raced to the hedge
and scrambled across it. Arthur jumped down the other
side, ready to catch Eileen. Unfortunately he failed to
look before he leaped and landed with a splash in a cold
muddy pond!

When the day came for Eileen to start her training at Mount Hermon Bible College, Arthur went with her. It was a college for ladies only, situated at Ealing in West London, and Arthur arranged to stay in the capital for a few days before travelling back to Devon

Some of the rules at Mount Hermon were very strict. The only free day was Saturday, and normally no concessions were made to get out of college at any other time. Their faces fell when they heard this; Arthur was only going to be around for two or three days and would then not see Eileen for the rest of the term. The college Principal took pity on them and told Arthur that he would be allowed to meet Eileen the next evening.

They decided to spend the evening at Kew Gardens. There were plenty of quiet places there to walk and talk, and the gardens were not too far away from the college. It didn't occur to them that the gardens might close at dusk. When the keeper came round with his bell to warn people that the gates were shutting, they were too engrossed in each other's company to take any notice.

A few minutes later, when it was time for Eileen to get back to college, they made their way to the gate only to discover that it was locked. The high wall around the gardens made escape a little difficult, even for someone with Arthur's adventurous spirit. Fortunately, as they stood there considering their predicament, a keeper came up on his bicycle. He took one look at them, laughed knowingly and unlocked the gate.

☆ ☆ ☆

The big day had finally arrived. Monday 11th July 1949. Arthur woke up with a sense of excitement and expectation. He was staying in Lewisham with Peter and Meg at the Westons' home. He pulled back the curtains to look out at a clear sunny day. He was very thankful. It had been a long wait, but now Eileen's course was finished and they were to be married at last.

Their two-year engagement passed more quickly for Eileen than for Arthur. She had been fully occupied in the day-to-day bustle and activity of college life. After lectures and study there was very little time in which to get bored.

For Arthur the terms would pass much more slowly. Much of his time was spent on his own, hidden away in the peace and quiet of his mother's Devon apartments. God was teaching him many things as he disciplined himself to get down to study day after day, but there were inevitably occasions when time dragged. He would write long letters to Eileen, telling her about the things he was studying and learning. How he looked forward to receiving her replies.

Whenever he could he found a good excuse to go to London and see her during term, but it was only really during the college holidays that they were able to spend much time together. Arthur had retained his love of sport and they were able to go to a number of sporting events together.

In the spring of 1948 they watched the University Boat Race on the River Thames. It was a particularly exciting event for Arthur because there was an Old Monktonian in the Cambridge crew. When the 'light blues' won a closely fought race he nearly fell into the river in his excitement!

During that summer the Olympic Games were held in Britain and they managed to get into Wembley stadium to see some of the athletics. Arthur was particularly thrilled to see the great Czechoslovakian runner, Emil Zatopek, winning the 10,000 metres.

It was good just to be with Eileen and to enjoy doing normal things with her, but Arthur knew that, if their marriage was going to be successful, it was important to develop a spiritual life together. Whenever they met during their courting days therefore, they would take time to pray with one another. They established a rule that they would not make any important decision without first talking to God about it.

Often when they were together Arthur would have to do some preparation for a talk he was to be giving. He always liked to make sure that this was done first before they went off to do anything else. They would find a quiet spot to sit, and he would get out his Bible and notebook and work on his sermon, discussing his thoughts with Eileen.

After two years of courtship they were now very eager to be married, and to be together all the time. Their friends urged them not to get married until they had found a home of their own. They found it hard to listen to this advice. After waiting quite long enough already, their patience was exhausted. They decided to set the wedding date first, and then worry about where to live. It would always be possible for them to live with Arthur's mother for a while until they found the right place.

Others, with more experience of the tensions that can arise between wife and mother-in-law, could see that this would not be the best way to start married life. Arthur and Eileen were deaf to their warnings. They were unable to find any suitable accommodation of their own, and so to live with 'Ma' initially was their only option.

Neither of them permanently belonged to a local church. By now Arthur and his mother were living in the little village of Talaton, about ten miles east of Exeter. They were in rooms within a farmhouse owned by Christians, and their regular church was a small Brethren Assembly in Ottery St Mary. When Eileen was at home in Southport, she also went to a 'Gospel Hall', but they did not feel they should get married there. Mr and Mrs Hemingway did not approve of Gospel Halls! They would only be happy with a church wedding.

As Arthur and Eileen had both been baptised at Duke Street Baptist Church in Richmond, it was a natural choice for the wedding. Eileen's parents were quite happy about this, so they contacted the Reverend Alan Redpath to make the necessary arrangements.

With her parents living up North, whereas she was in

nearby Ealing, Eileen had to make most of the arrangements for the wedding and reception. With rationing still in operation, she had to obtain a special permit to have a wedding cake made and the restaurant could only provide a very limited menu for the wedding breakfast. The only thing that was not rationed was the flowers!

In line with most evangelical Christians of the day, both Arthur and Eileen were strict teetotallers. They did not want to be toasted in wine or champagne. Eileen's father reluctantly agreed to this, but arranged to take some of his friends out to a hotel after the reception to enjoy a proper celebration!

Arthur decided to hire a top hat and tails for the wedding, although he did manage to save sufficient clothing coupons to buy a new suit to wear on his honeymoon. Eileen managed to purchase her wedding dress second-hand from a friend of Arthur's who had recently married, so she too was able to use her coupons to buy a new going-away outfit.

Peter was best man, and as they took their places at the front of the church Arthur found it hard to believe that the day had at long last arrived. There was no turning back now! After a few minutes the organ broke into 'Jesu, Joy of Man's Desiring', everyone rose to their feet, and he turned to see Eileen and her father entering the church.

She looked radiant as she walked slowly down the aisle to join him at the front of the church. He smiled at her reassuringly, and they stepped forward to stand together facing the minister. They sang a hymn and the wedding ceremony began. They took their vows, the ring was exchanged, and no one came up with 'any just cause or impediment'.

'I hereby declare that you are man and wife,' Alan Redpath pronounced, smiling at the happy couple. 'What God hath joined together let no man put asunder.'

'I'm now a married man!' thought Arthur to himself,

as Alan Redpath concluded his wedding address and Leith Samuel stood up to lead the congregation in prayer.

They sang a further hymn and the rest of the day passed very quickly: the register was signed, photographs taken, old friends greeted, food eaten, telegrams opened, the cake cut, speeches delivered and the car decorated! It was their day, and they enjoyed it to the full.

When they finally sat down together on the train at Euston station, it was with a mixture of relief and exhilaration. Everything had gone smoothly and the wedding formalities were now all over. Now they could settle down to the serious business of enjoying life as man and wife together.

They were travelling up to Lancashire on the first stage of their honeymoon en route to the Isle of Skye, off the west coast of Scotland. Mr and Mrs Hemingway were staying on in the London area, and so Arthur and Eileen had arranged to spend the first night at their Southport home.

The next day they continued to Scotland. At Glasgow they caught a local train out to Gouroch, a small town situated on the estuary of the River Clyde. Here they stayed with Mr and Mrs Murdoch, some old friends of Arthur's parents. The following morning Arthur and Eileen were taken out for a cruise around the Clyde estuary in the Murdochs' motor yacht.

From Gouroch, their journey north continued by steam-boat through Loch Fyne to Ardrishaig, where they boarded a coach for the trip up the winding west-coast road to Oban. From there they caught another steamer up through Loch Linnhe to Fort William. The weather was hot and sunny, and they were able to enjoy the rugged coastal scenery in ideal conditions.

Fort William is a beautiful highland town, strategically situated at the base of the Caledonian Canal which cuts from the west coast of Scotland up through Loch Ness to

Inverness in the north-east. Within a few miles of the town the rugged terrain rises over 4,400 feet from sea-level to the peak of Ben Nevis, the highest mountain in the British Isles. The view from their hotel window was quite breathtaking.

After just one night in Fort William they travelled by train a further forty miles through the highlands to Mallaig, where they caught a motor-boat across to the Isle of Skye. Here they had arranged to stay for a week at a small guest-house at Broadford.

The weather remained hot on most days, and they were able to see much of the island. They did not have their own transport, but got around by bus and coach and spent much of the time just walking and climbing amid the unspoilt highland scenery.

On the way back they spent a few more days with the Murdochs at Gouroch, who took them to see many of the beauty spots in the area. They then travelled south to Devon to take up residence with Arthur's mother at Talaton.

5

Country Life

The honeymoon was over. Arthur and Eileen settled down to life in the country with 'Ma' Wallis. The apartment where they were living was in a spacious farmhouse owned by some Christian farmers, Mr and Mrs Peters, who were members of the Plymouth Brethren.

Westcott House, as it was known, was a large residence in the heart of the Devon countryside, about a mile from the centre of the small village of Talaton. Behind the house were the farmyard and outbuildings which were reached by a rough untarred road; a separate long drive led to the front of the house which looked out across a large lawned garden to open fields.

The Peters lived in the side wing of the house and mainly used the back entrance which led out to the farm. Mrs Wallis rented a small kitchen, a living room and two large bedrooms at the front of the house. She also had the use of part of the garden where she could grow vegetables and keep a few chickens.

Arthur would spend the mornings studying in the living room while Eileen helped Ma with the household chores and preparation of meals. In the afternoon they would often go out and work in the garden, or collect firewood from the nearby copse. Eileen got quite handy with a cross-cut saw. She would take one end and Arthur would take the other, as they sawed the branches they

67

had gathered into logs. Meanwhile Ma gathered all the wood into piles to take into the house, and chopped up smaller pieces for kindling.

In the evenings they lit a log fire in the living room and sat round it working or reading. While Ma and Eileen occupied themselves with knitting or sewing, Arthur would often read from a book to keep them entertained.

Beneath the calm exterior of this simple lifestyle tensions were emerging. As far as Ma was concerned, Arthur and Eileen were part of her household and she was boss. They had no privacy and no real say in practical day-to-day affairs. This was particularly difficult for Eileen to cope with; she obviously wanted to get established in her role as Arthur's wife, and Ma's interference was particularly irksome.

Little things would annoy her. Food supplies were still limited, and coupons were required to buy tinned goods. Ma had established quite a horde of tins that she had received in parcels from friends in the States, but she still expected Arthur and Eileen to give her all their coupons. Eileen would have liked to have saved some up for when they started a home of their own.

Items like butter and sugar were strictly rationed, and so it was normal practice to take your own supply with you when you went to stay with someone else. Whenever Arthur went away for a few days Ma would give him a small supply of these necessities. Eileen would get upset if she considered the amount too frugal. There was some pride at stake here, for she felt this would reflect badly on her. Arthur's hosts would have no way of knowing that it was Ma and not Eileen who controlled the supply.

Mrs Wallis was quite a stickler for perfection when it came to housework. She expected things to be done her way. Eileen was not particularly practised or efficient at looking after a home and made many blunders. This led to a number of clashes between them. Ma would be stinging in her criticism of Eileen's shortcomings; Eileen on the other hand would stubbornly ignore her mother-in-law's instructions!

She dreaded being asked to go and buy some item of shopping. It was bound to be wrong. The food was not fresh, or it was underweight, or too expensive. It seemed to her that no matter what she did, Ma would find something wrong with it.

Of course it was not particularly easy for Arthur's mother. She had led a lonely life since losing her husband in her late forties. Throughout the war years she had lived on her own, and she had many fears and insecurities that made relationships difficult for her.

Arthur became increasingly aware of the tensions that were developing between wife and mother. He would often emerge from the peace and blessing of his morning's study to find that he could cut the atmosphere with a knife! He knew Ma was not an easy person to please, and he tried as best he could to shield Eileen from her. This was not easy, and he realised that the only real solution was for them to find a home of their own.

In some ways Arthur had some of his mother's temperament. He too was a bit of a perfectionist. He would find it much easier to notice things that were wrong than those which were right. During that winter, Eileen decided to make him a pair of slippers out of a thick piece of felt she had acquired. They turned out looking a little odd and somewhat amateurish, but she had put a lot of effort into them. Ma found them highly amusing and dismissed her handiwork with a few caustic comments, but Eileen expected a different reaction from her husband.

'At least Arthur will appreciate the effort that I've put into them,' she thought to herself as she presented them to him.

'Oh, thank you dear,' said Arthur, and a look of mock bemusement spread across his face. 'They look very interesting. What do they do?'

He did not seem to recognise Eileen's need for a bit of appreciation, even if her handiwork was slightly bizarre. It was as much as she could do to hold back the tears.

At times Eileen, too, could be a stickler for detail. Arthur would love to retell a story or incident in a graphic and dramatic way. He would not always bother to get the minor facts quite correct; they were usually incidental to the main story. Eileen however would chip in to put the record straight. This completely ruined the flow of the story, and irritated him considerably!

Their disagreements mainly took the form of minor annoyances of this sort. They found, as most young couples do, that married life is one of the most effective means of revealing where character and attitudes are not yet fully Christlike. Their differences of opinion did not usually result in a major quarrel, just many a niggle and the occasional heated argument. They learned to put matters right sooner rather than later, and were quick to apologise and pray together.

It was not long before they discovered that Eileen was pregnant. She had conceived while on their honeymoon, and her bouts of morning-sickness did not make it any easier to cope with the pressures of life with Ma. The need for a home of their own was becoming even more pressing.

They kept constantly on the look-out for rented accommodation, without finding anything suitable. Hopes rose when they went to look at one house near Claverham where Arthur spent some of his teenage years. Their friends, the Youngs, had made them aware of it, and the idea was that Arthur would help run the nearby mission hall. This plan did not work out, however, and they continued to look and pray for a home with no apparent success.

☆   ☆   ☆

Arthur was getting an increasing number of speaking invitations, and the basis on which he accepted or

declined such invitations became an important issue to
him. His main concern was to ensure that his itinerary
was directed by the Holy Spirit, and not by whether or
not there was a space in his diary or his need for income.
G.H. Lang had encouraged him to be discerning, and he
determined to take a radical stance in this area.

He would not agree unreservedly to an invitation
several months ahead, as he did not feel he could be
sure what God might have in store for him that far in
advance. In order to explain his philosophy, he produced a short paper which he would enclose when
replying to invitations.

An examination of the New Testament in general, and of
the Acts of the Apostles in particular, to find out the
principles of guidance by which the apostles and evangelists
of the early church conducted their ministry, revealed to me
that they were guided from place to place by the Holy Spirit
directly, and not by plans or arrangements they may have
felt led to make previously.

There were times when they did make plans, but these
were always subject to the over-ruling of the Lord, and to
later guidance that might be given, and that when such
differed from the original plan they were always willing for
the plan to be modified or abandoned that they might not be
bound by any person or any principle other than the person
of the Holy Spirit and the principles that God had revealed.

One of the open secrets of the train of blessing that
attended their labours, as has been true ever since of men of
God, is that they were 'the right men, in the right place, at
the right time', and being so perfectly in God's timings, their
lives and labours could not escape the blessings that
attended them.

Believing that these principles revealed were for my
admonition, I have felt compelled to abandon those methods on which I had previously worked and seek to conform
my principles of itinerary to the word of God. I fully realise
that such a course may often cut across the grain of present
evangelical methods.

I have decided that I must no longer be guided in
accepting or refusing invitations by a vacant or booked space

in my diary, or even by my common sense to appreciate the situation, but must wait until God does in fact reveal his will.

It has been interesting to discover that this was one of the governing principles in the life of George Muller, as no doubt of other great men of God—never to launch forth on any project, whether seemingly important or insignificant, until first convinced that it was the will of God, and never to assume the guidance of God without definitely seeking it.

I have determined therefore never to commit myself finally to any programme until the will of God is ascertained, but to make all arrangements provisional so that I am open to obey later instruction that the Lord may be pleased to reveal, even if this means confirming or cancelling at what may seem to be very short notice.

The value of following such a divine principle was brought home to me quite recently when, with my wife, I was conducting a fortnight's mission in the south-west. It was not until the second week that things began to move, so much so that we were asked to prolong our visit a further week. Being freed from a fixed programme, we were able to do this, and in some respects the third week was the most vital of all, not only for the further salvation of souls, but for the building up in the faith of several who had trusted Christ earlier. One felt that this was but an earnest of what God might do when we were prepared to follow the principles of his Word, abandoning twentieth century methods for the first century ones.

May I finally outline the practical outworking of all this as far as I am concerned, so that there shall be a clear understanding with those who have kindly sent invitations:-

1. That any further arrangements made re meetings etc are strictly provisional, and open to further leading from the Lord on both sides nearer the date.
2. That the one issuing the invitation is prepared for the possibility of the provisional arrangements being confirmed or cancelled at short notice.
3. That in the event of printing being involved, where my name is to appear as the speaker arranged, the announcement shall be qualified, so long as the booking is provisional, by some statement such as 'to be confirmed' indicating that the arrangement is tentative.
4. That I shall not be called upon to give beforehand a

subject or list of subjects, being seldom sure of the mind of God concerning an address very far in advance.

If it is now felt that these qualifications make the booking too precarious or uncertain, then I shall quite understand and appreciate the reason for making alternative arrangements.

This uncompromising stance did lay Arthur open to a certain amount of criticism and misunderstanding. In some circles the rumour went round that if you booked Arthur Wallis you could never be certain whether he would turn up!

There was of course a degree of financial security in having a full diary for several months in advance, but Arthur was determined not to be influenced by such considerations. He took great comfort from the words of Jesus in the Sermon on the Mount (Mt 6:25–33):

Therefore I say unto you, Be not anxious for your life, what ye shall eat, or what ye shall drink; nor yet for your body, what ye shall put on. Is not the life more than the food, and the body than the raiment? Behold the birds of the heaven, that they sow not, neither do they reap, nor gather into barns; and your heavenly Father feedeth them. Are not ye of much more value than they? ... Be not therefore anxious, saying, What shall we eat? or, What shall we drink? or, Wherewithal shall we be clothed? For your heavenly Father knoweth that ye have need of all these things. But seek first his kingdom, and his righteousness; and all these things shall be added unto you.

Arthur knew that to seek first God's kingdom and righteousness meant being sure that he was available for the things that God was giving him to do, and only accepting those invitations that he knew were in God's plan for him. He could trust his heavenly Father for the financial consequences.

☆　　☆　　☆

As the birth of their first child drew near, Eileen was getting increasingly concerned as to where they were going to live. The thought of still living with Ma with a small child was not a happy one, and she was in a quandary as to what arrangements to make for the birth. Arthur tried to reassure her that God had got just the right place prepared for them, but with nothing suitable on the horizon, her worries remained.

Eileen's parents were concerned that she should have proper medical care for the birth of her first child, and spoke to their doctor in Southport about it. Eileen had been his patient in the past, and he gladly offered to look after her provided that she made arrangements to be in Southport for the last six weeks of the pregnancy. She felt happy about this prospect and so they arranged for her to travel north at the beginning of March.

Arthur was booked to take quite a number of meetings that month, including an evangelistic mission on the Blackdown Hills. He stayed in Devon, therefore, and travelled up to Southport to join her at the beginning of April. Mr and Mrs Hemingway had booked Eileen into a private nursing home in Southport, and on 16th April 1950 she gave birth to a son.

Fathers were not permitted to witness a birth in those days, and so Arthur was admitted a few minutes after the event. He looked down on the tiny wizened features of his newborn son and heir with great delight. As he examined his little feet and hands, he was convinced that they had the same peculiarities of shape as his own. Eileen was not sure whether it really was a case of 'like father, like son' or wishful thinking!

They decided to name him Jonathan Reginald. Jonathan was a name they both liked, meaning 'gift of the Lord'; Reginald was in memory of Arthur's father.

As he prayed for his newborn son, Arthur did not only see him as a gift from the Lord. He also prayed that Jonathan would have the same spirit as his biblical namesake, a man who was born a prince, yet who humbly stepped aside when he recognised that the anointing for leadership was on another. Arthur was not too concerned as to whether his son would become a great preacher or leader; he was concerned that he grew up to be a man who served God with all his heart. He realised that his responsibility as a father was to build character into his son; he could leave the charisma to God.

A few days after Jonathan was born, Arthur travelled up to Capernwray Hall, near Carnforth. Major Ian Thomas, whom Arthur knew from his army days, ran a Christian conference centre there, and had invited him as the guest speaker that week. Having fulfilled this engagement, he got back to Southport just as Eileen and the baby were about to be discharged from the nursing home.

They still had no home of their own and decided to stay on with Eileen's parents for a few weeks. Mr and Mrs Hemingway were pleased to have them, but were obviously concerned that they should find somewhere permanent to live without further delay. Arthur and Eileen's need for a home was now desperate, and they continued to pray that God would provide the right place.

Within a matter of days they received the answer to their prayers. News came through from Ma Wallis that a house in Talaton had become available for rent, and the landlord was ready to offer it to them if they wanted it. Talaton was the last place on earth they had thought of finding a home, but this particular house did sound rather interesting.

'The Forge House' had been a blacksmith's home and workshop in the past. With four bedrooms, a box-room, bathroom, kitchen, and three living rooms, it sounded like a palace to Arthur and Eileen! Not only that, but the rent was only fifteen shillings a week. They were far too desperate for a home to mind the fact that it was back in Talaton. It sounded like a marvellous provision, and they agreed to take it.

A few days later they packed their bags, put Jonathan in his carry-cot, and made their way back to Devon in Arthur's old Morris 10 car.

Ma Wallis was looking forward to seeing her new

grandson and having them stay with her for a few weeks while they got organised to move into The Forge House. Unfortunately she had very fixed ideas on how to look after a baby which she immediately tried to impose on Eileen and it did not take long for old tensions to reappear. To make matters worse, she had decided that she did not want Arthur disturbed by the baby waking up in the night and had moved the beds around at Westcott House. Arthur was to sleep in one room on his own, and Eileen and Jonathan were to share the other bedroom with Ma. Not good news!

Although there was a fair bit of work to do at The Forge House, they decided to move in as soon as they could organise some essential items of furniture. They would get the place sorted out once they were living there.

On a bright warm day in May 1950 they moved into The Forge House. At last they were able to establish family life in their own home. Once they were no longer living with Ma, relationships improved. She became far more of a help to Eileen, and willingly looked after Jonathan whenever this was needed.

The Forge House was right in the centre of Talaton, next door to the little thatched cottage which housed the village post office. A little way behind the house stood the twelfth-century parish church, fifty yards down the road was the general store, and a little further on was the real centre of the social life of the area, the village pub!

In the main part of the house, there was a kitchen and two further living rooms, four bedrooms and a box-room. At first Arthur and Eileen seemed almost lost in all this space. They had very few belongings with which to fill such a large house and became regular attendants at any auction sales held in the area, gradually acquiring further items of furniture and household equipment. They had no cash for anything new. The house was rather drab and gloomy and not in particularly good condition. They did a little decorating and Arthur treated the worst of the damp, but in the main Eileen relied on curtains and other furnishings to brighten the place up and make it more welcoming.

There was no gas or electricity in the village. They relied on oil lamps for light and oil heaters or open fires for warmth. On arriving home on a winter's evening the first job would be to get the lamps and fires lit. It was a big house to keep warm, and there was no heating whatsoever in the bedrooms. But Arthur and Eileen had plenty of blankets, eiderdowns and warm clothing, and they were young and tough.

Outside the house they had no privacy. A common path led to the landlord's adjoining cottage, and the only place to sit out was a small patch of lawn next to the road and in full view of every passer by. Further back was a large outbuilding providing garage and storage facilities built with traditional cob walls of clay and straw. Beyond the landlord's cottage was a large plot where they were able to grow plenty of vegetables.

Mains water had not yet reached Talaton, and so they obtained their drinking water from a well at the back of the neighbouring post office. It provided a constant supply of lovely fresh water, but fetching it was hard work, definitely Arthur's job when he was at home!

The village shop stocked most provisions other than fresh food. All other regular requirements were delivered to the door by local tradesmen. One of the farmers in the village did the milk round; a baker used to come through the village daily; the butcher delivered three times a week; the fishmonger and the greengrocer called weekly; and every Friday night a mobile fish-and-chip van would set up outside the village pub.

Living in the country, with a good supply of homegrown fruit and vegetables, their cost of living was much lower than it would have been in a town or city. This was just as well; they had very little money. Arthur's ministry was steadily developing with many invitations coming from local chapels and a few from further afield, but very few of these places had any idea of giving to support a man in full-time Christian work.

Their motto seemed to be 'Lord, you keep him humble, and we'll keep him poor!'

Despite their simple lifestyle, the income Arthur received from his speaking engagements was insufficient for their daily needs. They had to trust God to supply the rest, and he did, mainly through unsolicited gifts. A number of friends and prayer partners asked to be kept regularly informed of their itinerary. These folk would pray for Arthur and Eileen, and many times God would prompt one or other of them to send a gift of money. This would generally arrive at a crucial moment when they were asking God to provide their needs.

Their income in the first year of marriage came to the princely sum of £236 (approximately £3,600 in 1990 values), but they were quite content. They determined never to go into debt, and God always provided their essential needs. Their faith would often be tested in their finances, but this invariably provided an opportunity for God to prove his faithfulness. Very rarely would they be unable to meet any payments that fell due.

On one occasion, Arthur was away and Eileen had no money for the weekly milk bill. Nothing arrived in the post and she was dreading having to tell the milkman that she could not pay him. For some reason when he delivered the milk that Saturday he did not knock at the door to ask for his money! By the following week she had sufficient to square the account.

Of course, by establishing home in the heart of Devon, they were rather off the beaten track. Some of their friends thought this was a big mistake; they were far away from the centre of evangelical church life. Wouldn't it have been better to settle down in a town or a city where much more was happening? Arthur and Eileen could never accept this view; they knew that God had led them to The Forge House, Talaton. For how long they could not tell, but they had no intention of moving for the time being.

They determined to find ways of sharing their faith

with the villagers. Not wanting to offend the local vicar, they asked him whether he would have any objection to them commencing an informal gospel service in their home. He did not mind as long as it did not clash with any of his activities. There were no services in the parish church on a Sunday evening, and so they decided to arrange a regular meeting at this time each week.

They distributed invitations throughout the vicinity, and were encouraged when over twenty people turned up to the first meeting. Eileen played the piano for a time of hymn-singing, and Arthur preached. Week by week a regular number of twenty to thirty villagers would attend, and if Arthur was going to be away he would arrange for someone else to come and speak.

The villagers who attended these meetings were quite happy to come along for a religious service and a friendly chat. But it became increasingly obvious that they did not really want to be faced with the challenge of the gospel. When the implications of commitment to Christ were presented they all fought shy.

Gradually the numbers began to diminish until after about a year only one or two people were coming along. Arthur decided to discontinue the meetings. They had served their purpose. Everyone in the village, whether they had come or not, now knew exactly what Arthur and Eileen stood for. The gospel had been clearly presented. Although no obvious fruit could be seen, a seed had been sown in many lives.

6

Power for Service

On a cold morning in February 1951, there was a knock on the door of The Forge House. It was Oscar Penhearow, the local colporteur. His job was to go around the district from door to door selling Bibles and Christian literature with the primary aim of sharing his faith and winning people for Christ. He had first called on Arthur and Eileen soon after their move to Talaton, and was by now a close friend.

Eileen brought him into Arthur's study, and they settled down for a cup of coffee and a chat.

'You know, Arthur,' he said, 'over the past few months I've become aware of something lacking in my ministry. As I've gone around the district talking with many people about Jesus and selling books, I have seen very little fruit from my labours. Much of the time my words seem like paper pellets bouncing off a brick wall.'

As Arthur struggled to find a word of encouragement for his friend, Oscar continued, 'I've come to the conclusion that there must be more. There must be some experience of spiritual power that I'm missing. You don't find Jesus or the Apostles having this trouble; their ministry was always effective.'

'Yes, but you must remember that they were living in a time of special awakening,' said Arthur, who was beginning to get stirred up by the need for revival. 'We must seek God for such times of outpouring, but you can't expect them to happen all the time. We are called to proclaim the gospel faithfully, even if we see no immediate results.'

'Yes, I accept that,' replied Oscar, 'but I still feel there's something more. I've been particularly challenged by an article I've just read by Dr R.A. Torrey on the baptism in the Holy Spirit. He describes this baptism as an experience of the anointing of the Holy Spirit that will transform your ministry, an enduement with power for service. In fact I have also written to Dr Martyn Lloyd-Jones on this subject and in his reply to my letter he agreed with Dr Torrey. In Acts chapter 1 Jesus says, "You shall receive power when the Holy Spirit has come upon you and you shall be my witnesses." I feel this is what I need, Arthur. What do you think?'

Arthur hedged. The question of the baptism in the Holy Spirit was a controversial one. He had never had any personal contact with Pentecostals, or with anyone who testified to such an experience. Not only that, but he had heard enough tales about pentecostalism to dismiss much of it as emotional froth. He certainly did not want anything to do with that!

Oscar clearly felt a great need for such an experience. Arthur did not. He was quite satisfied with his performance as a preacher. He was getting many complimentary remarks about his ministry, and receiving an increasing number of invitations. 'There may well be such an experience, Oscar,' he said, 'but I don't know that I need it.'

The words seemed to stick in his throat even before he'd uttered them! If such an experience was from God, who was he to say he didn't need it? He might have a full diary and a respected ministry, but that did not spell fruit. Didn't he need 'power for service' just as much as his friend?

Oscar was certainly not going to be put off. He was well and truly fired up by this issue, and Arthur's indifference did not dent his enthusiasm. He continued to unburden his deep desire for God to meet with him and to make his ministry truly effective. As they talked, something was stirring in Arthur's spirit. He was being convicted of his complacency and pride, and was beginning to see his own need of a deeper experience of the power of the Holy Spirit.

They both agreed that this was an important issue on which they needed an answer from God and knelt together in prayer, asking God to clearly show them his will. They resolved to search the Scriptures and to seek God for revelation, and promised to communicate if either of them received anything.

Before Oscar left, he took a quick look along Arthur's book-shelves, hoping he might have something that would help him on the subject. To his surprise he found a book by Dr Torrey entitled *The Baptism in the Holy Spirit*. The article he had just read was taken from this very book.

'I see you have a book here on the baptism in the Holy Spirit by Dr Torrey, Arthur,' Oscar said. 'Could I borrow it?'

'Of course, my brother,' said Arthur, magnanimously. Oscar had succeeded in getting him quite stirred up about this issue, and he would rather have liked to read it himself!

After his friend had gone, Arthur searched his book-shelves for anything else on the subject and spotted a book by Andrew Murray entitled *The Full Blessing of Pentecost*. 'That sounds good,' he thought to himself, and settled down to read it. He had no sooner opened the first page than he felt a clear restraint.

It was just as if God tapped him on the shoulder and said, 'Before you read what men say about this, would you care to read what I have to say?'

This was a challenge! Andrew Murray was put to one side and he got out his concordance. He had already done a study of the Holy Spirit during his two years of preparation, but did not even turn to his own notes. He wanted to approach the Scriptures with an open mind, and he set about going through the New Testament, looking up every reference to the Holy Spirit and taking particular note of any references to 'power for service'.

Although he had determined to look first at what God had to say on the subject, he was particularly interested to discover G.H. Lang's opinion. He decided to write to him, recounting his conversation with Oscar and seeking his views. 'Is there for the believer,' he asked, 'an enduement with power for service?' He knew that by the time he heard back from Mr Lang he would have completed his own search through the New Testament.

During the next three weeks, God gave Arthur a comprehensive seminar on the Holy Spirit. His original complacency was replaced by a strong desire for God to meet him, and Scriptures he had read many times seemed to strike him with a new force and relevance. He took particular note of the words that Jesus had spoken about the Spirit: 'If any one thirst, let him come to me and drink.' Previously he had approached the subject of the Holy Spirit intellectually, now he was thirsty!

God knew that Arthur would only open his heart to a new experience of the Spirit if he was first thoroughly convinced from the Bible. As he studied the New Testament, God led him to the inescapable conclusion that such an experience was not only valid but necessary. What finally persuaded him was the experience of Jesus himself.

He saw for the first time that it was only after the Spirit came upon Jesus at the Jordan that he commenced his ministry. Having been born of the Spirit, Jesus must surely have had the Holy Spirit in him during the first thirty years of his life, but he never preached a sermon, performed a miracle or won a disciple until after his Jordan experience. Only then was he able to say, 'The Spirit of the Lord is *upon* me.'

It was that little preposition 'upon' that struck Arthur. It was repeated in Acts when Jesus promised power to his disciples when the Spirit came upon them. If Jesus and the early Apostles needed such an anointing of the Spirit for their ministry, how much more did he.

God was also showing him areas of his life that needed cleansing—areas of pride, self-sufficiency and wrong ambition. He realised that before he could be filled he must empty himself of these things. As he meditated on the second chapter of Philippians, he saw that even Jesus had to empty himself, 'taking the form of a servant'.

For Jesus, of course, it was not a question of sin. As God, he had been entirely perfect and complete, but he emptied himself of his self-sufficiency, learned obedience, and became a servant. Arthur saw that for him, too, it was not simply a question of emptying himself of sin, but of consciously embracing the spirit of a servant. This surely was a key to being filled with the Spirit.

He had never heard anyone else connect Christ's emptiness and servanthood with the fullness of the Spirit, and was not entirely sure about this interpretation. Was this a little fanciful? He asked God to confirm it to him. A day or two later a letter arrived from G.H. Lang which provided just the confirmation he was seeking.

Mr Lang's response was very positive. He did believe that there was an experience of 'enduement with power for service', and referred to Isaiah 42: 'Behold my servant . . . I have put my Spirit upon him.'

'We must be servants,' he wrote, 'if we want the Father to entrust us with the power of his Spirit.'

Arthur needed no further convincing. He knew he needed the Spirit to empower him for ministry in the same way as Jesus. 'Lord, make me a servant,' he prayed, 'and endue me with the power of your Spirit.'

Nothing obvious happened, but a few days later, God challenged Arthur through his reading from *Daily Light*. It was the evening reading, 8th March, and it concluded: 'Believe ye that I am able to do this? . . . Yea, Lord. According to your faith be it unto you.' These words were taken from the incident of the healing of the blind man in Matthew chapter 9, and something happened inside Arthur as he read them. For the first time he realised that all he had to do was to believe it, and the blessing was his.

'I've got it!' he said to Eileen. He knew God had heard his prayer. Nothing obviously happened, but he stopped asking and started thanking God for the answer. Just thirty-six hours later, early on the morning of 10th March 1951, the Spirit 'came upon' him as he was alone in his study, praying. He experienced a strong physical sensation which he could only describe as 'being filled'. He did not speak with tongues, but he knew that the Holy Spirit had come in power.

When he contacted Oscar, he was delighted to discover that God had also met with his friend. A few days previously, Oscar was due to preach for the first time at Emmanuel Church, Sidmouth. Just two hours before the service, having completed detailed preparation of his sermon, God clearly spoke to him and said, 'Get rid of all your notes and trust me for tonight!'

Much to his wife's surprise, he took the notes he had so carefully prepared and threw them into the fire! As he stood up to preach he felt tongue-tied, but the Spirit suddenly came on him and he experienced an anointing of God's power. He had been baptised in the Spirit in the pulpit, and was already seeing a new effectiveness in his door-to-door witness.

During this time, as Arthur shared all that God was saying to him with Eileen, she was stirred to seek the baptism in the Spirit. She too was believing Jesus' promise to give the Holy Spirit to those who ask him, but had received no obvious sign that her prayer had been answered. Eileen was quiet and cautious and far more reserved than Arthur, but she longed for an experience of the Holy Spirit that was clear and unmistakable.

A few days later they were praying together, when suddenly Arthur lifted up his arms, as though prompted by some unseen force, and found himself placing them on her head and praying specifically for her to be filled with the Spirit. He had no prior experience of the 'laying on of hands', and it was completely spontaneous. To Eileen, this was sufficient to give her the assurance she needed.

Very soon the fruits of their experience of the Holy Spirit became apparent. Arthur's preaching took on a new dimension, and he began to see his ministry having a much greater impact on people's lives. Eileen, who was by now speaking at ladies' meetings in the area, found herself able to communicate far more effectively.

Both of them received a new boldness in sharing their faith. What they had done previously out of good Christian duty, they were now released to do in the liberty of the Spirit. Arthur even ventured into the village pub and began to speak to people about their need for salvation!

In their enthusiasm, however, they were not always as tactful as they might have been. They lost the friendship of some villagers they had got to know, who were far too embarrassed to continue associating with these religious fanatics. Being full of the Spirit did not alter the fact that they still had much to learn.

Their new experience of the Holy Spirit also had a significant effect on their prayer life. They found a new reality and power in this area, and began to grow in the ministry of intercession. Instead of dutifully going through the ritual of a daily 'quiet time', there was a new sense of enjoyment in talking to God and in reading the Bible.

The baptism in the Holy Spirit, they realised, was not so much a goal as a gateway. It was a beginning, not an end, an essential foundation for their future life and service.

7

Vision for Revival

The Sunday evening gospel service marked the culmination of a busy week of meetings, door-to-door evangelism and street work at the Etloe Road Brethren Church in Bristol. As a Sunday, it had hardly been a day of rest, and there was still a further week of mission to go. By the end of the service, Arthur was suffering from a slight headache. Feeling very tired, he would have liked nothing better than to return to the house where he was staying and climb into bed.

It was his first evangelistic mission since receiving the baptism in the Spirit, and he had been encouraged to see God at work throughout the week. Not only had people been converted to Christ, but something was stirring in the hearts of the believers.

News was coming through of a powerful revival which had broken out in the Hebrides. This had provoked a widespread desire within this Bristol church to see God move in a similar way somewhat nearer to home. When the service was over, instead of going home as usual, around thirty gathered to pray.

After a short break at 10 pm, some twenty returned, and they continued to cry to God to pour out his Spirit on their city. An hour later the numbers had reduced to seven, all young men, but the Holy Spirit came upon them in an unusual and powerful way. All feelings of tiredness disappeared and they prayed, praised and quoted Scripture with barely a moment's intermission for over four hours. They were few in number, but you had to be pretty sharp to get your prayer in.

At 3.30 am there was a knock at the chapel door. It was a policeman on his beat. Having seen lights in the building and heard the sound of singing, he came to investigate this phenomenon and was somewhat amazed to find a prayer meeting in full flow. They took this interruption as a signal to retire to their beds, and as he made his way home, Arthur realised that his headache was gone. He felt as fresh as the proverbial daisy!

It was one of the most remarkable prayer meetings that he had ever experienced. Although they did not see revival, the days that followed brought some answers to their prayers. Arthur began to realise, as never before, just how vital it is to spend time in waiting on God and intercession. He resolved to give these things a far more important place in his ministry.

☆   ☆   ☆

As the Highland bus made its way along the narrow winding road, Arthur looked out at the barren landscape and wondered why God should choose this place to pour out his Spirit. The surrounding countryside looked bare and bleak, strewn with rocks and boulders, and marked here and there with peat-banks.

He had travelled up to the Western Isles of Scotland in order to witness first hand the scenes of the revival that had broken out there. The bus route took him up through Lewis and Harris, the largest island of the Outer Hebrides, to the little village of Barvas on the north of the island.

Barvas was a small isolated place, comprising a few irregular clusters of crofters' cottages and bungalows. Standing alone, just beyond the edge of the village, was the plain stone-built 'kirk' which had witnessed the beginning of the 'Lewis Awakening'. Again Arthur knew the same feeling of awe and wonder he had experienced as a boy during his visit to the little schoolroom at Loughor in Wales. It was here in Barvas that God had come down in power in December 1949, and the effects of the revival were still being felt throughout the islands.

For months before revival broke out, the parish minister, the Reverend James Murray Mackay, and a small number of his congregation had prayed for an outpouring of the Spirit. That evening in the manse, Arthur enjoyed the warm Scottish hospitality of the minister and his wife and listened with intense interest as he related how God had so wonderfully answered their prayers.

God had shown Rev Mackay, while away at a convention in autumn 1949, that he should invite Duncan Campbell, the director of the Faith Mission in Edinburgh, to come to Lewis. When he returned to Barvas he was encouraged to find that God had spoken to one of the members of his prayer group through a dream. This indicated not only that revival was coming, but that Mr Campbell was the person God was going to use to bring this about.

In response to their invitation, Duncan Campbell arrived in Barvas in December 1949. He found a tremendous sense of expectancy among the members of the little congregation. They would not be disappointed. At the end of one of the first services at which he preached, the congregation gathered outside the church, reluctant to disperse. Suddenly from inside the building a loud cry was heard. A young man had stayed to pray. Pouring out his soul in intercession, he had fallen into a trance and was lying prostrate on the floor. Suddenly, moved by a power they could not resist, the congregation flocked back into the church. Deeply conscious of their sin, many began to break down, weeping and crying to God for mercy.

This meeting continued until the early hours of the morning. Such was the depth of repentance and the hunger for God that gripped them that they refused to go home. Some, who had not been at the service, spontaneously made their way to the church, moved by an unseen power, while others became suddenly aware in their own homes of the presence of God, crying out to him for mercy.

In the days that followed, this experience spread throughout the scattered villages of Lewis and Harris and some of the adjoining islands. The effects were still being felt in 1951, and Arthur felt privileged to be a witness to what God was doing. Unlike the widespread, sweeping movement of the Welsh Revival, the Lewis Awakening had been far more localised. Nevertheless, all the marks of a true revival were there. God *had* done it again!

As Arthur climbed into bed that night, many thoughts flooded his mind. If God could send revival to Lewis, was he unwilling to do it elsewhere? Why would he choose such an out-of-the-way, sparsely populated place to pour out his Spirit? Was the Outer Hebrides some sort of spiritual arena in which he was demonstrating in miniature that he could and would 'do it again'? Was this awakening, away in the Western Isles, the harbinger of a modern era of spiritual revival? With these questions filling his thoughts, he went to sleep.

He awoke early the next morning, and got down onto his knees to pray. Kneeling quietly in his bedroom, God gave him a vision. He saw a vast open prairie. As he looked across it, he could just see a small fire burning on the far side. It seemed to be coming slowly, very slowly nearer. The scene faded from view, only to reappear a few moments later.

This time the fire was much nearer. It stretched like a continuous wall right across the prairie as far as the eye could see. Slowly, inexorably, the wall of flame and smoke moved forward until again the picture faded from view.

When he looked again, the fire had gone. In its place was a vast and endless desert stretching away to the horizon. In the far distance a small dazzling object lay on the sand, shining like a star. As he watched, it grew larger and larger, filling out with blue as it did so, till even the shining framework was eclipsed by the blue. There in the middle of the desert was a lake of water. He immediately thought of Isaiah's prophetic words: 'And the mirage shall become a pool, and the thirsty grounds springs of water' (Is 35:7).

Rising from his knees, Arthur opened his Bible. As he commenced reading from Isaiah chapter 43, God spoke with great clarity and power:

> Ye are my witnesses, saith the Lord, and my servant whom I have chosen: that ye may know and believe me, and understand that I am he; before me there was no God formed, neither shall there be after me. I, even I, am the Lord; and beside me there is no saviour. . . . I will work, and who shall reverse it? . . . Thus saith the Lord, which maketh a way in the sea, and a path in the mighty waters; . . . Remember ye not the former things, neither consider the things of old. Behold I will do a new thing; now shall it spring forth; shall ye not know it? I will even make a way in the wilderness, and rivers in the desert. . . . I give waters in the wilderness, and rivers in the desert, to give drink to my people, my chosen: the people which I formed for myself, that they may set forth my praise.

This, surely, was the answer to his questions. God was not simply going to 'do it again', he was going to 'do a *new* thing'. This new thing would involve the fire of God's judgement, as he dealt with the sin of his people, but it would also involve the outpouring of the Holy Spirit to bring waters in the desert. A sense of wonder and excitement filled Arthur's heart. God's word to Isaiah was applicable to him! He too was chosen to be the Lord's servant. He would witness this 'new thing' that God was going to do.

God had chosen an autumn morning of 1951, in that little village of Barvas in the Outer Hebrides, to burn a deep conviction into Arthur's heart that he would never lose. It was a conviction that God was longing to release a great outpouring of his Spirit in his generation. He determined to devote himself to this vision and this cause. What, he reasoned, could be more important or more significant than to see God coming in mighty revival power? Some words he had once heard came to mind: 'If you would make the greatest success of your life, try to discover what God is doing in your time, and fling yourself into the accomplishment of his purpose and will.' He resolved to devote his time and energy to the accomplishment of this great purpose: to see an outpouring of God's Holy Spirit, not just in some remote island off the west coast of Scotland, but throughout the towns and cities of Great Britain.

During the remainder of his visit to the Outer Hebrides, all that Arthur saw served to deepen his vision and to increase his resolve. Duncan Campbell was in the Hebrides at this time, and Arthur managed to spend some time with him. He was greatly impressed by this godly Scot, a man whose self-effacing humility marked him out as one of God's truly great saints.

When he returned to Devon a week or two later, Arthur was a different man. He had been deeply inspired and envisioned by all he had seen and heard. When he left for Scotland, his vision for revival was like a glowing coal; it was now a burning flame. The effect of this was soon reflected in his ministry.

A few days after his return he was due to take an evangelistic mission at Chapelfield Hall, a Brethren Church in Whipton, Exeter. If God could bring revival in Lewis, why not here in Exeter? Full of all he had seen and heard in the Hebrides, he encouraged the people to believe for God to move in a similar way in their locality. Many of them found this impassioned young evangelist a bit much to take. When he called them to a day of prayer and fasting, this met with a fair amount of resistance. Prayer was one thing, but fasting? That was something else!

Even those who opposed Arthur recognised that there was something different about him. They could not deny that he was a man of prayer, a man who was straight and true, and a man who believed God's promises. They simply could not cope with his uncompromising intensity. However there was one man in the church with whom Arthur struck a particular accord, a school-teacher by the name of Jack Hardwidge. He introduced himself to Arthur at the end of one of the meetings, and immediately began questioning him about the Holy Spirit.

'I've been reading a book on the baptism in the Holy Spirit by Dr Torrey,' said Jack. 'Do you believe in such an experience, Arthur?'

This sounded familiar! 'Yes, I do,' he replied.

'And have you received it?' asked Jack.

'Yes, I received it back in March.'

'I want you to tell me about it. Can you come back for coffee?'

Arthur returned with Jack and his wife Daisy to their home, and they talked into the night. He told them how he had been baptised in the Spirit, and encouraged them to start believing that they would receive the experience themselves. Jack had many questions, but he was thirsty for God to meet him. Arthur knew that he had found a kindred spirit.

Despite the reticence of the church to respond, Arthur was still believing for an outpouring of God's Spirit. The next morning he was reading in the book of Hosea. As he got to chapter 6 the words seemed to jump out of the page at him:

> Come, and let us return unto the Lord: for he hath torn, and he will heal us; he hath smitten, and he will bind us up. After two days he will revive us: on the third day he will raise us up, and we shall live before him. And let us know, let us follow on to know the Lord; his going forth is sure as the morning: and he shall come unto us as the rain, as the latter rain that watereth the earth.

The words 'on the third day' struck Arthur with particular force. It was three days to the end of the mission. He took this scripture as a clear promise that something was going to happen on the last day.

As the final night's service approached, he still had no idea what he was going to say. God seemed to be challenging him to be truly radical. The great temptation was to prepare a sermon 'just in case', but he knew he should not do this. Anything he preached would only be effective if it was truly inspired by the Holy Spirit; he was not prepared to settle for anything less. He would simply trust God and see what happened.

Arthur was believing that the crowds would come in to fill the hall for this final meeting. It didn't happen. The service started without a single outsider present. When the time came for the sermon, he still had no message to preach. He would only have been preaching to the converted in any event.

Somewhat desperately, Arthur clung on to his belief that somehow God would break into the situation; he called the people to wait quietly before the Lord. Still nothing happened and God gave him nothing further to say. He felt increasingly uncomfortable. It seemed he had stepped out on a limb, and the limb had snapped. After a period of somewhat embarrassed silence, he closed the meeting.

The people at Chapelfield Hall did not take kindly to this episode, and he received a lot of criticism. As he thought through these events, he realised that out of his strong desire for revival he had jumped to false conclusions. His literal application of Hosea chapter 6 was a little fanciful to say the least. He saw that the coming of revival was in some ways like the return of Christ; he might have great assurance that it would happen, but only God knows exactly how and when.

It was also apparent to Arthur that the believers at Whipton were not ready for revival. Most of them did not want it or even see the need for it. He wrote the elders a letter apologising for any embarrassment he'd caused and admitting that his strong conviction had been mistaken.

Clearly not all Christians shared Arthur's concern for revival, but he was already meeting a number who did. Jack and Daisy Hardwidge were two such people. A revival was taking place in their hearts, if not in their church. Another couple who shared a deep longing for revival were Billy and Mary Ward. After serving as missionaries in India, they had now returned to England and were also living in Devon. Billy was a full-time preacher, working mostly among the Brethren assemblies.

If Arthur had learned one thing about revival, it was the vital importance of prayer. As Christmas approached he decided to invite a small number of friends to 'pray in' the New Year together. A total of seven men responded, including Jack Hardwidge, Billy Ward and Oscar Penhearow. They came together at The Forge House on New Year's Eve, spent some time sharing testimonies, and prayed into the early hours. It became clear to them that one New Year's Eve spent in this way was not sufficient. God was calling them to pray together on a persistent ongoing basis. The first Friday of every month was therefore established as the regular night for what became known as the Talaton Revival Prayer Meeting.

8

No More Children

It was January 1952, and Arthur and Eileen were eagerly
anticipating the birth of their second child. Eileen's
pregnancy had been trouble-free, and she decided to
have the birth at home. Her local GP arranged for the
district nurse to look after her; the doctor would only be
sent for in an emergency. Eileen was very happy with this
arrangement. Having been a nurse herself, she considered that, for normal births, a midwife was better than
a doctor!

As the baby was due in the depths of winter, a good
source of heat was needed in the bedroom. They decided
to give the room a thorough spring-clean and to test out
the fireplace, which they had never used. As it happened,
Eileen started labour several days earlier than expected
and these good intentions were never carried out. While
she gathered together all that would be needed by way of
sheets, towels, basins and baby clothes, Arthur hastily
cleared out the old fireplace and lit a fire. They tidied up
the room and just about managed to get everything
reasonably ship-shape before the midwife arrived.

For the next hour or two, Arthur's job was to go to and
fro fetching hot water and anything else that was
required, as well as trying to keep Jonathan out of
trouble. Not quite two years old, he was just at that
'getting into everything' age, and simply couldn't understand what all the palaver was about. Arthur was very

soon wondering whether this home delivery idea was such a good one after all.

Labour was obviously progressing very quickly, but the midwife soon became suspicious that all was not too well. She could not hear the baby's heartbeat, and had detected one or two abnormalities. Dr Sidebotham was called for, and he arrived just in time for the birth. Their baby, a boy, was stillborn.

Arthur and Eileen were stunned. They could not take it in at first. There had been no indications that things might not go to plan; the pregnancy had been seemingly trouble-free; it was a complete shock to them. The doctor and midwife did their best to comfort them, but there was very little that they could say to help. As soon as everything was cleared up, Arthur and Eileen just wanted to be left on their own.

As they sat on the bed, their arms around each other, the tears finally flowed. Jonathan did not understand what had happened, but he had been kept away from his mum for several hours; now he just wanted to give her a cuddle.

They had already decided that, if it was a boy, they were going to call him Stephen. As they prayed together, God gave them a deep sense of peace. They knew that little Stephen was now with the Lord; one day they would see and get to know him.

A few days later Dr Sidebotham called to see them. A little while before the birth he had taken a blood test on Eileen, something which he discovered was never done during her first pregnancy. The result had just arrived back from the lab. It indicated that her blood group was rhesus negative, whereas Arthur was rhesus positive.

He explained to them that this was the cause of the problem. It was something that did not affect the firstborn child. However the difference in blood grouping resulted in antibodies being formed which could cause subsequent children to be stillborn. He had consulted a specialist who strongly advised against any more children.

This piece of news was even more shattering to Arthur and Eileen than the loss of their child. Their main source of comfort over those few days had been the hope of further children to replace the one they had lost. Their dream was for a family of three or four children. Now it seemed that this would never be realised.

They prayed much about this over the weeks and months that followed. Should they ignore medical opinion and simply trust God for a miracle? Somehow they could receive no assurance from God to go ahead with another pregnancy. Eventually they came to the hard conclusion that the will of God for them was 'no more children'. Maybe he had other purposes for their lives that would be hindered by a large family. They could not understand the reasons; it was something they simply had to come to terms with.

☆   ☆   ☆

The regular gospel meetings at The Forge House had discontinued about a year previously, and Arthur felt the time had come for a fresh gospel outreach into the village. He decided to hold a tent mission in Talaton during the month of June 1952.

Only too aware of the need for this to be backed by much prayer, he invited a few supportive friends to participate in a week of prayer at the end of May.

WEEK OF PRAYER—MAY 26–31

Gatherings for prayer will be held at The Forge House, Talaton, every evening at 7.30, in view of the Tent mission commencing there on Sunday, June 1st. Only an outpouring of the Holy Spirit can meet the need. Even if unable to attend these prayer meetings—WILL YOU PRAY?

'Break up your fallow ground: for it is time to seek the Lord, till he come and rain righteousness upon you.' Hosea 10:12.

'Oh that thou wouldest rend the heavens, that thou wouldest come down, that the mountains might flow down at thy presence ... to make thy name known to thine adversaries, that the nations may tremble at thy presence!' Isaiah 64:1,2.

A number of the Prayer Meeting 'regulars' supported these meetings, and there was much prayer, in some cases well into the night. At the end of the week, Arthur, along with Jack Hardwidge and one or two others, erected a tent on the village common in the heart of Talaton.

Arthur was fully expecting revival to break out as the mission got under way. The reality was somewhat different. Many of the local Christians thought it was a crazy idea and were too embarrassed to support the outreach, and very few of the villagers dared to be seen entering the tent!

Meetings were arranged several nights a week, and a number of the other evenings were spent in prayer. It was a struggle. At first a small handful of outsiders came along, but as the mission progressed, on many nights no one came at all.

It was clear to Arthur that a spiritual battle was taking place and he continued to devote much time to prayer. Jack, who had received the baptism in the Spirit a few months earlier, was a great support and encouragement. Many nights he would cycle the ten miles out from Exeter to support the mission, and stay on to pray into the night before cycling back. On one such night it was 4.30 am when he set off for home. Daisy, who was at home looking after their young children, was very long suffering!

Some of their times of prayer were tremendously encouraging, others were a struggle. Their regular revival prayer meeting was particularly difficult that month; one brother poured cold water on the whole idea of the tent mission and the meeting was rapidly going nowhere. Arthur felt like asking the 'dear brother' why he'd bothered to come, but managed to restrain himself!

After four weeks of prayer, dogged persistence and considerable ridicule, they were approaching the end of the mission. Very few people had attended, and there was no apparent fruit for all this hard work. Arthur was somewhat bewildered by the whole thing; outwardly it appeared they had been bashing their heads against a brick wall. However, like the Apostle Paul, he was 'perplexed, but not driven to despair'. He knew the battle was not against 'flesh and blood' but against unseen 'principalities and powers'.

On Wednesday 2nd July, the final night, a man who had once professed Christianity attended the meeting with his son, but no other outsiders came. During a quiet moment in the meeting, a woman's voice was heard outside, loudly proclaiming, 'I'll be jolly glad to see the back of that ****** tent!'

After the meeting, they returned to The Forge House for a short time of prayer. God encouraged them with some words from Isaiah chapter 54:

'Sing, O barren, thou that didst not bear; break forth into singing and cry aloud, thou that didst not travail with child: for more are the children of the desolate than the children of the married wife,' saith the Lord. 'Enlarge the place of thy tent. . . . Fear not; for thou shalt not be ashamed: neither be thou confounded; for thou shalt not be put to shame. . . . For a small moment have I forsaken thee; but with great mercies will I gather thee.'

The words 'enlarge the place of thy tent' brought a smile to Arthur's face. He would not interpret them too literally! Despite the disappointment of seeming failure, God would bring fruitfulness in his way and in his time. He would not be 'put to shame', and his vision and commitment to revival in East Devon remained undeterred.

The next day, Jack came out to help take the tent

down. He felt it might be erected again at Talaton. Only time would tell.

Earlier that year, a letter had arrived in the post which had brought to a head a matter about which Arthur was becoming increasingly concerned. It was from the War Office. Although released from the army in November 1946, he had never resigned his commission. The letter was to advise him that, under the Reserve and Auxiliary Forces (Training) Act, 1951, he was likely to be called up for further military training.

Arthur recalled the serious doubts that he had had after the war about his position as a soldier and a minister of the gospel. Over the years his convictions on this matter had deepened. He now knew he could no longer participate in military service with a clear conscience.

It was something he had discussed at length with G.H. Lang who held very strong views on the subject. Mr Lang supported the traditional Brethren view that followers of Christ should not participate in military service. His arguments were mainly based on the fact that a Christian's allegiance was to a heavenly, not an earthly, kingdom.

The Bible describes Christians as 'sojourners and pilgrims' in this present world; in other words, aliens. Their citizenship is elsewhere. This view of 'citizenship' went much further in its application than the matter of military service. Most Brethren would take no part in politics, or even vote. Mr Lang not only subscribed to these views, but had produced a number of reasoned and biblical articles in support of them. Although not Arthur's main reason for conscientious objection, these arguments only served to strengthen his convictions.

He returned the forms to the War Office, clearly stating his objection to further military service on conscientious grounds, and requesting that he be allowed to resign his commission. At the end of May he received a reply from the Director of Personal Services. It was not encouraging.

> I am to inform you that you remain liable to call up for Army service till the statutory termination of the Emergency and that therefore you are not at liberty to resign your commission.
>
> In the event of circumstances arising which necessitate your recall, you will receive orders as to where to report.
>
> It is regretted that arrangements for dealing with matters in connection with your conscientious scruples cannot be entered into at this juncture.
>
> You will, however, be given the opportunity of putting forward your request to the appropriate authorities in the event of your recall during an emergency.

A few days later he received a notice to inform him that he would be required to undergo two weeks' training with the Territorial Army. This was to take place in early September at Barnard Castle, in County Durham. He replied promptly, urgently requesting further consideration of his objections. He was relieved to learn, a week or two later, that he was to be granted a hearing at the Bristol Conscientious Objectors' Tribunal on 25th July 1952.

In support of his application he prepared a statement outlining his position:

> For some years I have been wholly engaged as an evangelist (or lay minister of religion) working mostly among 'the Brethren' but also among other religious denominations. I have not had any secular occupation since I was released from the Forces in November 1946.
>
> Although as a youth of eighteen I volunteered for the Army in all good faith and served conscientiously at home and overseas, both in action and out during my five years' army service, and though during this time I was a convinced Christian, I had not given very much thought to the question of my duty to God in relation to National Service.
>
> During my time in the Forces, however, the question did

exercise my mind from time to time when I met with those who did not believe in Jesus Christ in the vital personal way that I did, but who remarked to this effect—'If I believed as you did I would never take up arms.'

It was however after taking up fully the work of an evangelist, and realising that Christ had commissioned me to preach the gospel to every creature, which applied not only to my own nation, but every nation—that I owed the gospel of God's grace to Germans and Russians as much as to British folk—that I saw quite clearly the inconsistency of my position. I could not reconcile my call to preach the gospel to every creature with a service commission which might at any moment insist on my taking to some of these creatures weapons of slaughter.

Dearly as I love my country, in such a question of conflicting loyalties, I feel that I have no alternative to put first and foremost my loyalty to God and to my commission as a messenger of the gospel of Christ, whatever the cost may be. My plea is the words of Acts 5 verse 29: 'We ought to obey God rather than man.' I do not judge others, but desire to be obedient to my own conscience.

I would therefore plead that I may be allowed to continue the work to which God has called me, and which may well be worth more to my country than whole battalions of soldiers.

Arthur was represented at the tribunal by George Harper, a lawyer who was an old friend of his father. His application was upheld by the judge who ruled 'that the applicant should be regarded as conscientiously objecting to performing military service'.

☆   ☆   ☆

Christmas was a time when the Wallis family enjoyed getting together, and 1952 was no exception. Arthur, Eileen and Jonathan, together with 'Ma', spent the festive season with Peter and Meg at their home in Ashford, Kent. Their family had grown rapidly. Ruth, their eldest child, was now five; Heather was a month younger than Jonathan, and their twins, Timothy and Mary, were just ten months old.

All in all, with three young children to get over-excited and two babies, it was a noisy Christmas! Like most good things, it was over far too quickly and, just before the New Year, Arthur and Eileen, together with Jonathan and Ma, set off in the old Morris 10 to return to Devon.

On the way home they decided to call in on a relative who lived near Windsor. This would help break the journey, a matter of particular importance for Jonathan, who was already asking if they were 'nearly there' after the first ten miles!

Travelling along the A25 near Redhill, they rounded a bend, only to find a parked car blocking the carriageway. With traffic approaching in the opposite direction, they could not pass and Arthur braked hard. There was a patch of black ice on the road, and although they were not travelling fast, the car skidded out of control and ploughed straight into the back of the stationary vehicle.

It was before the days of seat-belts, and Arthur was thrown forward onto the steering wheel. Ma, who was sitting in the front seat, was the most seriously injured, receiving a broken jaw and bad cuts to her face from the broken glass from the windscreen. Jonathan, who was sitting on his mother's lap in the back, hit his head on the front seat. Only Eileen was unharmed.

Some people from a nearby house kindly took them in until an ambulance arrived to take Eileen, Jonathan and Ma off to hospital. The car was a write-off and Arthur stayed to sort things out. When he joined the others at the hospital it was discovered that the impact of the steering wheel had cracked his breastbone.

The car had only been insured 'third party', and they had no money with which to replace it. They would just have to manage without one for a while. Public transport, particularly the train service, was very good, even in East Devon, and Arthur had a sturdy bicycle.

9

In the Day of Thy Power

During the autumn of 1952, as Arthur approached his thirtieth birthday, he first met David Lillie and soon discovered he had found another 'kindred spirit'. David was a stimulating and independent thinker who had, like Arthur, been strongly influenced by G.H. Lang and came from a Brethren background. Whereas Arthur was still closely linked and involved with the Brethren, David had left and was leading a small fellowship at Countess Wear, a housing estate on the edge of Exeter.

Arthur was fascinated to discover that David had not only received the baptism in the Spirit, but also spoke in tongues. He was far more sympathetic with the Pentecostals than Arthur, who still had reservations about such matters as tongues. Over the months that followed they talked and shared their experiences together and became close friends.

David had recently resigned from Barclays Bank for which he had worked for over twenty years. The bank wanted to transfer him to Leeds, a move he was not prepared to make. The fellowship at Countess Wear was developing, and he knew that that was where God wanted him to remain. He felt no specific call to full-time church work, and so, having left the bank, was looking for alternative employment.

Both men felt a bond with one another from the outset of their relationship, although their outlook and approach was quite different. Arthur's big interest was revival; he saw this as the primary answer to the needs of his day. David's major emphasis was the church; he had a clear vision for the restoration of church life to a New Testament pattern, and saw this as the key to the fulfilment of God's purposes.

Arthur found that David's views stimulated his thinking. He began to realise that the restoration of the church and revival were things that should go together; they were complementary areas. He also became much more open to receiving the gift of tongues; his subconscious fears about the gift were being dispelled; after all, David had received it, and he was still of sound mind!

Towards the end of May 1953, David and Arthur put on a small conference on the Holy Spirit, which was held at David's home in Countess Wear. Jack Hardwidge, Billy Ward and a number of other interested men and women were invited. Arthur took a non-Pentecostal stance, emphasising the baptism in the Spirit as an anointing of power for service and linking it to the believer's holiness of life. David emphasised the importance and place of the gifts of the Spirit in equipping Christians to serve God.

This was the start of a series of Saturday conferences which were held at Countess Wear about four times a year. Various speakers were invited to contribute, but the programme was never pre-planned. People attended, knowing there would be ministry, but with no guarantee of who would speak or on what subject. These things were left to the leading of the Holy Spirit on the day.

Arthur would regularly attend and participate in these conferences, and it was here that he began to get to know other men with more of a Pentecostal background and emphasis. Cecil Cousen from Bradford was one of the regular speakers. While a pastor in the Apostolic Church, he had received a deep experience of God's power through the 'Latter Rain' movement in Canada. When he returned home to share this with his own denomination it was not received, and he had left the Apostolic Church to form an independent fellowship.

It was during some of these early 'charismatic' conferences that Arthur first heard the gifts of tongues, interpretation and prophecy exercised publicly. Far from being put off, he had an instinctive sense that they were genuine. However, some of the Pentecostals he met maintained that unless you had spoken in tongues you were not baptised in the Spirit. Arthur strongly resisted this viewpoint and could see no scriptural justification for such a dogmatic stance. He had received no such gift, but knew he was baptised in the Spirit.

Early in 1953, God spoke to Arthur about the need to spend an extended period of time waiting on God. He felt that he should give up ministry for an indefinite period, stay at home, and give himself to prayer and seeking God.

When he shared this with some of his friends, they urged him to reconsider. Had he really heard from God? Preaching was his only visible source of financial support, and surely the scriptural principle was 'if a man does not work, neither shall he eat'. God expects us to work for our living, and Arthur had a responsibility to provide for his wife and son. He began to waver. Perhaps he had misinterpreted what God was saying. His friends certainly seemed to have some justification for their doubts. He asked God to confirm his will clearly.

In their living room, Arthur and Eileen had a calendar with a 'tear-off' Scripture verse for each day of the year. Within a few days God used this to give him the clear answer he was seeking. The verse for the day was taken from God's words to Elijah in 1 Kings chapter 17: 'Get thee hence, turn thee eastward, and hide thyself by the brook Cherith. . . . I have commanded the ravens to feed thee there.'

That sealed it! For a period of eight months Arthur took no meetings at all. They had no savings, and lived from hand to mouth. Day by day, God would provide their needs in different ways. Some friends provided personal gifts, others would drop by and leave some food, or a few logs for the fire. Most of these people had no idea of their circumstances.

Very soon any tins left in Eileen's cupboard were gone, and they had no reserves to fall back on. Jonathan was just three years old, but they always managed to ensure that he received the food he needed, even if they had to resort to fairly strange meals themselves.

For both Arthur and Eileen this was a significant time. Their faith was being tested, but they were proving the faithfulness of God. It was thrilling to see the many different ways he used to provide their needs. God was calling them to be radical in their obedience to him. If he told them to do something, then it was his responsibility to provide all that they needed. They did not always find it easy when dinner was potatoes and carrots yet again! But God knew their needs, and they realised he would not let them go hungry.

During this period, Arthur began to see that there was a great need for many Christians throughout the country to catch hold of the vision for revival and to start praying. Realising that there was very little reading material available that inspired and promoted this vision, he felt God prompting him to write something on the subject.

Not having written before, he thought initially in terms of a twenty-page booklet. However, he soon realised that it would be impossible to discharge this burden in so short a work; it would have to be a more substantial book. He began to plan, and looked out all the reading material he could find on the revivals of the past.

By the time Arthur felt God giving him the go-ahead

to start taking meetings again, they had run out of most of their essential supplies, and had no money to replace them. The cooker used bottled gas, which had all gone, and so they became adept at boiling the kettle and cooking on the log fire in the living room. Their meals were reduced to a very limited menu.

To make matters worse, Eileen's parents were due to come and stay with them for a few days. They found it hard to understand the concept of 'living by faith', and Arthur and Eileen were always careful to hide from them the fact that they often had no money. They felt it would somehow be letting God down if Mr and Mrs Hemingway were to discover just how little they lived on, and prayed that God would provide the finances to buy in plenty of food.

The day of their visit arrived, but still no money. Arthur and Eileen eagerly waited for the postman to come, but again—nothing! They could not see any way out of the situation. What did God have in mind? They felt severely tested in their faith, and Arthur, as the breadwinner, did not relish the prospect of having to explain their predicament to his in-laws.

Eileen knew that the first thing her parents would want on arrival was a cup of tea with sugar. They had none! The problem would be apparent within the first five minutes. As it got near the time they were due to arrive, Arthur occupied himself by cleaning the outside windows of the house. It at least gave an impression of some activity! He still wondered if some unexpected caller would turn up at the last minute, bringing miraculous provision. No one did.

Mr and Mrs Hemingway arrived, and Eileen put on the kettle. To stretch their legs after their journey, they decided to walk down to the village shop and spend their food coupons. A number of foods were still rationed, including sugar. They arrived back with no idea that they had just supplied the sugar to go with their long-awaited cup of tea!

When they saw that Eileen was boiling the kettle on

the fire, being 'townies', they just assumed that this was one of the hazards of country life. Eileen explained that the calor-gas had run out, and they probably thought it was difficult to get it delivered promptly to a little country village. She did not enlighten them. So far, so good, but they still had no money to buy any food for the next day.

As they sat around the fire in the living room that evening, Eileen's mother opened her purse and produced some money. Among Arthur and Eileen's wedding presents were two bone-china tea services, and Mrs Hemingway had offered to buy one of these from them so that they could get something more practical. By way of 'comfort' she assured them that they could have it back one day.

This was the least of their concerns; they just needed the money! It enabled them to buy the provisions they needed, and Eileen's parents never knew how close they had come to financial embarrassment.

☆　　☆　　☆

In 1955 Arthur finally completed his manuscript. His title was *In the Day of Thy Power—the Scriptural Principles of Revival*, and it had taken him over two years to write. It was a lengthy work of over 90,000 words, certainly not aimed at the casual reader. He asked Duncan Campbell if he would write the foreword, a request to which he willingly agreed.

In the Day of Thy Power was the expression of a deep, heart-felt burden. Arthur started the book with a description of the experiences that had triggered this burden for revival: his visits to Wales as a boy, and to the Hebrides in 1951. He then set out in the first chapter to define revival.

> Revival can never be explained in terms of activity, organisation, meetings, personalities, preaching. These may or may not be involved in the work, but they do not and cannot

account for the effects produced. Revival is essentially a manifestation of God; it has the stamp of Deity upon it, which even the unregenerate and uninitiated are quick to recognise. Revival must of necessity make an impact on the community, and this is one of the means by which we may distinguish it from the more usual operations of the Holy Spirit.

Revival is not always popular or universally accepted, but invariably arouses suspicion, fear and opposition in those who have not experienced it for themselves. Duncan Campbell made particular reference to this section of the book in his foreword:

> Readers will do well to ponder the contents of Chapter Two, 'A Sign Spoken Against'. Here Mr. Wallis cuts right across the popular approach and appeal. How arresting are his words: 'If we find a revival that is not spoken against we had better look again to ensure that it is a revival.'

One of Arthur's main purposes was to establish the scriptural basis for revival, and he related it back to the Old Testament promises to 'pour water upon him that is thirsty and floods upon the dry ground'. It is a sovereign outpouring of the Holy Spirit which is an essential part of God's divine strategy. There are a number of distinctive features of revival and, to outline these, Arthur took two chapters which formed the heart of the book.

> Divine sovereignty. . . . God is sovereign, and his sovereignty is revealed not only in the timing of every revival movement, but in the manner and measure of the Spirit's working.
> Spiritual preparation. . . . The word of God presents to us side by side the two foundation stones of every revival—the sovereignty of God and the preparedness of man. Because we cannot understand how they harmonise is no reason for emphasising one at the expense of the other.
> Suddenness. . . . In revival God works suddenly and unexpectedly.
> Spontaneous working. . . . It is the result of a divine and not a human impulse.
> God-consciousness. . . . Wherever the Spirit of God is

poured out saints and sinners alike are made acutely aware of the presence of the Almighty.

Anointed vessels. . . . A fresh emphasis on the person and work of the Holy Spirit.

Supernatural manifestation. . . . Never is the church nearer to the spirit and power of the first century than in times of revival.

Divine magnetism. . . . We may be sure that when God begins to work the people will be there, drawn not by invitation or persuasion, but by that divine magnetism that operates in revival.

Apostolic preaching. . . . spontaneous . . . anointed . . . fearless . . . Christ-centred. Apostolic preaching is not marked by its beautiful diction, or literary polish, or cleverness of expression . . . but operates 'in demonstration of the Spirit and of power'.

Superabundant blessing. . . . When God opens the windows of heaven and pours out such a blessing that there is not room enough to receive it.

Divine simplicity. . . . New wine requires new wine-skins. . . . A movement of the Spirit can only be contained by the organisation of the spirit, and that organisation is characterised by simplicity.

Having covered in detail the characteristic of revival, Arthur's next objective was to look at the conditions that God requires of his people before they can receive the outpouring of the Spirit. This section was based on the key scripture: 'Break up your fallow ground: for it is time to seek the Lord, till he come and rain righteousness upon you' (Hos 10:12).

'Break up your fallow ground'—that is heart-preparation; 'for it is time to seek the Lord, till. . .'—that is prevailing prayer; 'he come and rain righteousness upon you'—that is spiritual revival. Here then are set before us the two all-inclusive conditions: heart-preparation and prevailing prayer. We cannot rightly separate them, for, as the verse suggests, they are intimately related.

The section on prevailing prayer, which ran to sixty pages, could almost have been a book in its own right. After this, Arthur went on to deal with other aspects of the process of preparation for revival. He showed how God uses prophetic forerunners like John the Baptist to 'prepare the way of the Lord'. The message of the forerunner is primarily destructive:

> The very word 'prepare' contains the idea of casting out, emptying, and clearing as a field before planting. Destruction, ruthless and thorough, must precede the greater work of construction that is to follow. It takes a man who 'fears no one but God and hates nothing but sin' to proclaim the message of the forerunner.

Another essential aspect of the preparation process involves facing up to the fact that there is always a price to be paid in revival.

> It is an easy matter to pray for revival without realising what is involved, but it is quite another thing to pray with a clear appreciation of the price that must be paid. There may well be Christians praying for revival who, if they knew the implications, would be crying to God not to send it. With some there may be a willingness to face up to the question of sin, but an unwillingness to face up to the question of sacrifice; yet the latter is as much bound up with the conditions of blessing as the former.

A people ready and prepared for revival will not only manifest a willingness for sacrifice, but they will also have a spirit of expectancy. They will know how to discern 'the signs of the times' and will be tuned in to the fact that God is about to do a new thing. Arthur's final chapter was entitled 'The Solemn Alternative' and in it he warned that the only alternative to revival is the judgement of God.

> Strange though it may seem, there are distinct similarities between the ways of God in revival and in judgement. . . . There is an element of judgement in every revival. But it is also true that judgement is the solemn alternative to revival. The purifying and quickening of the people of God are a moral and spiritual necessity. Because of his very nature, God cannot and will not permit spiritual decline to continue unchecked. He is ever halting and reversing the trend of the

times by means of revival—or judgement. Where his people
are not prepared for the one, they shut themselves up to the
other.

He concluded with a call to God's people to give
themselves sacrificially to prayer and preparation for a
fresh outpouring of God's Spirit in revival power. It had
turned out to be a much longer work than Arthur had at
first anticipated, but he knew that in it he had discharged the burden and passion of his heart. He decided to
dedicate the book to the memory of his father, and
added a front page to his manuscript with the following
words:

To the memory of my father, REGINALD WALLIS,
through whose life and ministry I was drawn to Christ, and
through whose early death I was called to the work of an
evangelist, this, my first book, is affectionately dedicated.

As he sent it off to various leading Christian
publishers it was as if he was sending off part of himself,
and he felt somewhat vulnerable. He had exposed his
deepest desires and longings, and it left him feeling a
little naked. He awaited their response with a mixture of
eager anticipation and trepidation.

He had also sent the manuscript to several of his close
friends, including Leith Samuel and G.H. Lang. Their
overall appreciation of it was warm and genuine, and
any criticism was constructive. Both found that Arthur's
biblical exegesis was sound, but thought that prospective
publishers might find it rather too lengthy. Leith felt
that some of the later chapters, although great reading,
were not strictly relevant to the main theme. Nevertheless he considered that the book had the potential to
become a classic on revival.

The letters which Arthur received back from the
publishers were not encouraging. The fears that they
would find it too heavy and too long were justified, and
their initial reactions were summed up by the following
comments from one of their anonymous readers:

The main fault of this book is indicated in its dedication; it is a first book. Only the rare born writer can write a good first book of over 90,000 words. Mr. Wallis had put into this work of love three or four books, all of which might be of real value as separate works; but in its present form it is too heavy, too disconnected, too long. To include a manual on Christian living and on true prayer in a work on revival means an inadequate treatment of these subjects.

Arthur prayed much about these criticisms, but did not feel he should undergo a major restructuring of the book. To him, the sections on prayer and the other aspects of the Christian life were an important aspect of his theme. His purpose was not simply to provide a theoretical treatise on the subject of revival, but to inspire his readers to fulfil the conditions of revival in their own lives—to pray, to humble themselves before God, and to seek him for an outpouring of the Spirit. He felt that the critics had merely looked at it through publishers' eyes, and although he knew some of their criticisms were accurate, he felt they had missed the burden of the book.

Arthur began to look around for an alternative publisher, and was even prepared to forego his own royalties in order to get the book in print. His friends strongly discouraged him from doing this, assuring him that 'a worker is worthy of his hire'. After some consideration, he decided to try the Christian Literature Crusade. Although CLC was more of a faith-based mission than a publisher, they had begun producing a number of their own publications and he felt they would be responsive to the spirit of the book.

Their reaction was entirely positive. They felt the book conveyed a message that Christians needed to hear, and they enthusiastically took hold of it among their own workers. With limited financial resources, to publish a substantial work of this sort was a real step of faith for CLC, but they committed themselves to it wholeheartedly.

In June 1956, *In the Day of Thy Power* was published in hardback cover, priced twelve shillings and sixpence. Norman Grubb, the International Secretary of the Worldwide Evangelisation Crusade, wrote a prepublication review which CLC used in their promotional material.

> Thorough, balanced, soaked in the Scriptures which form his text-book, with plentiful quotations from eye-witnesses of revival, he has written what may become a classic on the subject.
>
> Others have given us adequate histories of revival, Arthur Wallis has given us the inescapable Biblical authority for such 'times of refreshing from the presence of the Lord'. . . . As I read the manuscript, it had the effect of confronting me with 'the word of the Lord' and demanding an answer. I gave it. I believe it will have a like effect on all who read it with 'ears to hear'.

In the Day of Thy Power received favourable reviews in much of the Christian Press.

> This is one of the most challenging books we have seen for years.
>
> *The Harvester*

> It would be a cold heart indeed that was not stirred by this book: stirred to acknowledge afresh the tragic state of Christ's church today; stirred to ponder anew the power and promises of our God: stirred as never before to plead with God to send the wind and the fire.
>
> *Intervarsity*

> Such a book as this should be read by every Christian; it should be read prayerfully and with the heart open to God's searching gaze. Then, surely, revival would come to the Church of God to accomplish the evangelisation of the world in this generation.
>
> *Floodtide*

This is a fascinating and soul-stirring book, but it should not be embarked upon by those who do not want to be challenged frequently and forcibly.

Crusade

In face of the challenge presented by this book, minor differences of Biblical interpretation are of small concern; if it were heeded, the great thing would happen.

Life of Faith

Perhaps even more encouraging to Arthur were the letters he began to receive which told of the effect that *In the Day of Thy Power* was having on those who had read it. Groups of ministers were using it as a basis for study and prayer, churches were taking its message to heart, and many individuals were beginning to believe and pray for revival. Whatever faults the book may have had from a literary point of view, God was using it to challenge and inspire many of his people to start expecting 'a new thing'.

10

Door-to-Door

Someone who became a close friend of Arthur's in the mid 1950s was Bill Patton. Bill worked for Devon County Council in Exeter and lived at West Hill, just outside Ottery St Mary. They first met in 1954 when Arthur was invited to speak at the small chapel that Bill attended. Many of the congregation were not born-again Christians, and so someone who came and preached a clear gospel message was just up Bill's street. He introduced himself after the meeting, and they established an immediate rapport.

Arthur was still very committed to evangelism in the Talaton area, despite the seeming unsuccess of previous attempts. He believed that a combination of prayer and ongoing evangelism would lead to revival breaking out in the area. Bill shared this conviction and they decided to work together in door-to-door visitation.

They defined the area they wanted to cover. It constituted about 100 square miles of Devon countryside broadly situated between the A30 road near Ottery St Mary and the A38 Exeter to Cullompton road. The area contained no towns, but a number of villages: Feniton, Payhembury, Plymtree, Clyst Hydon, Whimple, Clyst St Lawrence, Broad Clyst and Talaton, and many scattered houses and farms. Their aim was to visit every home with the gospel.

This work took them several years. Most weekends, if

118

Arthur was not away preaching, they would devote an afternoon to visiting. They systematically worked their way round the area, going from house to house on their bicycles.

At each house they would knock on the door and introduce themselves, making it clear they were not Jehovah's Witnesses but local Christians who wanted to speak about the Lord Jesus. They took a supply of gospel tracts and other Christian literature to leave with people. Arthur had a little book in which he would enter the name and address of anyone who seemed particularly interested.

The work had its hazards, most of which had four legs and a bark! On one occasion, the owner of the house was obviously out when they knocked on the door, although the growling noise from inside the door indicated that intruders would enter at their peril. As Arthur went to stuff a tract through the door, the dog, who had obviously practised on the postman, was ready for him. He just managed to withdraw his hand without losing any fingers. At the next house he turned to Bill and said wryly, 'You can do this one!'

One wet winter's afternoon they happened to call on a farmer who had obviously just sat down to relax and read his Sunday paper. He did not take kindly to his peace being interrupted by these two bedraggled strangers.

'I don't want anything to do with religion,' he said gruffly, and proceeded to set his dogs on them. As they beat a hasty retreat, Arthur called back, 'It is appointed unto man but once to die!' This elicited a further, unprintable response from the farmer, but fortunately Arthur and Bill were already peddling away rapidly down the lane before he had time to get out his shotgun.

There were only a limited number of suitable tracts and Christian booklets available, so Arthur decided to produce a gospel broadsheet. Getting the idea from The Forge House, they called it *The Anvil*, and several editions were printed and distributed around the area.

All this door-to-door evangelism resulted in three people turning to Christ. It was not much by way of immediate results for all the hard work and effort they had put in, but they were encouraged to believe that a lot of seed had been sown that would eventually bear fruit. Others had worked in the area before, and at one local farm a barn had been used to hold a weekly gospel meeting. They were surprised at the number of people they met who had been to these meetings in the past.

On one occasion Arthur and Bill visited a house at Payhembury and discovered that the lady living there had recently lost her husband in an horrific farming accident. He had been caught up in a threshing machine. They were able to talk and pray with her, and Arthur arranged for Eileen to visit her later.

Another area of outreach that Bill felt called to was to share the gospel among the down-and-outs at the Exeter 'Doss House'. He invited Arthur to join him and for a couple of years they visited the Doss House every week if they could, and sat and talked to the men about the Lord Jesus.

On the whole they were received well, and the worst part of the experience was having to drink the cocoa the men were given for supper. It tasted quite unlike anything Arthur had ever drunk or ever wanted to drink again! One man, Henry Hall, gave his life to Christ and they had the joy of baptising him in the River Exe at Countess Wear.

☆   ☆   ☆

The publication of *In the Day of Thy Power* was resulting in an increasing number of openings to Arthur to speak in various churches and prayer groups. In accepting speaking invitations he continued to bring each situation before God, asking him to confirm his will. He resisted the temptation to get fully booked for months ahead, still believing that it was important to leave room in his diary for the outbreak of revival and the unexpected opportunities that this might bring.

Not every unexpected opportunity was a result of revival, however, and one Thursday Arthur received an urgent telephone call from a Baptist minister in Bath. He had recently been appointed to the church and as part of his induction week a special series of meetings was being held, culminating that Saturday with a visit from Dr Martyn Lloyd-Jones.

He had just heard that the Doctor had been taken ill and was unable to come. As this meeting was to be the highlight of the week, he was understandably concerned as to whether he could find a suitable replacement at just two days' notice. Would Arthur be able to step in and take the Doctor's place?

It so happened that Arthur was free and so he agreed, but he couldn't help wondering how the congregation would overcome their disappointment at this last minute substitution. His trepidation at stepping into Dr Martyn Lloyd-Jones' shoes was not alleviated by the introduction he received two days later.

The chairman of the meeting had explained why Dr Lloyd-Jones was unable to come. 'It reminds me of a story I once heard,' he continued. 'A family were travelling in their car and were getting quite tired after a long journey. To their delight they spotted a sign which said "Afternoon Teas. Two miles ahead. Strawberries and Cream." This was just what they needed to revive their flagging spirits: strawberries and cream. Two miles later they pulled into the tea rooms and ordered their strawberries and cream. "I'm very sorry," said the waitress, "but we've run out of strawberries and cream. All we have left is prunes and custard."'

Arthur took the joke in good heart. 'Prunes and custard takes me back to my school-days,' he said as he started his address. 'We always thought that prunes were rather like missionaries: noble specimens sent into the dark interior to do good!' As the laughter died down he added, 'It may not be strawberries and cream today but, by the time we're through, I trust you'll feel that the prunes and custard have done you good!'

In August 1957, a group of friends decided to go on a week-long evangelistic 'trek' through some of the Devon villages. There were five in all, Arthur, Jack Hardwidge, David Lillie, Billy Ward and Terry Mitchell, a local builder. They set out, trusting that God would cover all their expenses. Jack kept a record of this expedition in his diary.

Monday 12th August

Travelled by bus and van to Blackborough where we all met.

Left at 1.10 pm and walked to Uffculme, contacting very few people and having lunch in a field nearby.

Met Bill Bedford—worked in Uffculme from 3 pm to 5.30—worked in pairs—invited in a few times—of six contacts, two seemed to be believers.

Left at 5.45 and walked to The Lamb—visited all the houses we could see—no outstanding contacts.

Walked on to Burlescombe, calling on the way—arrived at Canonsleigh Barton at about 8.45—Mr & Mrs Woolway received us well—retired after supper.

My feet have lasted well—walked about 10 miles today—the Lord has provided £4 12s 6d in the kitty.

Tuesday 13th August

Rose early—had a time in the open with the Lord—after a good breakfast from Mrs Woolway we set off over the hill.

Had a meal in the open after prayer and meditation on Revelation 1.

After 2 pm pushed on to Holcombe Rogus where we began visiting—morning visiting is not good—evening is best of all for contacts—energy is not sufficient to work all day—Billy and I found the going barren, so we sought the Lord and he brought us to a woman with a ready heart—she left us intending to go in and receive the Lord—praise him!

Working with Arthur we had a mixed reception—one man in a cycle-shop we hope was helped—two spiritists turned us out, she was clearly possessed, probably he as well—we ought to have witnessed directly of the victory of Christ—am learning much—one woman, a churchgoer, listened embarrassed but took a 'Becoming a Christian'.

Tea was taken outside Holcombe Rogus—we still have some of the food we brought with us. Then Arthur and Terry did Westleigh while Billy, David and I did Burlescombe—good contacts with a farmer's wife and a young labourer—the butcher ahead of us was not helping, so we broke off and sought the Lord—on returning we met a young woman, Mrs *****, in the first Council House, and left her inclined to trust the Lord.

Back to Canonsleigh Barton at 9.15—7 miles today.

Wednesday 14th August

Left Burlescombe soon after breakfast and a little prayer—the Woolways have been most kind to us.

Walked to Holcombe Rogus and saw Mrs ***** who said she had received the Lord, but had no evident joy.

Had lunch under a haystack on a farm—a make-do meal—did visiting in Hockworthy—David and Billy met Mr ***** who seemed inclined to throw his ability and life into Christian service—a one hour talk—we had pushed on—good contacts at Staple Cross—spoke with an old woman whose mother had been a believer—she seemed moved.

The way seemed long—hoped for a lift but no cars came—had a doughcake and some jam tarts from a baker on the road—entered Bampton at about 6.15—too late to buy food, but the Lord provided a bed and breakfast where we stayed the night—they gave us a meal of steak and kidney pie, beans, gooseberries etc.

Visited in evening—found two Christians and met the Baptist pastor—Arthur and Billy met a pair of Christian West Indians—David had a good talk with a boy—contact with folk in the streets until late.

10 miles today.

Thursday 15th August

Left bed and breakfast at about 10.30 to walk to Dulverton—it rained a little all the way—reached

Dulverton—just caught the shops, which were closing for early-closing day—had lunch by the river—deposited our packs at the lodgings.

Walked to the new housing estate—the sun shone—it was cold, but the Lord gave us a wonderful time—many were most receptive—no-one turned us away—good contacts which may lead to conversions—were not impressed with the Congregationals we met.

Returned to town to get a meal—all closed, but the Lord is good, one man cooked a meal in his tea-shop for 3 shillings a head—we each put £1 in the kitty.

Talked to people in the streets—then to bed.

Friday 16th August

Left the lodgings quite early—met Mr and Mrs **** near the town-hall, he gave us £5, Hallelujah—found a 10 shilling note on the street which we handed in to the police station—hoped to get this back, it would just meet our needs, but a woman claimed she had lost it.

Left Dulverton—had lunch by the stream at Brushford—a hot day—Billy stayed to do Brushford and then returned from Dulverton station—we pushed on to Bampton and did the housing estates—worked with Arthur and had a toughish time, but one woman, Mrs ****** said she was moved to accept Christ—we stopped as people were having tea, and went into Bampton to get Billy's hat and some pop—afterwards finished the remaining houses—one good contact.

Returned by train, praising God, with 4 pence left after all fares were paid to Taunton, Exeter and Exmouth—a wonderful experience of God's power—arrived in Exeter at 8.30.

They came away, having enjoyed the experience, but feeling that God was saying something more. Although it was good to preach the gospel and see people saved, this was not enough. They needed to find some way of looking after them, providing ongoing care, and building them up in their new-found faith. They had set out on their 'evangelistic trek' with no thought or plan as to how this was to be achieved. It was becoming apparent to each of them that the most effective form of evangelism, certainly in terms of lasting fruitfulness, is that which is based on a local church which can provide ongoing contact and support.

11

A Vision for the Church

During the first few years of their marriage, Arthur and Eileen attended the local Brethren Assembly in Ottery St Mary, about four miles from Talaton. As Arthur's views on the baptism and gifts of the Spirit developed, it became increasingly difficult to remain 'in fellowship' at a Brethren assembly which strongly opposed these things. The problem was that they had no car and there were very few other evangelical churches within walking or cycling distance of Talaton.

The nearest alternative was the Sidmouth Junction Union Chapel at Feniton, about two miles away. This small Baptist chapel had sprung out of a mini-revival among the railway workers in the nineteenth century, at the time the Waterloo to Exeter railway line was built, and was just a hundred yards from Sidmouth Junction railway station. Unusually for a Baptist chapel, it had no baptistry and no pastor, but was run by two elderly ladies, Mrs Syms and Miss Ridge. They booked evangelical preachers Sunday by Sunday and had been praying for new people to boost the tiny congregation. Arthur and Eileen both felt it was right to leave the Brethren and start attending here.

The services followed a traditional Baptist pattern, not exactly in line with Arthur's vision for a New Testament church, and he explained that they were only coming temporarily until something started in Talaton.

Nonetheless they were received and welcomed very warmly, and rumours began to circulate that Arthur Wallis had left the Brethren and joined the Baptists. The truth, but not quite the whole truth!

The whole question of the church and how it should function was becoming increasingly important in Arthur's thinking. He could see that, before any revival could become lasting and effective, a considerable shake-up in church life and structure was needed. David Lillie played a considerable part in influencing Arthur's thinking in this way, and during the summer of 1957, he called in on Arthur to share an idea which was buzzing around in his mind.

'Arthur,' he said, 'I feel there's a need for the vision for the church to be shared among a wider circle of men. While I was up in Oxfordshire last week I started to write down a list of people I think we should invite to come to a residential conference for a few days to discuss this whole issue.'

Arthur looked down David's list and laughed. Many were well-known evangelists and Bible teachers, busy men with successful ministries. 'Who are we that we could invite these men?' he replied.

David was still convinced it was a good idea, and so Arthur promised him he would pray about it. They met several times during the remainder of the year and Arthur gradually became more and more enthusiastic about the concept.

'I have been thinking again about your idea of a conference. How about getting together for half a day to pray about it?' he suggested to David one day. 'Perhaps we could book some provisional dates at a conference centre and then write to the people we want to invite. We would quickly assess whether the reaction was sufficiently positive to go ahead and confirm the booking.'

Early in 1958 they met together to pray and plan. They had found some suitable dates in May of that year when Croylands Conference Centre at Exmouth was free, and put together a convening letter.

Many thoughtful Christians are feeling the challenge of the present world situation, and are burdened by the immensity of the spiritual need on every hand, and the apparent inadequacy of the church to grapple with the task. . . . One wonders how the present social order can survive apart from a spiritual revival.

And the churches, what are they doing? One hears on every hand reports of spiritual decline, internal strife, world conformity. . . . Ministry has become light and lifeless. Scriptural principles are being abandoned and unspiritual features introduced to attract new adherents. . . .

Thank God, however there is another side of the story. Faced with the challenge of the cross, and the need of the hour, some of God's people here and there are being driven to their knees by an earnest desire to know God's mind for themselves and their ministry, and to receive further light on the larger issues affecting the church, its function, mission and destiny. Undoubtedly, God has been speaking to many hearts. . . .

Thus, we find ourselves compelled to test the traditions which have so largely conditioned our thinking by the clear, unequivocal teaching of the Word of God. Much which hitherto we had accepted without question, has thus proved to be unsound. . . .

There is a growing conviction that God will yet grant, in response to believing prayer, another gracious visitation of the Holy Spirit in reviving grace. Many are being stirred to pray to this end. . . . It is also our conviction that God is raising up men, taught of the Spirit according to the Word, who will thus be . . . qualified to cherish and feed the flock of God in the day of visitation.

Suggestion was then made of holding a conference at Exmouth from 7th–10th May 1958, in order that various men might come together, spend time praying together, and exchange ideas. The conference title was 'The Church of Jesus Christ—Its Purity, Power, Pattern and Programme in the Context of Today'.

The response was positive, the conference arrangements were confirmed, and around thirty men came together on Wednesday 7th May 1958. That evening David Lillie gave an introductory talk based on Ephesians chapter 1. He maintained that the supreme function of the church of Jesus Christ was 'to be to the praise of his glory'. Only a church of purity and power could fulfil this great purpose, but it must also be a church built according to God's plan, a 'holy temple'.

> So here the figure of a building is introduced, and reflecting upon that, we realise that this building has an architect, and that he is building according to his own specifications, and not according to ours; and he has a programme. . . . We may be sure that the great architect who has begun this programme is going to see it through to completion. . . .
>
> I believe that we are at the dawn of a new day of restoration when God's blessing shall rest increasingly upon the ministry of churches which, though local in setting, are a true expression of the one church, which is his body.

The conference programme was designed to leave plenty of opportunity at the end of each session for discussion, and ample free time for informal fellowship and exchange of ideas. A lively discussion developed on the first night about the implications of the conference programme and the need to bring church practice back to the test of Scripture.

The next morning Arthur spoke on 'The Purity of the Church'. He believed strongly that holiness and purity of life were foundational areas that needed to be addressed, and a vital prerequisite to God's power being released. He outlined the means by which our lives are purified—the blood of Jesus, the water of the Spirit, and the fire of God, and concluded his message by challenging his audience to seek God's purity in the way they thought, the way they lived, and the way they prayed.

On Thursday evening, Cecil Cousen spoke about the power of the Spirit. His message centred on the baptism of the Holy Spirit as the means of equipping the church with power. He brought out the fact that God's promise of the Spirit is based, not on our own righteousness, but on our inheritance as sons of God.

> We are not weak and useless and helpless and ineffective, leaving undone all the things that we ought to do, and doing those things that we should not do; miserable offenders, year after year after year. We are the sons of God in Christ Jesus, and we are anointed with the Holy Ghost that we might minister in his name, and bring the anointing of God and the power of God and the kingdom of heaven into the lives of men and women.

Not all who attended the conference were 'pentecostal' or 'charismatic' in persuasion, but God was at work, mainly behind the scenes, in opening men up to the Holy Spirit. Cecil Cousen's address was an important catalyst in this, and although there was no public prayer for people to receive the baptism, there was a lot of private 'ministry' involving Cecil in particular.

Before the conference, David and Arthur had decided that there would be no display of spiritual gifts. They felt that this would be likely to embarrass some who, although seemingly open in their minds, were certainly not pentecostal in their experience. Arthur was somewhat surprised therefore when, in the middle of one of the times of prayer, David suddenly started speaking out in tongues! It seemed totally out of keeping with his character; he was normally very level-headed and well controlled. Evidently God's intentions were somewhat less restrained than theirs! The Holy Spirit had come upon David in such a powerful way that he felt compelled to exercise his gift rather than risk disobeying God.

On Friday the two sessions were taken up with 'The Pattern and the Programme of the Church'. In the first of these, Metcalfe Collier based his talk on the Gospels and the Acts of the Apostles. In the second, Roger

Forster took a detailed look at this theme in the epistles. There was much talk about the need for a right pattern of church life to accompany the great commission to 'go and make disciples of all nations'.

After the conference Arthur and David took on the task of going through the tapes of the proceedings and putting together a conference report to circulate among the delegates. It was a helpful way for them to crystallise the key things that God had been saying. The general feedback they received was very positive and only one person reacted visibly against the 'pentecostal element'.

In 1961, the time came for Jonathan, now aged eleven, to start his secondary school education. Until now, he had attended the village primary school at Talaton, a small country school run by two spinsters. This school was just a hundred yards from The Forge House, in a small thatched building containing just two classrooms, one for each teacher.

With an age range of five to eleven, and only one class for infants and one for juniors, the education at Talaton School was rather limited although the atmosphere was very personal and friendly. The fact that Jonathan attended the local school helped Arthur and Eileen to integrate into village life and become more accepted by the locals.

Arthur had seriously considered sending Jonathan to his old school, Monkton Combe. This would have been a real step of faith, as he and Eileen did not have the necessary money, and he eventually decided against it. It would be preferable (and cheaper!) to send his son to a local school where he would be exposed to normal life and could receive sound spiritual training at home.

After considering the various possibilities, they decided to try and get Jonathan into Exeter School, a 'direct grant' school. Although essentially a private school, the direct grant system provided a means whereby the state would cover a proportion of the fees, dependent on the parents' income. There were separate entrance examinations for the school, and Jonathan needed to take extra study courses in preparation. The teachers at Talaton were very helpful, Arthur and Eileen disciplined him to get down to a regular programme of study, and he did well enough in the exam to be accepted into the school. As Arthur and Eileen's income was very low, they qualified for a full grant to cover the school fees.

In the summer of 1961, David Lillie arranged a house-party at Heatree House at Manaton, on Dartmoor. It was intended to be more of a family holiday than a conference, but a meeting was arranged each evening. There was plenty of opportunity for informal fellowship among the adults, and a variety of activities organised for the children. Along with David and Kathleen Lillie and their two children, the Wallis family was there in force, Ma Wallis, Arthur, Eileen and Jonathan, and Peter and Meg with their five children, Ruth, Heather, Mary, Timothy and Richard, who was just a baby.

In the relaxed holiday atmosphere at Heatree House the Holy Spirit began moving in a remarkable way, and a key figure was Edgar Trout. Edgar was from a Methodist background, but had come into an experience of the baptism and gifts of the Holy Spirit after being miraculously healed of a fractured vertebra following a car accident. In 1960 he had gone into full-time Christian work, and was being particularly used by God in deliverance and exorcism.

One couple who were significantly touched by God at Manaton were Graham and Sylvia Perrins. Graham had attended the 1958 Exmouth conference and was working full time with the Brethren. As he was in his bedroom at Heatree House, praying in preparation for the evening meeting, God baptised him in the Holy Spirit and he suddenly found himself speaking in tongues.

Later that evening a group, including Arthur and Eileen, gathered for prayer in the lounge. Most were on their knees, but Edgar Trout was pacing up and down restlessly, looking as though he was ready to pounce on someone.

'Continue what you've been doing,' he suddenly said to Graham, who was praying silently. Graham immediately started speaking out loud with his newly acquired gift of tongues, and gradually became increasingly fluent.

'Now interpret that!' commanded Edgar, and Graham obeyed, speaking out the words that God gave him. Edgar then got him onto his feet. 'Right,' he said, 'now go and prophesy over Eileen Wallis.'

Feeling as if he'd been thrown in at the deep end, Graham moved across the room and prophesied a word of encouragement over Eileen. Both she and Arthur were 'earnestly desiring spiritual gifts'; although they had been baptised in the Holy Spirit for over ten years, neither had spoken in tongues or prophesied. They had been prayed for many times about this, but had received no such gift.

God had dealt with their fears and prejudices over spiritual gifts, and tongues in particular, and now they were genuinely open to receive this gift. Although God seemed to be meeting and blessing those round about them, they were still not 'breaking through'. At the end of the holiday they returned to Talaton somewhat frustrated, but all the more determined to continue seeking God until their prayers were answered.

☆   ☆   ☆

Arthur and David were feeling that the time was right for a further conference to pursue and develop the theme that had been started three years earlier at Exmouth. In June 1961, therefore, they sent out a convening letter.

More than three years have elapsed since a few of us met for a three day conference at Exmouth. . . . Many of us feel that we are still far from seeing a dynamic New Testament Church in action, either locally or on a wider scale.

Meanwhile, as we look out on the world around us, an ominous pattern of 'things to come' is clearly emerging. . . . We witness the rising tide of godlessness, with a decline in moral standards which is indeed alarming.

Where, then, is the true Church of Jesus Christ which should be facing this challenge? . . . Must it continue to be obscured and dishonoured by all the impedimenta of denominationalism, by its unbelief, its worldliness, its apathy?

Convinced that revival is the only answer we turn again . . . to the word of prophecy. Before us, from the pages of the New Testament, there rises THE CHURCH OF JESUS CHRIST, a glorious church, not having spot or wrinkle or any such thing. . . .

This, surely, is the Church which must arise at this hour through the mighty operation of the Holy Spirit! If this is our conviction, then we must be open, both individually and collectively to experience a mighty enduement of the Spirit of God in revival power . . . .

Feeling the need for this enduement and for clearer instructions regarding the function of the Church in the divine plan, it is felt that the time is ripe for some of us to come together to wait upon God and confer over these matters. . . .

And so, on Wednesday 27th September 1961, some forty people gathered together for a further conference at Cleve House, Belstone, near Okehampton in Devon. The house was ideal, completely secluded with a beautiful garden and magnificent views over the moors. The title for the conference was 'The Divine Purpose in the Institution of the Church—an Enquiry'.

As at Exmouth, a lot of time was allowed for prayer, waiting on God, and discussion, and the basic programme comprised four main sessions, geared to developing this theme from the Scriptures. Arthur was taking one of these sessions, and his talk, based on the epistles, was called 'The Divine Idea of the Local Church'.

The theme of his address centred on Paul's description of the church as the *body* of Christ. The more Arthur studied the church of the New Testament, the more he realised how much the modern-day church had moved away from true biblical principles. His message expressed a deep-felt longing for a return to a New Testament pattern of church life.

> I want to fasten our attention on this figure of 'the body'. . . . It is a figure that Paul loved and constantly used. . . . It applies primarily to the church universal, but since the church local is a microcosm or miniature of the church universal, it has its application to the local church also. . . .
>
> A body is a means of expression. . . . Though the Lord Jesus hàs returned to heaven, he still has a body here on earth to continue what he himself began to do and teach. . . .
>
> The figure of the body also suggests an organism rather than an organisation, and that is most important. An organisation has a kind of order, but it is the order of the creature; an organism possesses the order of the Creator . . . .

Arthur could see that, as human beings, we have a propensity to build up structures and organisations, and he wanted his listeners to understand the principles necessary for the functioning of 'the body', rather than to dwell on matters of outward practice. A right understanding of God's principles would soon reveal those practices which were clearly unacceptable. By the same token, differing practices may be equally acceptable expressions of the same underlying principles.

He started by looking at 'The Unity of the Body'. The true concept of the local church involves a group of believers deeply 'bonded and knit together'. Each member of a local body should have a real 'sense of belonging'.

> It avoids the situation so often seen today: folk loosely connected with a fellowship, tending to drift hither and thither sermon tasting; or a believer leaving his church and going elsewhere because he doesn't like the ministry, or the

preacher, or because he can't get on with his fellow Christians.

The next section of Arthur's talk was entitled 'The Completeness of the Body'. He felt strongly that each local church was intended to be complete in itself in union with Christ as head.

> For Christ is not only head of the universal church, he is also head of each local church. In him the local church is to be self-sufficient; it is to be self-governing, self-supporting, self-edifying, self-propagating.

Arthur could see no place for a denominational church structure:

> The church is to stand on its own feet and manage its own affairs. It is not to be dependent upon outside control, though warmly welcoming outside fellowship, and holding loving communion with other believers and other fellowships of believers. . . .
> This vital principle of the self sufficiency and completeness under Christ of each local church could save us from the formation of another denomination, from which may the Lord deliver us.

Arthur was not denying that there are men to whom God has given a ministry to the body of Christ as a whole, the 'Ephesians 4 ministries' of apostle, prophet, evangelist, pastor and teacher. However, these ministries did not overrule the fact that the prime responsibility and control of the local body lay with the local leaders.

> A body displays orderliness and control. The control is by the head, but it is effective through nerves and other organs. There are, in the local church, chosen and fitted leaders, by which the heavenly head exercises his control over the local body. Rule in the church is not to be a dictatorship—a one man rule, nor a democracy—any man rule; it is to be an oligarchy—the rule of the few. New Testament churches were governed by a team, a select body of men called elders.

How then are elders to be appointed? It is clearly important to know God's principles, and Arthur was keen to stress the prime importance of the ministry of the Holy Spirit in selecting and anointing men for this task:

> Notice these elders were not appointed by a vote of the church, or by any other human method, they were appointed by the Holy Spirit—'The Holy Spirit hath made you overseers' . . .
>
> In newly established churches it is usually the church planters who recognise and indicate whom the Holy Spirit has equipped as elders . . .

Arthur felt that this principle of a 'team' controlling and governing the church was vital. It provided a shared responsibility, without too much pressure falling on the shoulders of any one man, and it guarded against partiality and errors in judgement. Dictatorship is avoided and decisions are reached with a sense of unanimity.

Having talked about 'The Control of the Body' he then went on to consider 'The Function of the Body'. Every member of the body has a vital part to play, and a mature and successful church would be one where each member was encouraged to take up and fulfil his or her God-given role.

> The local church is not to be a passenger train where there are a few vital members—the driver, fireman, guard etc, doing a job of work while the rest are carried along; but it is to be a battleship where every man down to the newest able-bodied seaman has got a job to do, and knows what it is.

Arthur had believed for a long time that the baptism of the Holy Spirit was a vital experience for every believer. He was beginning to see now that this 'enduement with power for service' should primarily find its expression in and through the church. The gifts of the Spirit were given for the edification and building up of the believers, and for the expansion of the church through evangelism.

He could see that God was beginning to speak to people in various denominations and fellowships about the need for churches to follow the New Testament pattern. This was not without its dangers, and any 'new movement' could easily make the same mistakes as the movements of the past. God's people had repeatedly received revelation on new areas of truth, but then, instead of remaining open for God to continue to reveal new things, they became 'stuck' on the revelation of the past and a new denomination is formed. Arthur made particular reference to what he referred to as 'the twin dangers' of 'brethrenism' and 'pentecostalism'.

Firstly Brethrenism. Not everything that has found its way into 'Brethrenism' stems from the Word of God. As in all such movements there is an admixture of what is scriptural and what is traditional. There has been insistence on a certain pattern of procedure, a certain outward form. There is the supposition that what was revealed over a hundred years ago was God's last work on church order. This has all too often resulted in a sectarian spirit on the part of those who claim to be free from sectarianism.

The Brethren movement as a whole has rejected the enduement of the Spirit as a definite and distinct experience, and with it of course the supernatural gifts of the Spirit which, it is asserted, died with the apostolic age. This of course makes 1 Corinthians 14 with its teaching on the regulation of the gifts a museum piece. . . .

Closely associated with this is their silencing of the sisters in the general gatherings, so that 'the priesthood of all believers' becomes 'the priesthood of the male members'. . . .

Then Pentecostalism: God has used this movement to re-emphasize the baptism of the Holy Spirit, and to pioneer again in these end times the supernatural gifts of the Spirit. It has remained fundamental and evangelistic, but I am sure that we are all aware that there have been extremes and extravagances, both doctrinal and experimental. These have occurred largely because, with the emphasis upon the Spirit, there has not been sufficient emphasis on the Word. . . .

All too often a fetish has been made of one gift, such as tongues or healing; or the gifts of the Spirit have been emphasized at the expense of walking in the Spirit. There has not always been a willingness to bring all that is said or done, ostensibly in the Spirit, to the test of Holy Scripture. The Word is our only standard and by it everything must be judged.

Alas, there has often been a simulation of the movement of the Spirit; things have been worked up by human ingenuity, so that experiences have been soulish or superficial, rather than spiritual. . . . I would testify that I am open, wide open, to all that comes down from heaven, but I am fearful of that which man can work up.

As with 'Brethrenism' and church order, we must not assume that 'Pentecostalism' has received all the light there is on the Holy Spirit and spiritual gifts. There is more truth yet to break forth out of God's Holy Word.

Arthur concluded his address with a summary of his vision for the future. He felt that God was preparing his church for two main things: revival and persecution.

This divine idea of the local church is essential for the hour of revival. In its very nature it is a vessel shaped to receive such an outpouring of the Holy Spirit, and to conserve the fruits.

A few years ago God poured out his blessing on the Hebrides. As far as the churches are concerned the effects have largely disappeared. Why? I believe that one major reason is ecclesiasticism. When the Holy Spirit falls upon humble believers, they often receive gifts of power that they did not have before . . . Instead of finding opportunity to exercise their gifts within the sphere of the local church, the manifestation of the Spirit is quenched and suffocated by ministerial authority.

Then I believe that persecution is coming, perhaps greater persecution than this favoured land of ours has ever known. When the powers that be are determined to crush the church, or what may be more dangerous, to control it, I am convinced that it is only churches of this stamp—simple, spiritual, self-governing, endued with power and gifts of the Spirit, bonded and knit together, giving allegiance to Christ

alone—only such churches will survive the shocks and
afflictions of the time of the end.

Arthur's talk had been radical, and a lively discussion
took place. There were many practical questions
regarding the implications for church order and structure. The thorny issue of whether believers should leave
their denominational churches in order to join themselves to a 'New Testament church' was also touched
upon. They did not find ready answers to many of these
questions. The key thing, in Arthur's view, was that they
remained open to the leading and direction of the Holy
Spirit in seeking to put these principles into practice.

As he and David reviewed the Belstone conference,
there was a sense of excitement and expectancy in
Arthur's heart. He thought back to the vision that God
had given him, ten years previously, on the Island of
Lewis and the words from Isaiah chapter 43: 'Remember not the former things, nor consider the things of
old. Behold I am doing a new thing; now it springs
forth, do you not perceive it? I will make a way in the
wilderness, and rivers in the desert.'

God was doing 'a new thing'. It was going to involve
far more than just an isolated revival, and would encom-
pass a restoration of New Testament church life. Arthur
was convinced that this alone could pave the way for a
greater and more lasting revival than the church had
ever known before.

12

New Zealand Calling

In July 1962 a letter arrived from New Zealand. It was from the Committee of the Willow Park Easter Camp in Auckland.

> In praying and planning for Easter 1963, your name has been laid on the hearts of a number of our committee members. None knows you personally, but several have been blessed by reading your book *In the Day of Thy Power*.
>
> After prayerful consideration, the committee have unanimously agreed that we should write to you saying that you would be warmly welcomed as a speaker at Willow Park Camp next Easter, should the Lord direct you to New Zealand.

Arthur was surprised to receive an invitation from the other side of the world and could immediately see practical difficulties standing in the way of acceptance. The most important was the fact that Eileen was two months pregnant.

After the stillbirth in 1952, they had come to terms with the medical verdict of 'no more children', but never lost their desire for a larger family. On learning that advances in medical science had now made it possible to overcome the 'rhesus negative' factor, their hopes had risen and they consulted a specialist who confirmed this positive view. In his opinion there was no reason why

Eileen would not be able to have a successful pregnancy, but the baby would need to be closely monitored.

It did not prove to be as simple as that, however. Over the months that followed their consultation, Eileen suffered several miscarriages, and the consultant advocated a minor operation. This proved successful, and her latest pregnancy was proceeding satisfactorily.

With the baby due the following February, Arthur did not feel that he could accept this invitation. There could well be complications, and it would hardly be fair to Eileen if he disappeared off to New Zealand a couple of months after the birth. After praying about it, he wrote to the Willow Park Committee politely declining. That was that, or so he thought.

☆   ☆   ☆

In September 1962, Arthur and David held a third conference. This time the theme was 'The Present Ministry of the Holy Spirit'. The venue was Mamhead Park, a spacious country house situated between Exeter and Dawlish. As a conference centre it had room for more people than Belstone, and about seventy attended, half of whom were 'newcomers' who had not been at the previous conferences.

Among these newcomers was Bryn Jones, a young Welshman in his early twenties. He had first heard Arthur preach in 1956 when, as a teenager, he attended a meeting at the Bible College of Wales in Swansea. Bryn came from a South Wales coal-mining family. After his conversion to Christ in his teens he felt clearly called to Christian ministry and went to Bible school. He then went as an evangelist to Cornwall, working in close association with Edgar Trout, and was seeing a large number of people turning to Christ.

Both Arthur and David were concerned that the conference programme should be sufficiently flexible to allow the Holy Spirit to work in unexpected ways. They also wanted to give plenty of opportunity for ministry to individuals.

> Many will undoubtedly come seeking above all a deeper experience of the Holy Spirit. We shall thus be quite prepared to modify or abandon, as the Spirit leads, any or all of the syllabus, so long as God has his way. Our concern is that our coming together shall not be merely for mental exercise, but an occasion for the mainfested presence and undisputed authority of the Holy Spirit.

Cecil Cousen took a session on 'The Holy Spirit and the Personal Need of the Believer', Arthur took a session on 'The Holy Spirit Vitalising our Witness', and David led two open Bible studies on 1 Corinthians chapters 12 and 14. There was another session called 'News and Views' where several speakers covered different aspects of their experiences of the Holy Spirit.

A particular feature of the conference was a far greater freedom in worship than they had experienced in the previous gatherings. At times, as Cecil Cousen played the piano, it seemed as if the Holy Spirit was coming over them in great waves, and many were deeply touched by his power.

There was inevitably a certain amount of 'turbulence' caused by people from different 'streams' of the church coming together, but the overall feed-back was positive. Arthur and David asked everyone to complete a questionnaire to help them to assess reactions more thoroughly, and to provide a guideline for future arrangements. After the conference they circulated a summary of their findings.

> Many testified to a real sense of unity and love among those present. This was all the more remarkable because it appears that a few were not really expecting any manifestations of the Holy Spirit through spiritual gifts. One or two seemed to be disturbed to find that the beliefs of some of their brethren regarding the baptism of the Holy Spirit and the exercise of such gifts as tongues or prophecy were not just theoretical.

The main criticisms centred on what was seen as excessive and unrestrained vocal expression by some of the more Pentecostal delegates, particularly during the worship times. Arthur and David recognised that this was bound to cause difficulties to those for whom it was unfamiliar, and addressed this problem in their comments:

> Let us not forget that silence can be carnal as well as spiritual —there is the silence of the grave-yard! Some would remind us of the verse 'Be still and know that I am God' (Psalm 46:1), but forget that two verses on we have, 'Clap your hands, all ye peoples, shout to God with loud songs of joy'.
>
> It must be faced that the quietness and undemonstrativeness of some believers are due to reserves and inhibitions which are not spiritual. 'Noisy carnality' comes in for a good deal of justifiable criticism, while 'quiet carnality' often gets away with it.
>
> It is surely a fact, however, that when believers come into a new experience of the Spirit and of spiritual gifts they are usually liberated from unspiritual reserves and inhibitions, and lose much of their inbred self-consciousness. That in itself is surely a good thing. But it is vital that we exercise self-control, and keep a short rein on our emotions, that they are not allowed to run away with us.

Despite Arthur's acceptance of spiritual gifts, he was still seeking to experience such gifts for himself, and the breakthrough did not come during the conference, but a week or so later, while he was staying with Graham and Sylvia Perrins in Cardiff. Cecil Cousen, who frequently prayed with Arthur over this, had told him, 'When it happens you will not only speak in tongues but you will prophesy.' This proved to be the case.

Before Arthur went to bed, Graham laid hands on him and prayed for a release of God's Spirit in his life. He went to bed and fell sound asleep, but at about 3 am God woke him up. Lying in his bed he began to pray, and suddenly the Lord filled him with the Holy Spirit, just as he had done in 1951. It was just as if he was being filled up by a 'river' of the Holy Spirit, but he felt as though there was a 'dam' holding the waters back. Suddenly the dam burst and he began to speak in tongues and prophesy.

He had been through a long struggle to come to this place of release, but God had allowed this struggle for a very real purpose. The general emphasis among pentecostal believers was 'unless you've spoken in tongues, you've not been baptised in the Spirit'. Arthur felt that this dogmatic stance should be strongly resisted. He came across many believers who were earnestly seeking the baptism, but who were hung up over the question of tongues. The Bible did not say 'you shall receive tongues', but 'you shall receive power' when the Holy Spirit comes. His own experience only served to reinforce this fact, and he would always encourage people to 'earnestly desire spiritual gifts' but not to get too preoccupied with the gift of tongues.

Although Arthur had coped without a car for nearly ten years, there was no doubt that it was a little restrictive to be so reliant on public transport. From time to time he would pray about this; he did not have the money to buy a car, and so it would be up to God to provide one if this was his will.

In 1961 this prayer was answered when God prompted David Lillie to buy Arthur and Eileen a small light grey Ford Anglia. With Eileen now pregnant, this gift was proving particularly timely.

In November 1962 Arthur turned forty. It was not a milestone that bothered him; he was too committed to the prospect of revival to be worried about middle-age. A few weeks later the family travelled to Sussex to spend Christmas with Eileen's parents who had retired there. Eileen's brother Ken and his family were also living nearby. Over the Christmas period, the weather turned cold and it began to snow so heavily that most of the roads in the country became impassable. When, on Saturday 5th January, they were finally able to return home, they found that many of the roads around Talaton were still blocked by snow-drifts.

Among the pile of post that was lying inside their door was a letter from New Zealand. It was from John Massam, Secretary of the Willow Park Easter Camp Committee.

> Dear Mr Wallis,
> Since I wrote to you last in regard to your visiting New Zealand next Easter to coincide with the Willow Park Easter Camp, the members of the Camp Committee have been much before the Lord to know his clear will and direction.
> About a month ago we spent time in prayer to specifically bring the matter of a speaker before the Lord. The original exercise that we had in regard to your name was clearly confirmed and it was agreed that a letter should be sent to you, telling of our unanimous conviction that you come to Auckland next Easter. . . .
> We know that if you come it will be at the direction of the Lord and Master whom we both serve, and for the purpose that he has in his divine will previously ordained, and so this letter will, I pray, be used to confirm a conviction that is already in your own heart.
> Enclosed please find a return air ticket for your use. The Lord has individually convicted members of the Committee and laid aside the means for your coming. . . .

Accompanying this invitation was a further explanatory letter from Blyth Harper, another Willow Park Committee member, and a telegram from BOAC in London, asking Arthur to call them.

'The impertinence!' thought Arthur, who was somewhat surprised and put out by this unexpected development. 'Who do they think they are? And if they are right, why hasn't God told *me*?'

Immediately, all the practical obstacles sprang to his mind. The baby was due next month; what if there were complications? It did not seem to make any sense, and yet the fact remained that an unknown group of men on the other side of the world had been so convinced that this was the will of God that they would not take 'no' for an answer.

Early the next week, Arthur called BOAC who confirmed that they had received the money for the air fare to New Zealand and wanted to know when he would be travelling. He explained that he could not give them dates or even confirm that he would definitely be going. They assured him there was no urgency as he was not going to be travelling until April, and he promised to let them know as soon as the details were confirmed. He then sat down to reply to the committee.

The contents of your letters were a tremendous surprise, as I had taken it for granted that my reply to your original invitation had concluded the matter as far as I was concerned, and had given the matter little further thought.

The question that leapt into my mind as I read your letter was, 'Is this a subtle temptation to step out of the will of God?' Over against this was the plain fact that spiritual men with a real burden for the glory of God and for the reviving of his people had issued this further invitation after a prolonged season of waiting on the Lord, and with the conviction that this was the will of God, and had also made available the passage money, no doubt at considerable sacrifice. I could only spread the whole matter before the Lord again, not without some perplexity, and seek to take my hands off, that the will of the Lord might be made known.

There are two or three practical difficulties in my coming, though I realize that these could be removed in answer to prayer, if the thing is truly in the will of God. One of them is that my wife is expecting a baby next month, and there is the liability of complications, and even of the birth having to be prematurely induced. Just what the situation might be in April is impossible to say.

Then there are meetings in process of being arranged for April that would have to be cancelled, local responsibilities that would have to be cared for etc. You will appreciate that I need to be very sure of the will of God before committing myself.

Another important question is 'How long would it be for?'

This of course is probably impossible to know at the moment, assuming that it is his will that I come. Again I envisage difficulties in being absent for more than 3 or 4 weeks.

Where am I at the moment? At the point where I am willing to come if the Lord will make it clear to me as you believe he has made it to you, and this will involve the removal of the practical difficulties, and the peace of God umpiring the heart, both for my wife and myself. I may say that my wife is wholly willing for me to come, if the Lord makes it clear.

He concluded his letter with a report of his conversation with BOAC and a promise to write again as soon as the way became clear.

☆   ☆   ☆

Eileen had been visiting the specialist in Exeter for regular check-ups throughout the pregnancy, and everything seemed to be proceeding normally. Her blood-pressure was a little high however, and towards the end of January the doctors decided that she should be brought into hospital for complete rest and regular monitoring. So that Arthur could be free to be with Eileen as much as possible, he made arrangements for Jonathan to stay with Ma Wallis, who by now was living in Exeter.

A day or two later labour suddenly commenced and, during one of the regular checks, the midwife found that she could not hear the baby's heartbeat. Arthur was called in to be with Eileen throughout the labour. They kept hoping and praying right to the end, but another baby boy was stillborn.

This was a major blow, and their grief was very deep. It seemed they would finally have to come to terms with 'no more children'. Arthur had for some time felt a strong desire for a daughter. He knew now that this would never be realised.

Most of their Christian friends were very sympathetic and supportive, but they did receive one letter of 'comfort' from a 'friend' expressing his opinion that it had happened as a result of someone's sin. The very morning this letter arrived, Eileen had been reading in Luke chapter 13 where Jesus said: 'Do you think that these Galileans were worse sinners than all the other Galileans, because they suffered thus? I tell you, No.' That word 'no' convinced Arthur and Eileen that this man was quite wrong in his judgement. They determined to believe God rather than man.

Because abortion was still illegal in Britain at that time, the whole issue of when life starts had not been thought through by many Christians. Arthur and Eileen were amazed to hear one Christian leader express his view that no baby is a living soul until actually born alive. It would seem that, as far as he was concerned, their two stillborn sons were 'non-entities'.

They could see no scriptural justification for this view. In fact, to them, all the biblical evidence pointed strongly the other way. Passages like Psalm 139, and the story of John the Baptist 'leaping' in Elizabeth's womb, convinced them that their stillborn babies were 'real people'. They found great comfort in the fact that both their sons were alive with Christ and one day they would see them. In fact, Eileen's earlier miscarriages meant that there were other children waiting for them in heaven as well.

Clearly one of the potential obstacles to Arthur's trip to New Zealand had now been removed. It had not happened in the way they wanted or anticipated, but as they prayed together over the next few days, God gave them both a clear sense of peace that he should go. In mid February he wrote back to the Willow Park Committee accepting their invitation.

13

Into the Cauldron

On Saturday 6th April 1963, Arthur stepped off the BOAC plane at Auckland Airport, blissfully unaware that he was walking onto the centre stage of an intense controversy. It was his first overseas ministry trip, and he was approaching it with a sense of expectancy and excitement. Just before leaving England, Edgar Trout had written to him, sharing his conviction that this visit to New Zealand was going to significantly change the whole course of Arthur's ministry.

A good friend of Arthur's, Campbell McAlpine, was already in New Zealand. Campbell, like Arthur, was from a Brethren background, and they had first met back in 1957. Their experiences of the baptism of the Holy Spirit were very similar, and they had established an immediate rapport. In 1959 Campbell and his family moved out to New Zealand to work mainly among the Brethren Assemblies in teaching and evangelism.

Arthur knew that Campbell was involved in a certain amount of controversy among the Brethren in New Zealand over the question of speaking in tongues, and was rather hoping that God would not direct him to talk about this subject! He certainly did not realise the extent to which this issue was already causing division, or that his visit had become the focal point of a bubbling cauldron of contention.

The Chairman of the Willow Park Committee, Leo

Clarke, and one of the other committee members, Blyth
Harper, were there to greet Arthur, and he was driven
back to Blyth's home where he would be staying. God
had spoken to Blyth's wife, Jan, about preparing a room
in their Mount Eden residence for him to use as a
bedroom study. On entering this room Arthur knelt to
pray and asked God to bless Blyth and Jan's home
during his stay. His room soon became known as 'the
prophet's chamber'.

'Arthur, I know you're probably very tired after such
a long flight,' said Blyth as they sat relaxing that
evening, 'but we were wondering if you would feel up to
giving a brief message at our church tomorrow
morning.'

'I'd be very pleased to,' replied Arthur, 'provided the
Lord gives me something to say. I'll certainly pray about
it and let you know in the morning.'

Over breakfast the next day, Arthur was feeling
refreshed after a good sleep. He told Blyth that he
would gladly speak to the church. Blyth was the reserve
speaker in case Arthur was too tired, so he was particularly pleased!

The first half of the morning service at Wiremu Street
Chapel followed a traditional Brethren pattern with a
time of open worship followed by breaking of bread.
Then Arthur spoke from John chapter 12 and centred
his address on the cross of Christ. If Blyth needed any
confirmation that Arthur was 'God's man for the hour'
this was it. As reserve speaker, he had prepared a
message for that morning; it was on the same theme,
and based on exactly the same passage of Scripture!

Blyth was just a few years younger than Arthur, and
managed the BTI Bookroom in Auckland, a Christian
literature arm of the New Zealand Bible Training Institute. After lunch he took Arthur for a drive to show him
some of the sights of Auckland. Sitting in the car on One
Tree Hill, a high point which overlooks the beautiful
city with its 'harbours of two oceans', he began to tell
Arthur all about the background to his visit and to give

him some details of the areas of controversy that were developing.

Historically the Brethren Assemblies in New Zealand had been at the heart of the evangelical life of the country. The whole Brethren movement was very outward-looking and evangelistic, and had been involved in the organisation and support of a Billy Graham Crusade that took place in the country in 1959. This proved to be a great success, and around 18,000 people had stepped forward to commit or rededicate their lives to Jesus Christ.

The evangelistic momentum that started in the crusade continued in the years that followed, with many young people turning to Christ. There was a great need for ongoing training and teaching among all these new converts, and so a group of Brethren youth leaders came together to pray about launching an Easter Camp at Willow Park, Eastern Beach, Auckland. This camp and convention centre was owned by a trust on behalf of about thirty-five Brethren Assemblies in the area.

The first camp took place at Easter 1961, led by Blyth. The purpose was to encourage and to deepen the spiritual lives of all who attended. It was mainly, but not exclusively, geared to young people, and proved to be a time of great blessing. Soon afterwards the committee got together to start praying and planning for another camp in 1962.

They decided to invite Campbell McAlpine as one of the main speakers. Campbell was linked to Howe Street Chapel, the central Brethren Assembly in Auckland, and was travelling widely throughout the country. He was just about to launch the Tell New Zealand Crusade, a programme aimed at distributing a copy of John's gospel to every home in the country, when controversy arose.

Campbell had been baptised in the Holy Spirit back in 1954 and exercised the gifts of the Spirit in his private devotions, although he had never made a big issue of it. One day he informally shared with a colleague from

Howe Street Chapel his personal conviction that the gifts of the Spirit as listed in 1 Corinthians chapter 12 were not extinct but were relevant to the church today, and mentioned that he exercised the gift of tongues in his private devotions. This news came as a bombshell to the elders at the Chapel, who included Robert Laidlaw and Dr William Pettit.

Robert Laidlaw was one of the leading figures among the evangelical life of New Zealand. He was a successful businessman and a gifted preacher and teacher, internationally renowned among the Brethren. He was a close friend of Campbell, and so this revelation, being contrary to his own deeply held convictions, was particularly painful for him.

Dr Pettit was an earnest contender for evangelical doctrine and for the distinctive beliefs of the Brethren. He was well known for his vigorous attacks on liberal theology and the ecumenism of the World Council of Churches, but his latest 'bone of contention' was the phenomenon of speaking in tongues, which was reportedly being experienced by a growing number of Christians. Both he and Mr Laidlaw strongly contended that this, and the other gifts of the Spirit referred to in 1 Corinthians chapter 12, had passed away when the New Testament canon was completed.

Their teaching allowed no possibility that any modern-day gifts of the Spirit could be genuine. In their minds, therefore, speaking in tongues could only be regarded as either meaningless noise or demonic counterfeit. That someone so clearly spiritual as Campbell McAlpine confessed to using this gift was very perplexing. They were determined that such false teaching and practice should not penetrate the closely knit Brethren assemblies, and decided to react firmly.

Their first step was to bring strong pressure to bear on the Willow Park Committee to withdraw Campbell's invitation. After much heart-searching and prayer the committee remained fully convinced that it was God's will for Campbell to speak at the Easter camp. Still unhappy about the situation, the elders asked Campbell if he would be prepared to stop speaking in tongues.

His initial reaction was 'not on your life', but he promised to pray about it. When he did, the Lord spoke to him quite clearly.

'Which is more important to you, Campbell, speaking in tongues or the unity of my people?'

'It's got to be the unity of your people, Lord,' he replied.

'Are you willing to lay this gift aside for a while then, for the sake of unity?'

'Yes, Lord.'

Campbell went back to the elders and told them that, although his convictions had not changed, he was prepared to stop using this gift in his private devotions for the sake of unity. They were reasonably happy with this, and he promised that if and when God released him to use the gift again he would let them know.

Robert Laidlaw offered to speak at the Easter camp together with Campbell, and it again proved to be a time of great blessing. Campbell stopped using his gift of tongues for several months, but later in the year felt God releasing him to start using it again. He communicated this to Robert Laidlaw, and was called up in front of the Howe Street elders. Dr Pettit had a letter prepared for him, telling him that as far as the Brethren were concerned his ministry was finished, and he would not be permitted to speak in their churches any more.

Despite their differences, Campbell found that God gave him a real love for all these men, and in particular Robert Laidlaw, whom he continued to hold in the highest regard. In many ways this development couldn't have happened at a worse time for him, just as the Tell New Zealand Crusade was getting underway. Some support for this work from Brethren circles was withdrawn, but God still provided him with over 100 dedicated young men and women who served to get the job done.

The Willow Park Committee were by now making

their plans for 1963. A number of them had read *In the Day of Thy Power* and they reached the firm conclusion that they should invite Arthur. This conviction remained, despite his initial refusal, and it was agreed that John Massam, the committee secretary, should write again. As John prayed about it, God clearly indicated that, in addition to writing, they should also provide the air ticket.

The committee were initially reticent about this, but agreed that if the funds were provided over the next few weeks then this would be a sign that John had got his guidance right. Over this period several of the other committee members came to share this conviction, and they received all the money required. After the problems over Campbell the previous year, they made sure the elders who were on the Board of the Camp Trust were kept fully informed.

In February 1963 they finally heard that the way had opened for Arthur to come. By this time, however, other problems were developing. One of the committee, a gifted Bible teacher by the name of Milton Smith, had reached the conclusion that the Brethren view on the gifts of the Spirit was untenable. He had just published a paper giving a careful exposition of 1 Corinthians chapters 12 and 13, concluding that the 'sign gifts' had not ceased because 'the perfect' had not yet come. Milton had already been asked to lead the morning teaching sessions.

The publication of this paper resulted in an urgent request from the Willow Park Trust Board for the committee to withdraw their invitation to Milton. As if this was not enough, another bit of disturbing news arrived via the Brethren grapevine. Robert Laidlaw received a letter from England from Ransome Cooper, a Brethren evangelist who had received the published text of a message Arthur had given at Eastbourne in early 1962. In the course of his address on 'Revival and Reformation in the Church', Arthur had made the following remarks:

Thoughtful Christians, who are not blinded by prejudice, are coming to realise increasingly that the Pentecostal movement in the providence of God has come to make its special contribution to the great unfolding of God's truth.

Ransome Cooper was aware of the tensions in New Zealand over pentecostalism and, as soon as he heard that Arthur had been invited there, wrote to warn of his 'neo-pentecostal leanings'! This put Robert Laidlaw and the other elders in a difficult position. They had welcomed Arthur's acceptance, his fare was paid, and by now his flight booking was confirmed; they could hardly turn round at this late stage and withdraw their invitation. They did insist, however, that Milton Smith be barred from the public platform.

News of these developments spread rapidly through the 'bush telegraph', and some of the Auckland Assemblies advised their young people to stay away from the Easter camp. The registrations of just over 200 were lower than expected.

As Arthur listened to Blyth's account of these events, he couldn't help feeling that God had rather successfully 'dropped him in it'. It was somewhat bizarre. These dear brethren had unwittingly paid for him to fly half way round the world to speak at a conference, whereas local men had been excluded for holding views with which Arthur whole-heartedly concurred!

'Well, I trust you know what you're doing, Lord,' he prayed.

'I do hope that the messages that you have for the Easter camp won't add fuel to the fire, Arthur,' said Blyth.

God had given Arthur a series from the Sermon on the Mount that would fit in with the theme of the camp which was 'Christ Indwelling and Enthroned'. This did not sound too controversial, which was quite a relief.

The Easter camp commenced the following Thursday evening, with great expectation and some trepidation. Each evening Arthur taught progressively from the

Sermon on the Mount. His ministry was accompanied by a clear sense of God's power and anointing, and Blyth was amazed to observe that he preached without notes. The Brethren leaders who came along to observe could find nothing more controversial in his messages than the fact that he read from the *Revised Standard Version* of the Bible!

The conclusion of his message at the evening meeting on Easter Sunday was marked by a clear sense of the presence of the Lord across the hall. No one moved as Arthur finished speaking and you could have heard a pin drop. Suddenly, a Christian leader got up and walked down to the front of the hall and prostrated himself on the floor in front of the platform. Blyth, who was chairing the proceedings, closed the meeting but invited anyone who wished to pray to stay behind.

Nearly everyone remained in their seats, and the Holy Spirit began to work. The silence turned into a torrent of sound as people poured out their hearts to God; a number wept openly under the conviction of sin, and some came forward to speak out the things God was saying to them. Blyth felt totally out of his depth, and asked Arthur to take over the leadership of the meeting. Towards midnight, after nearly two hours in which the Spirit of God moved powerfully and spontaneously, Arthur finally closed the meeting and sent the campers off to bed to get some rest before the final day of the camp.

Not everyone was impressed by this open display of the Holy Spirit at work. As Blyth was leaving the meeting he was approached by Dr Pettit, who had been closely observing the events of the evening.

'Blyth,' he said, 'what we have just seen is nothing short of pentecostalism. Women were taking part, there was a lot of emotion, and the camp leader handed over his responsibility to Arthur Wallis. Someone could even have spoken in tongues here tonight!'

After the Easter weekend was over, the phone started ringing with invitations for Arthur to speak at meetings across the city. Many of the Brethren Assemblies, who had heard of his 'neo-pentecostal tendencies', were closed to him, but other doors began to open. Robert Laidlaw, despite his reservations about Arthur's views on the Holy Spirit, generously loaned him a car in which to get around during his stay.

It did not take Arthur long to discover many 'kindred spirits' in the area, people who shared his burden for revival and who were open to the Spirit of God. One such couple, with whom Arthur quickly established a close relationship, were Jim and Joy Dawson. In 1960 Ivor Davies, the leader of the Worldwide Evangelisation Crusade in New Zealand, had started a regular prayer meeting for revival, and this now took place weekly in Jim and Joy's home.

A couple of weeks after Easter, Arthur came together with the camp committee to pray about the possibility of an evangelistic campaign in Auckland as a follow-up to the Tell New Zealand Crusade. Arthur was proposed as a speaker along with Muri Thompson, a Maori evangelist, but as they prayed together God seemed to shut the door on this possibility.

Instead, it became clear that Arthur's ministry in New Zealand was to be primarily that of 'lighting the lamps' of local groups and churches. Any city-wide outreach should come from revived local churches. The new wine of the Spirit needed new wine-skins to contain it.

The vision for the church, something that had for some time been dominating Arthur's thinking, along with that of David Lillie and others, was going to be central to his ministry in New Zealand. As they prayed, Arthur's hopes began to rise. There was a readiness and an expectancy among many of God's people in New Zealand for a fresh outpouring of the Spirit. Perhaps here he would see his vision for revival and the restoration of church life become a reality. It also seemed that he was in for quite a long stay.

Arthur settled well into the routine of the Harper household, and became 'Uncle Arthur' to Blyth and Jan's three sons. Some of his habits particularly intrigued them. He was always an early riser, and would get up at 6 am for his cold bath!

This somewhat masochistic habit was instilled into him during his schooldays at Monkton Combe. The idea was not to lie in the water for too long (that would have been going too far!) but just to have a quick dip. He found that getting in to a cold bath was a good test of his will power, and the sudden shock to the system did wonders for his circulation. The warm glow after towelling down made it all worth while.

Another thing which intrigued the Harpers was Arthur's regular cup of 'content'. This was a simple unflavoured combination of milk and hot water in much the same proportions as a cup of tea. Arthur and Eileen had always drunk very little tea or coffee, which they felt to be unhealthy. This was one of their standard alternatives.

Arthur quickly got into a regular weekly routine, and would normally keep Friday as a day of prayer and fasting when he could prepare for weekend services. Saturday was his regular day for recreation when he would drive up to the hills west of Auckland and go for long bush tramps, or enjoy the sea breezes at one of the city's many beaches.

He wrote regularly to Eileen and Jonathan back in England. He would give Eileen lots of detail of all that was happening in his ministry, the difficulties and controversies he was facing, the people he was meeting, and the things God was saying to him. To Jonathan he wrote much more about the practical aspects of life in New Zealand.

God provided faithfully for Eileen and Jonathan back at home, and they received all the money they needed to live on. In addition to the regular amounts Arthur was able to send back from New Zealand, friends in England continued to provide gifts and support.

Neither Arthur nor Eileen had any real idea how long he would be away. It was becoming increasingly obvious, however, that the 'three to four weeks' he envisaged before leaving was going to be a serious underestimate.

14

The Pitcher Is Broken

The 'tongues controversy' was not going to go away, and Robert Laidlaw was getting many letters from bewildered leaders in Brethren assemblies throughout New Zealand, asking what his position was on this issue. Dr Pettit and others encouraged him to make a written statement on the matter, and so he drafted a booklet entitled *Is the Gift of Tongues for Today?* aimed at giving a definitive statement of the Brethren position.

As manager of the BTI Bookroom, Blyth was responsible for the printing and distribution of this booklet, but its contents disturbed him. The conclusion was that the gifts of tongues and healing had ceased, and that anyone holding the opposite view should be barred from Brethren platforms. Blyth felt that the interpretation put forward was not backed by Scripture, and that the recommendation violated the autonomy of each local church.

Mr Laidlaw was keen for the members of the Easter camp committee to endorse his statement, but Blyth did not feel able to do this. Instead he wrote his own paper, taking a more moderate position, and circulated this among the brothers concerned. He concluded that there was no scriptural basis for excluding the modern-day receipt of such gifts, and that any problems resulting from their use in the local church lay with the elders of that church.

When Dr Pettit received his copy of Blyth's paper, he immediately telephoned him. He was clearly unhappy about the views Blyth had expressed, and wanted to arrange a meeting of the Easter camp committee, together with a few other men, in his consulting rooms the following Monday evening. He intended to show them conclusively that these gifts had ceased, and that the 'tongues movement' was creating havoc among Christians in New Zealand.

'By the way, Blyth,' said Dr Pettit as he concluded his telephone call, 'I would like Arthur Wallis to be at that meeting. Could you please invite him to come?'

☆   ☆   ☆

In the early hours of Friday morning, 3rd May 1963, Arthur suddenly awoke with a very real sense of the fear of God surrounding him. Immediately, the words came into his mind, 'Tell him, "The pitcher is broken at the fountain."'

He realised that this was a message from God, and with it came a very strong impression that it was to do with Dr Pettit. Arthur did not attempt to understand the implications of this, but committed it to God in prayer and went back to sleep.

In the morning he got up to pray, and began to ponder just what this strange impression could mean. Was God telling him to pass this message on to Dr Pettit? Although the doctor had been present at some of the Easter camp meetings, Arthur had never met him, and he shrunk from the thought of conveying such a message.

He found the verse of scripture quoted in Ecclesiastes 12 verse 6, and the context was one of death: 'Man goes to his eternal home . . . the pitcher is broken at the fountain . . . the dust returns to the earth as it was . . . the spirit returns to God who gave it.'

Arthur remembered that this phrase was also quoted

in *The Pilgrim's Progress*. The pilgrims, awaiting their time to cross the river to the Celestial City, received different messages from this passage of Ecclesiastes. Arthur could not remember to whom this particular message had been given, but it did occur to him that there was one character in the book, Mr Valiant-for-Truth, who aptly fitted Dr Pettit.

Could it really be that God had given Arthur a message to convey to Dr Pettit that predicted his imminent death? It would certainly seem that this was the obvious interpretation. He was understandably fearful about the consequences of delivering such a message, and felt considerably perplexed about the whole matter. Why would God ask him to convey such a message to an elderly man he had never met? Dr Pettit was in his late seventies, and it would be sure to cause worry and concern to him and his family. On the other hand, he realised that he had been instructed simply to deliver this message, not to interpret it. Nevertheless, he felt in need of some clear independent confirmation that this really was from God.

'Lord, if this message is one you want me to deliver to Dr Pettit,' Arthur prayed, 'I need you to confirm it in two ways. First, let this message be the one given to Mr Valiant-for-Truth. Secondly, may I not have to take the initiative to go and see Dr Pettit, but may he make contact with me.'

His first confirming sign was easily obtained when, later that day, he consulted *The Pilgrim's Progress* and found that this was the message given to Mr Valiant-for-Truth. The very next evening, he heard that Dr Pettit had requested his attendance at the meeting scheduled for the following Monday to discuss the question of spiritual gifts. Arthur now knew beyond any doubt that it was for real.

About a dozen men gathered in the doctor's rooms in central Auckland the following Monday evening. Dr Pettit stated his case against the gifts of the Spirit in a gracious but uncompromising way, and there was a certain amount of discussion. As the meeting was nearly at an end, Arthur felt that the time had come to deliver the message that God had given him.

'Dr Pettit,' he said, 'I want to pass on a message that the Lord has given me. It is "Tell him, the pitcher is broken at the fountain."'

The doctor paused, turned red, and finally said 'I will pray about that.'

The meeting ended in an electric atmosphere, with a number of those present feeling that a prophetic word had been spoken, involving judgement from God against Dr Pettit. Arthur considered that the words were a message to be passed on, rather than a prophecy.

Clearly this incident was not destined to win Arthur any friends among the Brethren movement in New Zealand, and was likely to add to what was already a situation of deep controversy and division. He knew, however, that this was not really the issue. Sometimes God's purposes can only be achieved through division and, ultimately, the only thing that really matters is obedience to God. The message had been confirmed in a way that left him without doubt that it was from the Lord. He would just have to leave the consequences with his heavenly Father.

☆   ☆   ☆

Soon after his arrival in New Zealand, Arthur had got in touch with Campbell McAlpine and visited him on several occasions. Campbell had been led by the Lord to start a long fast towards the end of April, and Arthur was able to join him in prayer several times. They both shared a deep concern for New Zealand, and felt that God was doing something very special in the nation.

Campbell's fast lasted three weeks, and during this time God was speaking to him and dealing with his attitudes over many issues. The climax of this period occurred after he had started to break the fast. He was waiting on the Lord in prayer, when God gave him a vision of New Zealand.

There is a large volcano, Mount Tarawera, on the North Island and this had unexpectedly erupted towards the end of the nineteenth century, resulting in great loss of life. In his vision Campbell saw this volcano erupting, with lava pouring out over the two islands. He knew this represented the judgement of God, and began to cry out to God with an intensity of intercession he had never experienced before, pleading that God would have mercy and withhold his judgement until revival came.

This period of intercession lasted about an hour, but Campbell knew that the whole of his twenty-one day fast had been a preparation for this brief period. (Arthur was later to include extracts from Campbell's diary of this fast in his book *God's Chosen Fast*.)

At this time, God was speaking to Arthur in a very similar way, and he felt that many other Christians in New Zealand were being called to pray, fast and intercede for the nation. At a meeting of the Auckland Christian Businessmen's Association, a gathering which included many leaders from the Brethren and other evangelical churches, Arthur shared a solemn word from Joel chapter 2. The alternatives facing New Zealand were God's judgement, or repentance and revival.

It was apparent that an important work was opening up for Arthur in New Zealand, and he was in for a long stay. A number of his New Zealand friends were beginning to feel that Eileen should come out and join him for a while, and this became the focus of much prayer. Over the next month or two Arthur began to receive gifts towards her fare.

Back at home, Eileen too was praying about this possibility, and in July she received a clear confirmation from the Lord when she was given £45 by a friend 'to

help with the expenses attendant upon your going out
to join Arthur'. Arthur's mother was happy for
Jonathan to come and stay with her in Exeter, where she
lived conveniently near his school, and so the way was
opened for Eileen to come and a flight was booked for
September.

Eileen had never flown before, and she felt a great
sense of excitement as Peter and Meg took her, with
Jonathan, to London's Heathrow Airport. She said
goodbye to Jonathan, indicating that she and Arthur
would probably be back for Christmas, and settled down
for the long flight.

It was not a good introduction to flying for her; the
aeroplane hit turbulence and at one point felt as if it was
dropping out of the sky. Fortunately a doctor friend had
given her some tablets to calm her stomach during the
flight. These were effective, but she arrived in Auckland
feeling very drained and rather unwell.

For their first few days together, Arthur and Eileen
stayed with Christian friends in the North of New
Zealand where Arthur was ministering at the time.
They were then offered the use of a seaside holiday home, known as a 'bach', which was owned by
the Mayor of Dargaville, a Christian. It was a simple
wooden bungalow on raised foundations, quite old, a
little damp and dark after the New Zealand winter, but
in a lovely position on the edge of a beach several miles
outside Dargaville. They were grateful to have somewhere to be on their own together and it soon became
home.

They were able to relax and enjoy the refreshing sea
air, but the bach was rather isolated, particularly with no
car. Friends would regularly visit, bringing supplies of
food and other necessities. Arthur's programme of
meetings was much quieter now than prior to Eileen's
arrival, but whenever he was speaking somewhere she
would travel with him.

They had very little money, and most of what they
received provided the regular amounts they needed to

send Arthur's mother for Jonathan's keep. They lived very simply, and trusted God for their essential day-to-day needs.

After a couple of months in the bach, a local farmer provided them with alternative accommodation, somewhat nearer to Dargaville. It was a simple country cottage, starkly furnished with just the basic essentials. Just before Christmas Blyth Harper and John Massam arrived to see them.

John owned a car dealership in Auckland, and God had led him to give Arthur and Eileen the gift of a small Ford Prefect. He and Blyth had come to deliver it, and to discuss with Arthur their plans for Easter 1964. The little cottage was not designed for guests. There were only two dining chairs and two sets of cutlery, and so Eileen had to serve lunch for the four of them in two sittings!

Because of the continuing controversy over the tongues issue, the Trust Board was not prepared to allow the committee to invite Arthur to be a speaker again, and so they had decided to invite him as a study group leader instead. He was quite happy to serve in this way, but said he would pray about it.

It was certainly a great benefit to have a car in which to get around, particularly for their monthly trips to Auckland where Arthur helped to lead a regular day of prayer for revival. He was still firmly of the conviction that he would see revival break out in New Zealand before he returned to England. Eileen's hopes of them both returning for Christmas were clearly not going to be realised.

Many New Zealanders spend Christmas Day at the beach, and this was a new experience for Arthur and Eileen. A Christian family from Whangerei invited them to spend the day with them at their seaside bach. As well as enjoying a festive meal, there was the opportunity to swim and relax in the sun, which made it a somewhat more healthy and invigorating day than the average British Christmas.

In early January, Arthur and Eileen moved back to Auckland and stayed with Jim and Joy Dawson, who had turned their basement into a guest suite. Joy had a very clear ministry of intercession and had learned a lot about the ways of God in this area. She exuded a tremendous enthusiasm and spiritual intensity that was beautifully balanced by Jim who was quite laid-back in comparison, and blessed with a great sense of humour.

Arthur had felt God leading him to start the new year with a three-week period of fasting and prayer. Some Christian friends who were going away for an extended period made their home available just outside Auckland, and he decided to stay there for the duration of his fast, while Eileen stayed on with the Dawsons and visited him daily.

Eileen decided to go onto a restricted diet during this three-week period, so that she could identify with Arthur while remaining reasonably 'normal'. Physically it was not an easy time for him, and after the first few days he found it difficult to sleep at night, but he persevered and kept in good health in all other respects.

Both Arthur and Eileen prayed a great deal for revival during this period, and God gave Arthur some clear direction regarding his future work in New Zealand. One of the areas he prayed about was the Easter camp, and he felt God telling him to have no direct involvement in the camp, but to give himself to intercession over the Easter period.

One of the benefits of the fast was a great clarity of mind and an enhanced spiritual awareness, but by the end of the three weeks Arthur was looking very thin, and Eileen carefully supervised the breaking of the fast. This was in many ways more difficult than the fast itself. At first he took just fruit juices in small quantities, and then gradually moved onto solids over the next week. After a long fast of this kind it was very important to move back to normal eating slowly at his body's own pace, and Arthur's digestive system took longer than most to get back to normal.

Once the fast was over, they moved to Howick, and continued to spend much time praying and seeking God together. They were planning to travel together to the South Island, and didn't know where or how God would lead them. Arthur just had one or two people he knew to visit, and they prayed much that God would open up the right doors for them.

It was at this time that Arthur came to the conviction that Eileen would have to return to England on her own, and that he should stay on in the expectation of the outbreak of revival. He said nothing to her, however, as he wanted her to hear this from God for herself. She was longing to be able to write to Jonathan and tell him when they would both be flying home, and would find it very difficult to come to terms with the thought of returning home alone.

Eileen had still not received the gift of tongues, and this was another matter to which they devoted much prayer. One evening, a few days before their trip to the South Island, Arthur felt that the time had come to claim this gift for her. They got down on their knees to pray and determined that they would not get up until she had received it!

To their surprise, as they prayed and waited on God, Eileen began to laugh uncontrollably! It was something very foreign to her reserved nature and provided a clear indication that the Holy Spirit was at work. 'I think you just have to step out in faith and to begin to speak out the words which God gives you,' said Arthur. 'There is absolutely no reason why you can't speak in tongues.'

She simply spoke out the few strange words that God had put into her mind. It didn't seem nearly as exciting as laughing in the Spirit, but it was a start! The next day, as they prayed together, she interpreted a tongue that Arthur had spoken, and began to prophesy.

Just before they left Auckland, they were given a much newer car, and were able to sell the little Ford Prefect. Eileen had come to terms with the fact that she would have to return to England for Easter without Arthur, and he decided that she should take the money from selling this car to live on once she got home.

At the end of March, Eileen kissed Arthur goodbye and boarded the flight for London. During her six months' absence, Jonathan had not got on particularly well with his grandmother and was very pleased to see her. He tried hard to hide his disappointment that his dad had still not returned.

Arthur and a few friends gave themselves to intercession over the Easter period. He was still expecting to see revival in New Zealand.

☆   ☆   ☆

On Friday 17th July 1964, while staying in Howick, Arthur received a visit from Dr Pettit. The doctor had been shaken by the message Arthur had spoken to him some fourteen months previously, and had taken it seriously. Not wanting to upset his wife, he had said nothing to her about it.

'From my own reading of Ecclesiastes and *The Pilgrim's Progress*,' said Dr Pettit, 'I can only conclude that the message meant that my life was about to end. I'm not afraid to die, Mr Wallis, and at the age of seventy-nine it would not be particularly extraordinary if I were to do so, but here we are, fourteen months later, and I am still in good health for which I thank God. Can you explain to me why your prophecy has failed?'

'I have always maintained that it was a message to be passed on, rather than a prophecy,' replied Arthur, 'and I believe the Holy Spirit specifically prohibited me from offering any interpretation of this message. I cannot confirm or deny the conclusion you have reached regarding its meaning.'

Arthur then proceeded to reiterate the objective way in which the message was confirmed to him. Dr Pettit pressed him to offer his interpretation of it, but this he would not do. The doctor conveyed the deep distress with which he viewed the inroads of 'neo-pentecostalism' into the Assembly life of New Zealand, and although the meeting was cordial, it was clear that the two men were poles apart in their thinking.

Before they parted, Arthur agreed that an account of the message from Ecclesiastes should be put in writing, and Dr Pettit said he would do this and send a copy to Arthur for his approval. A week or so later, Arthur received a gracious letter from Dr Pettit thanking him for the meeting, and enclosing a statement for Arthur to check for accuracy. There were certain minor inaccuracies and omissions, and so Arthur retyped his own account, which he returned to the doctor.

☆   ☆   ☆

Arthur was increasingly convinced that revival in New Zealand was going to be accompanied by a restoration of Spirit-filled New Testament church life, and he was finding many others who shared this conviction. One was Frank Carlisle from Wellington. He had been so disturbed by Mr Laidlaw's pamphlet on the gift of tongues, which he felt misinterpreted the teaching of the Bible, that he wrote his own pamphlet in reply, challenging the Brethren to be genuinely obedient to Scripture.

> If we cannot produce a valid case from the Scripture against the presence of the gifts in the church today, then we must adopt a positive attitude to all the relevant scriptures and apply them in our fellowship.

Frank had by now left the Brethren, and Arthur had got to know him well. Together they decided to convene a conference on the subject of 'The Building of a Spirit-filled New Testament Church', and this was to be held towards the end of August in Massey University,

Palmerston North. Campbell McAlpine, who had moved back to England in December 1963, agreed to return for this conference as one of the main speakers.

In their convening letter, Frank Carlisle and Arthur outlined the purpose of the conference:

> There is increasing conviction in ever widening circles that only New Testament churches, unfettered and unfederated, can survive the storms that are soon to break upon our world . . .
>
> The time has come for a larger coming together to share the great vision that the Spirit of God is unfolding. The time has come to stand shoulder to shoulder for what we believe are God-given convictions, and God-given experiences, to strengthen each other's hands in God, and to discern God's fingerposts that point out the future way . . .
>
> We believe, with many others, that God wants to bring his church into the experience of New Testament Christianity, recovering not only the full blessing of the Holy Spirit, but also . . . New Testament church practice and principles—the new wineskin that must contain the new wine of the Holy Spirit's operations . . . The familiar minister-congregation arrangement is too brittle to contain the potent new wine that God is preparing to pour out. The Holy Spirit is waiting to work in Apostolic power through a fully-functioning local body, fed and led and governed by spiritual elders, amongst them those with special gifts and callings as 'pastors and teachers', each company linked only to Christ the Head, not to a federation or denomination.

This convening letter provoked a strong and vigorous response from Mr Laidlaw, Dr Pettit and others, and they circulated all the Brethren leaders warning them of the 'real purpose of the conference' which they considered to be underhand and divisive. This hastily compiled circular contained some allegations regarding Arthur which were based solely on hearsay and quite untrue.

In a letter to Dr Pettit, Arthur expressed surprise that 'those who are numbered among the leading brethren in the Assemblies of New Zealand should have been willing to append their signatures to a letter which makes allegations based on hearsay, without prior reference to the brother concerned'.

Arthur felt that this was a very serious matter, 'serious not for me, as I am content to leave the Lord to take care of my reputation, but for those who have appended their signatures to this untruth, without giving the person concerned the opportunity to confirm or deny'.

Dr Pettit's reply was apologetic but uncompromising. Regarding the Massey conference, he urged Arthur to use his 'utmost influence to establish separate groups completely independent of our assemblies'. He felt that both Arthur and Campbell had used 'surreptitious' and 'dishonourable' methods to 'secretly infiltrate groups of our young people and others with ideas regarding tongues and healing which are contrary to assembly teaching during the past 135 years'.

☆   ☆   ☆

Details of Arthur's message to Dr Pettit became well publicised in Brethren circles. Arthur was said to have prophesied the doctor's imminent violent death for opposing pentecostal views, and yet the doctor was still fit and well. The conclusion reached was fairly predictable: Arthur Wallis was a false prophet.

In fact Dr Pettit lived for a further twenty years, and finally died soon after his 100th birthday! Arthur was always at pains to stress that he had never predicted his imminent death, although on the face of it this seemed the obvious interpretation of the message. It was certainly something of a mystery at the time, and it was some years before Arthur came to understand that the message was not meant for Dr Pettit personally, but for what he represented and stood for so vigorously.

As I look back over the years, I have no doubt in my mind that the message was not personally for Dr Pettit, but for the whole Brethren movement, if they could receive it. 'The pitcher' is the Brethren movement in New Zealand. 'The fountain' was the outbreak of the Spirit at that time, that could have brought such life, release and blessing to all the assemblies.

15

Disappointment

It had been a long day, and Arthur was feeling tired and hungry as he sat down to enjoy his evening meal of roast lamb. He was based at Howick, a few miles outside Auckland, and was in the middle of a busy schedule of meetings. Many Christian homes have the sort of telephone that invariably rings the moment you sit down to eat, and he had just taken his first mouthful when it rang! It was a friend from Auckland wanting to speak to him.

'Arthur, we've got a difficult situation here, and we were wondering if you could help us. We've got Joe here, a brother who clearly needs deliverance from demon spirits. We've spent some time in prayer with him, but we just don't seem to be achieving any sort of breakthrough. Could you come down and help?'

'I'd be very glad to help,' Arthur replied, 'but I've just sat down to eat. Would you be able to bring him out here? It would give me the opportunity to finish my dinner before you arrive.'

'Yes, that would be fine, Arthur. Thank you. We're on our way.'

Arthur explained to his hosts what was planned, and sat down to finish his meal. God had been using him to help such cases during his time in New Zealand, and he felt confident that he could be of assistance.

Soon after he finished eating, his friend arrived with

Joe. They sat down together in the lounge, and Arthur began to probe.

'Tell me, Joe,' he asked, 'what has been your problem?'

Joe began to open up. He was obviously very keen to be set free from the power that was oppressing him, and it seemed a straightforward enough case. Arthur could not help wondering why his Auckland friends had been unable to see Joe delivered.

'Let's pray,' he said. 'I'm sure that God is going to set you free, Joe.'

They knelt down and began to pray. Absolutely nothing happened. Arthur felt as if all his spiritual authority had somehow drained away from him, and after a few minutes it was clear they were making no progress whatsoever. Joe had risen from his knees and was sitting in his chair with a look on his face that spoke volumes. It was as if he was saying 'What on earth is going on?' and 'Why did I bother to come out here?'

'We're clearly not getting through,' said Arthur. 'Let's spend some time quietly before the Lord and ask him to reveal what is holding things up.'

As Arthur knelt down and opened his heart and mind, God began to speak.

'The problem's not Joe, but you, Arthur,' the Lord said. 'There is pride in your heart. I know what you were thinking, "Here is a problem these brothers cannot solve, and so they have to come out to Arthur Wallis, the big-shot!"'

'I'm sorry, Lord.'

'Not only that, but you were more concerned about finishing your dinner than you were about helping this brother. You're not going to make any progress until you repent and humble yourself.'

Arthur humbled himself before the Lord and confessed his pride and selfishness.

'Now confess your sin to these brothers,' said the Lord.

He obediently shared with them the matters over

which God had convicted him. Before he had even finished speaking, Joe was flat on his face on the floor under the power and conviction of the Holy Spirit. Arthur commanded the evil spirits to leave him, and he was instantly set free.

This incident was part of a deep purifying work that was taking place in Arthur's heart during his stay in New Zealand. It was as if he was going through a refiner's fire, with the heat of God's dealings constantly bringing impurities to the surface.

Sometimes he would be reminded of things that had happened long ago, which he had not put right or dealt with properly at the time. One such incident was that of the Italian peasant woman whose goose his men had killed during the war. Although not directly involved himself, the Holy Spirit convicted him of failing to take action over this at the time. There was no way he could now make restitution for what had taken place so long ago, but he was able to put the matter straight before God.

☆   ☆   ☆

A variety of delegates were expected to attend the conference at Massey University, representing a wide spectrum of Christians. Some were from a mainstream pentecostal background, some were Baptists, and some had their origins in the Brethren; all had a deep desire to see the power of the Holy Spirit at work in the church.

A few weekends before the conference, Arthur, Frank Carlisle and a number of others met together to pray and seek God. During this time God brought a prophecy warning them of a false prophet. They were to be on the alert, all would seem to be well on the surface and they would find no fault with anything he did or said, but they would know him by his fruit.

This warning of the devil's activity only served to

heighten their sense of expectancy that God was about to work in a very special way. They wanted to stress that the conference was not a call to set up a new denomination but a call to unity. Undoubtedly many people came hoping for the establishment of a new movement or church. In some respects this was also what the Brethren leaders would have liked to see, so that the 'neo-pentecostals' could be totally separated from the Assemblies. Arthur was at pains to dampen any such expectations in his opening remarks:

> This conference has not been convened to call any individual to leave his denomination, church, assembly or fellowship. This conference has not been convened to form anything, a new movement or a new church. If any of these things are involved, then God must do them; the onus is upon the Almighty. We would not presume to raise a little finger to precipitate anything.

There were particular times during the conference when the sense of God's presence was quite awesome. In one of the sessions Campbell spoke on 'The Holiness of God', and at the end of his message called the people to silence, to wait on God. The presence of God was keenly felt, and they remained in silence for about an hour. It was just as if God was walking up and down the aisles, stopping here and there, dealing with people, convicting of sin and meeting needs.

This was more than some of the more pentecostal delegates could cope with, and Campbell had to silence them when they started to interject the odd 'Praise the Lord' and 'Hallelujah'.

No new movement or church was started at the Massey Conference, and no false prophet was revealed, but there was a great sense of God's presence and blessing on all those attending, and most came away with

a new sense of vision and purpose for what God was
going to do in the church.

☆   ☆   ☆

Much of Arthur's time during the month or two after
Massey was spent in the South Island where he was
based at Wakefield. During this period he received a
telephone call from Joy Dawson in Auckland.

'Arthur,' she said, 'I think you'd better come up here
as soon as you can. There's a man who has being doing
the rounds of all the charismatic groups in the Auckland
area. He's apparently very gifted in the word of knowledge and has performed some amazing healings and
miracles, but some of us have our suspicions. We feel he
may be the false prophet that God warned us about.'

Immediately Arthur made arrangements to fly back
to Auckland. A meeting was arranged in Jim and Joy
Dawson's home to which the man concerned was
invited. A number of other mature Christians were
present including Ivor Davies and Milton Smith. The
brother in question had suddenly appeared on the
scene, and there was nothing obviously wrong with his
ministry, or off-beam about the things he said. However
a number of Christian leaders had, for no apparent
reason, been through attacks of depression after coming
into contact with him.

Arthur was given the task of confronting him, and
when he did so the real fruit of his life became apparent.
His countenance changed, and his language became
foul and abusive. In a bitter outburst of anger, he put a
curse on Arthur, who seemed to be transfixed to the
spot, unable to move.

Ivor Davies immediately had the man removed from
the meeting, and joined with Milton Smith and Joy
Dawson to pray for Arthur. As they gathered around
him, calling on the Lord, and resisting Satan's attack in
the name of Jesus, the oppression lifted and Arthur

experienced no further repercussions. The false prophet disappeared off the scene as quickly as he had come.

☆   ☆   ☆

In late November 1964, various friends of Arthur met in Jim and Joy Dawson's home in Auckland to bid him farewell. The time had come for him to return home, his original 'three to four week trip' having extended to nearly twenty months.

Arthur shared with them his conviction that God was going to bring revival to New Zealand. He believed this was imminent, but was cautious about the exact timing. He paralleled what was happening with the days of Esther when there was a long period of preparation, but in the day of crisis God was ready and able to move.

Deep down, Arthur was having his own private battle with the Lord. Throughout his period in New Zealand he had felt a build-up of hope and expectancy that he would see revival before he left the country. He had found many 'kindred spirits', people alert to the hope of revival, devoting themselves to prayer and claiming God's promises. But it had not happened. He was a deeply disappointed man.

On the long flight home, he poured out his heart and soul to God. The only reason he had stayed so long in New Zealand, away from home and loved ones, was because he wholeheartedly believed he would see the fulfilment of this hope. Why had God not responded to his expectations?

On the way home Arthur had arranged to visit various contacts in the United States for a week. At San Fransisco he spent some time with John Myers of *Voice in the Wilderness* magazine, and in Los Angeles he met David du Plessis. His time in the States coincided with Thanksgiving Day and he succeeded in receiving two traditional turkey and pumpkin pie dinners, one on the plane to Detroit, and the other once he had arrived!

The last weekend of his stopover in the States was spent in New York where he visited the work of the Teen Challenge Centre led by David Wilkerson. He then flew from Kennedy Airport back to Heathrow, where Eileen, Jonathan, Peter, Meg and his mother were all waiting to greet him.

In the days and weeks that followed, his joy at being reunited with friends and family was tinged with a deep sense of disappointment that the passionate desires of his heart over the past year and a half had not been fulfilled. Although not naturally given to depression, this was a low point in Arthur's life. God was continuing to put him through the refiner's fire. He had allowed bitterness and resentment to creep into his heart and needed to repent and humble himself before the Lord.

As he took time to do this, God began to restore his spirit. Perhaps New Zealand was not yet ready for revival? He could not pretend to understand the ways of the Almighty. He could only acknowledge, by faith, that God's timing is always perfect.

As Arthur settled back to life in England, he soon discovered that the Brethren grapevine had been working with more than its usual efficiency. Not only was he a false prophet, but he was responsible for splitting the Brethren churches in New Zealand 'from Cape to Bluff'. Furthermore, following Eileen's return to England, the news was circulating that Arthur Wallis' wife had left him!

Edgar Trout's prophecy that this trip would completely alter the course of Arthur's ministry had been fulfilled. Previously open doors were now closed to him, but this was something of a relief. He was no longer happy to minister in churches which were resistant to the message of the Holy Spirit, and for each door that closed, many new ones were opening.

16

Home and Abroad

Throughout the United Kingdom, many Christians from all denominations were developing a strong interest in the baptism and gifts of the Spirit, and this provided many new opportunities for Arthur. At the beginning of 1965 he, Campbell McAlpine and Denis Clark were the main speakers at a Prayer and Bible Week arranged by Denis at the Greenhills Baptist Youth Centre in Worthing.

The first such week had taken place the previous year in Denis' home, and similar weeks were to take place for several further years during the New Year period. They proved to be a seed-bed of much that developed later in the church, and were attended by men such as Peter Lyne, Terry Virgo, Barney Coombs and John Noble, who were to become well-known church leaders.

Denis Clark was undoubtedly the dominant personality. A South African by origin, he was a man of outstanding zeal, totally radical and 'sold out' for God. He also had a tremendous sense of humour which came out strongly in his ministry. At times he would leave his listeners quite paralytic with laughter, a state which he would rapidly follow up with a hard-hitting application. When asked about this he would explain, 'I get everyone laughing, and then while their mouths are still open I ram the truth down their throats!'

There was a sharp cutting edge to Denis' ministry to

the point where, to some, he appeared ruthless and abrasive. Campbell, together with Arthur, certainly brought a softer edge to the proceedings. Campbell's friendship with Denis went right back to the late 1940s when they had met in South Africa where Campbell was working at the time. In 1955, after receiving the baptism in the Spirit, both men felt God wanted them to move to England with their families.

Most of the teaching at these Prayer and Bible Weeks came from Denis, Campbell and Arthur, jokingly referred to as 'the three musketeers'. Each was very different in style but they developed a strong friendship, appreciation and dependence on one another and together formed a very powerful and effective trio.

They genuinely were *Prayer* and Bible Weeks, with some of the sessions devoted solely to prayer and waiting on God. The gifts of the Spirit would be frequently exercised in the meetings and any prophetic messages would be weighed up and taken seriously.

The 1965 conference centred on 'deliverance' and Arthur shared some of his experiences in this realm while in New Zealand.

Later that January, Arthur and Campbell spoke at another conference, this time arranged by Michael Harper under the auspices of the newly founded 'Fountain Trust'. This conference, which took place at High Leigh Conference Centre, was mainly attended by Anglicans, many of whom were baptised in the Spirit.

While Arthur was in New Zealand, Michael, who was one of John Stott's curates at All Souls, Langham Place in London, received the baptism in the Spirit. He resigned his curacy and founded the Fountain Trust which was established to encourage the many within the Anglican church and the other historic denominations who were seeking the Holy Spirit.

Many new doors were opening for Arthur, but one invitation which took him completely by surprise came from the Rector of Talaton, who asked him to preach at the parish church for three Sunday evenings during

Lent. As he donned a Geneva gown and climbed into the pulpit of the old fourteenth-century church it seemed quite a contrast to his more usual charismatic setting. On the final Sunday he invited all those interested in finding the way of salvation to take a copy of John Stott's booklet *Becoming a Christian*. About a dozen people responded, including the Rector!

In April 1965, David Lillie, Campbell McAlpine and Arthur convened another conference which was a follow-up to those held previously at Exmouth, Belstone and Mamhead Park. The subject was 'The Apostolic Commission, The Message, The Men and The Methods', and the venue was Herne Bay Court in Kent.

The convening letter gave a brief summary of the previous conferences, and explained how the theme for this conference had been sparked off by a short message given by Roger Forster at Mamhead Park.

> Referring to Matthew 24:14 ('And this gospel of the kingdom will be preached throughout the whole world as a testimony to all nations, and then the end will come') he suggested that each generation of the church had had the opportunity to become the divine instrument to bring in the kingdom by the fulfilment of this command . . . but no such generation had yet risen to its opportunity. Would our generation be the one to tackle the task and see it through? The challenge has been ringing in the ears of many of us since the conference. . . .
>
> In the light of the Divine Commission . . . how can 'evangelical' believers remain 'unevangelistic' and still hold up their heads? The call to evangelize is insistent and irresistible. 'Evangelize or perish' is seen to be no mere slogan but a statement of sober fact. We are being compelled to face up to the subject of evangelism in the light of the whole counsel of God, and it would seem that there is a greater desire at this present time to do this than at any previous period in this century.

The letter then referred to all that was currently happening in the area of evangelism through Operation Mobilisation, and through American evangelists such as

Billy Graham, Oral Roberts and T.L. Osborn. There was much cause for encouragement.

> We are coming into a wonderful new era, and like men emerging from a dark tunnel we are somewhat confused and perplexed. We need to take time to pray over these matters and to ponder them in the light of the Word of God. The spiritual climate is getting warmer and we are finding that some of our garments of tradition are becoming too heavy for us.

About 100 people were present, and Arthur was later to write that the conference was marked by 'a growing sense of God's presence, great unity and love, ministry in power and authority, and many coming into release and blessing'. As well as Arthur, Campbell and David, Cecil Cousen was again involved in the ministry of the conference, and also a veteran missionary pioneer from the Congo, William Burton.

At home in Talaton, Arthur and Bill Patton continued to run a Bible class for teenage boys, who would come to The Forge House each Sunday morning before church. Jonathan was now fifteen, and the handful of boys that regularly attended the class were his friends from the village.

For a number of years Eileen had held an afternoon Sunday School, and this was thriving with as many children as she could cope with. There was nothing for children run by the local parish church, and their parents seemed only too glad of an hour's peace on a Sunday afternoon!

The monthly Talaton Revival Prayer meeting, started way back in January 1952, still took place on the first Friday of every month. Some of the faithful 'prayer warriors' who had been in at the start were still involved, but God was continually bringing new people along, and fitting them all into the front room at The Forge House was an increasing problem.

A new pattern of ministry was developing for Arthur. He had been invited onto the advisory council of the

Fountain Trust, and was getting an increasing number of invitations to conferences, churches and revival prayer groups around the country. Invariably people would quiz him about the baptism and gifts of the Spirit, and the implications of these things for their church or fellowship. He would always strive to bring his answers back to the basic teaching of the word of God, and this gave many people confidence in the counsel he was able to give them.

These increasing demands on his ministry left Arthur with less time than he wished for writing. During 1966 an address he gave on the prayer life of Jesus according to Luke's gospel was published as a booklet under the title *Jesus Prayed*, and his second full-length book was at long last nearing completion.

While in New Zealand, Arthur had felt that there was a lack of written material on fasting and had set about addressing this subject. He saw fasting as something that had been neglected by many Christians, and aimed to approach it in a balanced and biblical way. The result was *God's Chosen Fast*, a spiritual and practical handbook on the subject. He outlined the purpose of the book in his introduction:

It is not a major biblical doctrine, a foundation stone of the faith, or a panacea for every spiritual ill. Nevertheless, when exercised with a pure heart and a right motive, fasting may provide us with a key to unlock doors where other keys have failed; a window opening up new horizons in the unseen world; a spiritual weapon of God's providing, 'mighty to the pulling down of strongholds'. May God use this book to awaken many of his people to the spiritual possibilities latent in the fast that God has chosen.

Several friends read the manuscript, including one or two in the medical profession, and their comments were encouraging, but at the end of 1966 Arthur still felt the book needed more work on it. He was finally able to complete it early in 1967, and decided to submit the manuscript to Hodder and Stoughton, who were the largest publisher of Christian books in the country at that time.

In mid 1967, he heard back from Hodder, declining to publish his manuscript. One objection to the book was its size, and Arthur decided to go through the manuscript again to reduce it where possible. He was disappointed by this decision, and asked God to show him clearly whom else to approach when he had completed his editing.

In fact he did not have to approach anybody, but was contacted by Hugh Fuller, the Managing Director of Victory Press. He had heard of Hodder's decision and was writing to express interest. Victory Press (which in 1976 merged with Coverdale House Publishers to form what later became Kingsway Publications) was a much smaller publishing house, but Arthur felt this was an answer to prayer.

In September he submitted his revised manuscript to Victory Press and it was accepted for publication, finally coming into print in 1968 with the American edition being published by CLC. It was generally well received as, to quote one reviewer, 'a fair-minded book that brings to the fore what may well be a much neglected means of blessing'.

☆   ☆   ☆

Often when Arthur and Eileen were praying together, God would speak to them from the Bible or through a word of prophecy. They would always carefully note this down and seek to implement any directions given. During a prayer time in mid 1966, Eileen brought one such word that was to prove particularly significant.

In this prophecy God spoke about the needs of those whom he had called to serve him overseas. They were often in need of upbuilding and encouragement in order to be able to minister the gospel effectively to the people in those lands. 'I will give you the tools,' God said, 'that those I have sent might have the tools.'

At the time they did not understand just what was really meant by this word, but a letter from Indonesia later that year was to bring about the fulfilment of this prophecy. The letter was from Keith Liddle, a man Arthur had met in New Zealand. Both Keith and his wife Belle were in their mid sixties but, at a time when most people would be thinking of retiring, they had been clearly led to serve the Lord in Indonesia.

Their obedience was being richly rewarded, and they had found themselves in the middle of a revival which was breaking out all over Indonesia; many thousands were turning to Christ as the gospel was proclaimed with healings, miracles and even some attested cases of the raising of the dead. Keith was working to establish a radio broadcasting ministry, and he was in urgent need of some of the recording equipment required to fulfil this ministry. For some inexplicable reason he felt impressed to write to Arthur about this.

Arthur and Eileen could not understand why. They had no financial resources for purchasing such equipment, but Arthur began to make inquiries. He was advised that it would be best for Keith to buy the equipment himself in Singapore. As Arthur shared the need with various people, he quickly collected the £100 required and sent this off to Keith.

This simple incident, in which a need was shared and met, resulted in a vision being born in Arthur and Eileen for something far bigger. They began to think of the many missionaries Arthur met at conferences around the country. 'If only we could have teaching like this when we are abroad,' he would hear them say. 'We seem to be constantly giving out and seldom taking in.'

Surely there was a need of supplying 'spiritual food' to missionaries while they were abroad, not just on their visits home? Arthur and Eileen began to see that this could be done through tapes and literature. But that was not all. As well as meeting spiritual needs, there was also a need to provide for physical needs. In many lands there were food shortages, and essential supplies were difficult or expensive to obtain.

As they prayed about these ideas, they became convinced that God was calling them to initiate something in this area. They had by this stage totally forgotten about Eileen's prophecy, but when they came across it again in their notes, it provided clear confirmation. They decided to operate under the name of 'Supplyline' and began to share the idea with others. All were very encouraging, and a number gave financial support.

In January 1967 they sent off their first food parcel, a 20lb package for Keith and Belle Liddle. They knew the diet in Indonesia was mainly rice and vegetables, with very little protein, so they packed it with tins of meat and processed cheese, as well as vitamins, and a few luxury items of biscuits and chocolate.

It was an expensive parcel to send, and by the time they had sealed it securely and filled in all the customs forms they felt the need to pray and lay hands on it, asking God for its safe arrival as a real seal to the work they were commencing.

A few days later, Arthur was speaking to the students at the London Bible College on the subject of revival. He mentioned the revival that was taking place in Indonesia, and was approached afterwards by a lady missionary who had just come back from the Far East. He told her about this parcel to which her immediate response was, 'Oh, that will never arrive!'

Seeing a look of horror come across Arthur's face she qualified her statement. 'At least, if it does arrive safely, it will be a miracle. We never receive parcels.'

'In that case, we'll be asking God to do a miracle,' replied Arthur. As he thought over this 'chance' encounter, he could not help but smile at the Lord's sense of humour. Without this knowledge, God could have done a miracle without their recognising it!

They continued to pray regularly for the safe arrival of this parcel, and eventually they heard from Keith. Not only had the parcel arrived completely intact, with no customs duty charged, but the timing was perfect. Belle was about to return to New Zealand for a period, leaving Keith in Indonesia, but she was worried about his health and how he would manage without her to prepare his meals. The parcel arrived the day before she left. It provided just the reassurance she needed that there was no cause for worry. God was in control.

Meanwhile Arthur and Eileen had written to about a dozen friends who were overseas, sharing the idea with them, and asking for their comments. All were most enthusiastic and positive. God was clearly giving the go-ahead, and they began to make contact with various missionaries who they felt could benefit from Supplyline, asking them to complete a questionnaire identifying their main areas of need. This was particularly important when it came to food parcels as needs varied greatly from place to place.

By the end of 1967, Supplyline had rapidly developed and over forty missionaries were on its books. One of the bedrooms at The Forge House became the Supplyline room, and was soon filled with tape-recording equipment, stored food, shelves of books and packaging. Initially most of the work fell on Eileen, but gradually a small team of local helpers developed around her. The vision had come to birth.

☆   ☆   ☆

One of the inevitable results of the development of Supplyline was an increasing number of invitations for Arthur to travel overseas, and in the autumn of 1968 he set off on a visit to India. The invitation had come from a group of missionaries based at Landour, who used to travel up into the Himalayan foothills near Dehra Dun for an annual conference.

Arthur, now in his mid-forties, was able to include a visit to Nepal, Pakistan and Afghanistan on his itinerary, and planned to be away from home for about two months. On the way out he decided to stop off for two days in Rome, and to visit an Italian Count he had met during the war. It was here that his trip got off to an unfortunate start.

At Heathrow, instead of taking his briefcase onto the plane as hand luggage, he allowed it to be taken with his main luggage into the hold of the plane. On arrival at Rome airport, he collected his suitcase, but there was no sign of his briefcase. All enquiries proved fruitless and the airline could only assure him that as soon as it was found they would notify him and send it on. In his missing briefcase were his Bible and sermon notes, and the only manuscript of a new book he was working on, *Pray in the Spirit*. It is easy to be wise in retrospect, but he really kicked himself for allowing this to happen. All he could do now was to commit the situation to God. As he prayed, God clearly brought into his mind the words 'David recovered all'.

This phrase is found in 1 Samuel chapter 30, where David and his men returned to their home town of Ziklag to find that, in their absence, the Amalekites had raided the town, carried off their wives and children, and set fire to their homes. David's men were so distressed that they threaten to stone him, and he turned aside to pray. At God's direction he led his men in pursuit of the enemy, with the outcome that 'David recovered all'.

Arthur took hold of this verse as God's promise that he would recover his briefcase, and fully expected it to turn up when he arrived in India. Despite intensive enquiries on his arrival at Delhi airport, however, there was still no sign of it and he made his way north to Dehra Dun without having recovered anything.

As if that were not enough, he arrived in the hill country to find that he'd lost his passport. He knew it was in his possession on arrival at Delhi, but now it was nowhere to be found. This was embarrassing to say the least. The loss of his briefcase had been beyond his control, but the passport could only be put down to his own carelessness.

A number of missionaries were praying that Arthur would get his briefcase back, but his passport? That was something else. A British passport was worth a lot of rupees on the black market, and they urged him to apply to the British Embassy for a replacement.

Nevertheless, the more Arthur prayed about it, the more he felt God repeating the words, 'David recovered all', and he became increasingly convinced that this promise included his passport as well as his briefcase. He determined not to make any application for a new passport. To do so would be a denial of his faith.

A few days later, back in England, Eileen's mother received a letter from the controller of the airport at Lagos, Nigeria, telling her that he had a 'missionary briefcase belonging to a Mr Wallis'. Could she advise him what to do with it? Arthur's home address was evidently unclear from the contents of the case, and he had picked her name at random from his address book. Eileen contacted the airline, who arranged for the briefcase to be forwarded to Delhi, and sent Arthur a telegram.

As for his passport, it transpired that he had left it at the bank at the airport when he had changed some money on arrival. Eventually after a month without his Bible and sermon notes, and just in time for his onward journey to Nepal, a friend who was travelling down to Delhi was able to collect both items, and 'David recovered all'.

☆   ☆   ☆

The work of Supplyline was growing rapidly and there was no danger of The Forge House becoming too quiet or of Eileen finding herself at a loose end when Arthur was away. There was much for her to do in the day-to-day running of the ministry, and a constant buzz of helpers was going to and fro.

When they were home, Arthur and Eileen were still

attending the little Baptist chapel at Sidmouth Junction
on a Sunday morning. This church was now being run
by Jim Kelly, an income-tax official from Honiton. They
were warmly received here, but God was beginning to
speak clearly to Arthur and Eileen about establishing a
new church in East Devon which would reflect the move
of the Holy Spirit that was taking place throughout the
country.

On Sunday evenings, a small group of friends occasionally met at The Forge House for Bible study, prayer
and fellowship, although none of them really saw this as
'church'. A young married couple, Mike and Penny
Stevens, began to come along, and they proved to be a
significant catalyst in the development of this group.

Mike was an officer in the army, and had recently
been posted on special assignment to the Royal Marines
base at Lympstone near Exmouth. He and Penny, who
were expecting their first child, were looking for a
regular church to attend.

'Arthur, we've found our church,' said Mike as they
shared tea together one Sunday afternoon.

'Oh, where's that?' inquired Arthur.

'It's here!' said Mike. 'This is where we're getting fed.
This is where our friends are. This is where we feel at
home. This is church!'

'Well it's interesting you should say that, Mike,' said
Arthur, who was shortly to leave on a two-month trip to
South America. 'The other day I felt God saying that by
the time I return to England there will be a church
meeting in our home.'

It was a small beginning, just a handful of committed
people. Gradually more were added, and there was a
steady growth in love and unity as well as numbers.
They continued to meet on a Sunday evening, but
would often gather together at The Forge House during
the afternoon for informal fellowship together, each
bringing their contribution to a communal tea.

The meeting was normally led by Arthur or Mike, but
would follow a very open format, with everyone free to

participate. Time would be given to praise and worship, and to prayer and seeking God, and often Arthur, Mike or others would give a talk. With such few numbers it was always very relaxed and informal, and open to the leading of the Holy Spirit.

When Arthur was at home, he and Mike would meet regularly for prayer each week. This was important to Arthur, for he looked on Mike as the main one to assist him in carrying the responsibility for the infant church.

At times Mike found their prayer times quite an education. Arthur had just completed the manuscript of *Pray in the Spirit*, a book which dealt specifically with the Holy Spirit and prayer. One of the chapters was about prayer 'without words', a reference to the Spirit interceding with 'groans that cannot be expressed' (Rom 8:26). Arthur had begun to experience this kind of prayer, and when Mike first witnessed him groaning, prostrate on the floor, he was a little taken aback!

It was very much a father-and-son relationship. They would take time to relax as well as to meet for prayer, and on one or two occasions went sailing together on the Exe estuary. Mike was able to borrow a sailing boat from the Marines, and Arthur thought this would be a great opportunity to do some bird-watching, one of his great loves.

As they sailed up the estuary, with Mike manfully struggling to control the sails and steer the boat, Arthur would be seeing what birds he could spot through his binoculars. It reminded Mike of the incident in the New Testament when the disciples got caught in a storm on the lake, with Jesus fast asleep in the boat, seeming oblivious to their predicament. He could identify with those disciples!

'Look Mike,' Arthur would exclaim excitedly, 'a pair of cormorants.'

'Over there! An arctic tern. . .'

'Now that's an unusual gull. . .'

'I've not seen any geese quite like those before. I'll have to look them up in my book. . .'

'Oh yes, how wonderful Arthur,' replied Mike, wishing the Lord had given him two extra pairs of hands.

☆   ☆   ☆

In 1970, *Pray in the Spirit* was published by Victory Press. It was not intended to be a general book on prayer, but as Arthur said in his preface:

> It concentrates on the ministry of the Holy Spirit in relation to prayer. It investigates the deeper meaning of that apostolic injunction, 'Pray in the Spirit.' It analyses our many weaknesses in prayer and the spiritual and practical difficulties we encounter and shows us how the Holy Spirit helps us in our weakness and makes up for all our deficiency. It encourages us to yield ourselves to Him and allow Him to pray through us. We need have no fear that this will make us unbalanced or extreme. The more fully we submit to the Holy Spirit the more Christ-centred we become, and the more truly God is glorified in us.
>
> What tremendous possibilities there are when we have lunged into that river of the Spirit which is full of water. Here are 'waters to swim in'. Prayer in the Spirit suggests new avenues waiting to be explored, new resources to be tapped, new power to be released. And when we have begun to enter into all that is opened up in these pages, we shall realize how much there is of 'the deep things of God' still waiting to be discovered.

The book contained testimonies of various people to whom God has given a specific ministry of prayer and intercession. Some had been led by the Spirit in remarkable ways, experiencing similar physical sensations to those they were praying for many miles away. Some readers reacted adversely to the recounting of these experiences, but many others wrote to Arthur saying what an inspiration the book had been to them.

☆   ☆   ☆

Arthur was in India when, in the autumn of 1968, Jonathan first went away to Birmingham University, but towards the end of his first term he made the time to spend a night with him in Birmingham.

As they were getting ready for bed, Jonathan told Arthur that he had started writing to Sylvia Courtney, a young lady he had met at Beacon Heath Chapel in Exeter, where her father was an elder. Many of the young people in this Brethren Assembly had been filled with the Holy Spirit, and Jonathan went there regularly. Sylvia was at college in Cardiff studying physiotherapy, and he had arranged to go down there at the end of term and spend a weekend with Graham and Sylvia Perrins in order to visit her.

Thinking of his own impetuosity in proposing to Eileen on their first date, Arthur cautioned his son to 'make haste slowly'! Jonathan had at this stage simply written to Sylvia, but he believed that God had clearly spoken to him that it was right to start dating her.

Arthur was only too well aware that it is not easy to hear 'the word of the Lord' objectively when it comes to matters of the heart! However, the friendship blossomed. Before long Jonathan brought Sylvia to The Forge House to meet Arthur and Eileen, and they too became assured about the relationship.

Sylvia's parents had heard many of the rumours that came back from New Zealand about Arthur and were understandably cautious at first. However, as they got to know Jonathan, and then Arthur and Eileen, their fears were gradually allayed.

With Jonathan now away at university for most of the year, Arthur and Eileen should have become a lot more free to travel away from home. God seemed to have different plans however, and other family commitments were to place a significant restriction on them over the next few years.

Eileen's father died in December 1968, and during 1969 her mother spent much of the year staying with Arthur and Eileen at The Forge House. Eventually her home at Shoreham-by-Sea was sold, and she decided to buy a flat at Worthing, near Eileen's brother. By this time, however, Arthur's mother was becoming a cause for concern.

Ma Wallis had been living on her own in a small house on the outskirts of Exeter, and was still physically very fit. Unfortunately her mind and memory were failing, and it was no longer safe for her to be living alone. Arthur and Peter took their responsibility for their mother seriously, and during 1969 decided that she should sell her house and come and live with them, spending two months with Arthur and Eileen, and then two months with Peter and Meg in Ashford.

Virtually as soon as Mrs Hemingway had gone back to Worthing, Ma moved into The Forge House for her first two-month stay. At first she would not hear of the idea of selling her house. She agreed to come and stay with her sons, but in her mind she was just on a visit. It was well into the next year before Arthur and Peter's powers of persuasion prevailed and her house was put on the market.

The fulfilment of this responsibility toward his mother placed an increasing limitation on Arthur's ministry. Ma's state of mind was steadily deteriorating and he knew it was not right to leave her alone with Eileen, particularly with Jonathan away at university. For six months of the year, therefore, he would not accept any speaking engagements that would involve staying away from home.

It was a restriction that he believed God had allowed for a purpose, enabling him to give much more time to the development of the local church in Talaton, and to the work of God in the Devon area. He was also able to give time to the writing of his next book, *Into Battle*, a manual on spiritual warfare which was published in 1973.

In the summer of 1971 Jonathan graduated from Birmingham University and married Sylvia. The wedding took place at Belmont Chapel in Exeter. Mike Stevens performed the wedding ceremony, and Allan Pavey, one of the youth leaders at Beacon Heath, gave the address. Arthur gave an emotional speech at the reception, sharing that he and Eileen had always wanted more children. He in particular had always wanted a daughter. He did not look on Jonathan's wedding day as the day when he lost a son, but as the time when at last he gained a daughter.

17

The Seven

The whole issue of biblical prophecy and its interpretation was becoming a matter of increasing concern to Arthur. There was no doubt in his mind that God was unlocking several important keys that were to be of prime significance to the church in the end times. One was clearly the baptism and fullness of the Holy Spirit; another was the restoration of New Testament church pattern and structure. A right understanding of prophecy would, he believed, be a third.

Biblical eschatology (the study of the end-times) was a subject about which there were more divergent theories and opinions than virtually any other aspect of theology. Matters like the place of the state of Israel in God's purposes, the great tribulation, the rapture of the church, and the millennium were all subjects of great debate and argument between Christians, each determined to fit these things into their own particular eschatological viewpoint.

Arthur had his own thoughts and ideas on many of these issues, but had never felt sufficiently certain about any one school of thought to take it on board unreservedly. His mind was open, and he was becoming convinced that God intended to impart some fresh revelation and understanding of these matters.

Arthur did not believe that biblical prophecy could ever be properly interpreted on a purely intellectual basis. God seemed to have deliberately surrounded the subject in a shroud of mystery. It was the job of the Holy Spirit to lead God's people into the truth, and it would only be through the revelation of the Holy Spirit that these things would be made clear.

With these thoughts in mind, he decided to gather together a group of like-minded men to spend a few days in prayer and waiting on God; he hoped they would make some progress in understanding this subject. This 'Mini Conference on Prophecy' was convened for 8th–11th February 1972, at The Forge House.

Five men were invited: Bryn Jones, Peter Lyne, David Mansell, Graham Perrins and Hugh Thompson. All were by now fully involved in the 'charismatic movement' and deeply committed to seeing all that God was saying about a 'New Testament church' outworked in practical terms.

They were a radical group of characters, each involved in full-time ministry among the new fellowships and groups that were emerging out of the charismatic movement. None of them was prepared to settle for the 'status quo', believing that the outpouring of the Spirit would be dissipated if it was contained within man-made church structures and institutions.

Bryn Jones had got to know Arthur well since the Mamhead Park Conference in September 1962. After a spell of missionary work in Guyana in the mid sixties, he was now based at Bradford in Yorkshire where he was leading a small newly formed church.

Peter Lyne and Hugh Thompson were living in Bristol and were both involved in independent fellowships. Peter came from a Christian background, but had rebelled as a teenager. He had come back to God at Loughborough University while studying for a physical education degree, and had experienced the baptism of the Spirit at one of Denis Clark's early Prayer and Bible Weeks. Denis, Arthur and Campbell had each been a great influence on him.

Hugh came from a Brethren background and had first heard Arthur speak as a teenager. To a young intellectually orientated Bible student, Arthur's message was disappointingly straightforward, and yet through it God touched and challenged him on an altogether deeper spiritual level. A few years later, as a young Brethren evangelist, he read a report of Arthur's baptism in the Holy Spirit, and began to seek after this experience for himself. He was baptised in the Spirit at a conference in 1964 and this had effectively burned his boats with the Brethren.

As a young man Graham Perrins also heard Arthur speak while he was studying at the South Wales Bible College. Not long after leaving college he had visited G.H. Lang in Dorset, and happened to meet David Lillie there. This encounter resulted in an invitation to the 1958 Exmouth Conference, which was the beginning of a developing friendship with Arthur. Graham lived in Cardiff where he led a small fellowship.

David Mansell's contact with Arthur was the most recent. He had been converted in the Brethren, baptised in the Holy Spirit in 1970, and had then met Arthur at a conference in Exeter. Arthur's message on 'God's three keys for the end times', the Holy Spirit, the church and the prophetic, had made a deep impression on David, who lived on the outskirts of London. Not long afterwards he launched out into full-time Christian ministry as an 'independent'. He had no obvious support or financial backing, just a sense of God's calling.

Arthur wrote to each of these men in December 1971 to set out the objectives for the mini conference and to encourage them to come prepared. Rather than invite specific contributions, he wanted each man to give some time to seek the Lord and to come ready to share whatever God showed him. There were various basic questions, however, which Arthur felt would provide a solid foundation for further investigation:

1. What is the nature of biblical prophecy? Is it merely 'history written in advance' or is there more to it, as would

be implied by the statement 'the testimony of Jesus is the spirit of prophecy' (Rev 19:10)?

2. What are the purposes of biblical prophecy? How does it apply to those to whom it was first given, to those who will see it finally fulfilled, and to those living in between?

A consideration of these questions would perhaps throw some light on the main question:

3. What are the keys to its interpretation? Are there lessons to be learned from fulfilled prophecy? Where the prophecy is detailed and specific, does this mean the interpretation is to be detailed and specific, or could it have a more general and figurative meaning?

Arthur outlined these and other questions in order to stimulate thought and get the ball rolling. He also decided to invite Lance Lambert from Richmond to join the conference. Lance led a fellowship at Halford House in Richmond, and Arthur felt that his strong views on Israel would add an extra dimension to their deliberations. Lance was keen to come, but was unable to do so due to illness.

On Thursday 8th February 1972, the six of them gathered together at The Forge House. Right from the start there was a sense that God was going to do something very special, and as they began to pray a most remarkable prophetic spirit came upon them. As God started speaking, they experienced a rising sense of excitement and anticipation, and it soon became clear that the Holy Spirit was leading them in a way they had not expected. It is true that they did receive some insight into the nature of prophecy, but the main emphasis was on the person of the prophet. God was speaking to them about men and ministries rather than doctrines; about relationships rather than theories.

God spoke about the fear of the Lord, and the fact that his secrets are only revealed to those that fear him, showing them that the interpretation of prophecy is deliberately veiled and hidden so that it cannot be understood on an intellectual level.

You have wondered at the mystery of my prophetic word. You have wondered at the secrets so seemingly hidden in darkness. And I have ordained it so. . . . For the blindness that is upon you all is a darkness that is essential, for it is the shroud of mystery. For if I would have made it clear and plain, then there would have been no hidden counsel, no hidden wisdom. Men would have quickly forgotten the glory of the Lord. Men would have swiftly lost the fear of me . . . they would have lifted themselves up as gods because they know all. I say the hidden and the secret and the darkness is essential.

But I have ordained that in your generation there shall be those to whom I will draw aside the curtains and the shrouds, and they shall be permitted to see, not to see all, but to see that which I shall have ordained for them to speak forth. For you shall witness in this season the arising of prophets that are to speak forth with an anointing of word that shall capture the attention of my people far and near. . . . And the word which shall come forth from their lips shall be a word so anointed . . . that it shall come as revelation and shall burn in its coming and bring life in its flow, for they shall be prophets of the word.

And there shall be prophets of manifestation and their ministry shall be exercised not in what they say but in what they do; for they shall demonstrate the signs and the wonders of the kingdom. . . .

And there shall be prophets that are meant solely to be a prophetic voice in what they are, so that as men view their life and the disciplines of their life . . . the prophet indeed shall be the message. . . .

And there shall be prophets who will write and they shall be slow of speech . . . but they shall write my word and it shall be sent into all the earth so that my purposes are made known unto my people far and near.

Do not think that I speak only through him that speaks. I speak through him that writes. I speak through him that performs. And I speak through him that simply is what I am saying at this time.

The Holy Spirit was concentrating their thoughts on the ministry and person of the prophet rather than the interpretation of prophecy. In fact God warned them that when revelation came, they were to be prepared to hold it to themselves.

> It is not the time to share all that I will whisper; for I will prove my prophets. If they are the men to bear my secrets then they must hold them, for too much has been too hastily spoken and so swiftly lost.
> Learn to hold until I declare to you the time to speak, and then the very word that would have crushed will build, then the very word that would have injured if you had run too soon will now illuminate that others might see . . . learn I counsel you to hold my secrets, says the Lord.

Each of the men present felt an overwhelming sense of God's presence among them, and an exhilaration that comes from the impartation of God's word and of fresh vision. David Mansell, for one, did not get much sleep; such was the sense of the Spirit's anointing that he kept getting visions in the night. Peter Lyne didn't get much sleep either, he was sharing a room with Dave!

Arthur surprised one or two of the others by producing a bottle of wine for their evening meal. Both he and Eileen had been completely teetotal when they were first married, but they now realised that there was no scriptural basis for taking a legalistic stance over this issue. Paul encouraged Timothy to 'take a little wine for your stomach's sake', and Arthur could see that a little wine in moderation was no bad thing.

God continued to speak very clearly over the remainder of the three-day period. His purpose, he said, was to bring his prophets together.

> It is my purpose that my servants, the prophets, should meet together and should share together . . . and seek my face together, that the secret of the Lord shall be confirmed to their hearts together as a body; that they might be joined together as one; that they shall speak with one voice and one heart . . . recognising one another . . . knowing one another . . . spiritually knit together in the bonds of love and fellowship; that the voice of God may sound through many

trumpets, through many sounds, but yet in one harmonious voice and word to the church. . . . I am not going to raise up one man or two men, but a great multitude of prophets shall arise.

It was in order for this 'coming together' to happen that God had delayed the unfolding of his truth. 'Be patient and hold with patience that which I speak to you; for the delay is part of my divine purpose so that with oneness of voice and oneness of heart the prophets shall speak.'

God encouraged them not to feel limited or restricted by their local church situations, but to realise that God had given them 'a wider calling'. They were living in a time of preparation in which God had deliberately hidden his prophets. 'Think not that the prophets have vanished from the church . . . but I have hidden my servants in this my hour of preparation.'

God was at work in the lives and circumstances of his prophets in order that his message might become part of them. What was important in their current circumstances and situations was 'not what you are contributing in the situation, but what I am working in you through that situation. . . . For this is the purpose of the hiding of my prophets, that I might work the word into the man, so that the man and his message are one as he comes forth.'

God was taking 'infinite care and patience' over the preparation of his vessels.

I am not in a hurry, says the Lord. I have eternity at my disposal! . . . What I am doing in your lives I am doing in the lives of scores of my servants. . . . I use upon them the hammer of circumstances, that they might be shaped and made fit vessels; and so the circumstances that I weave around their lives become the hammer with which I am shaping them into what I want them to be.

And I would not have my servants to faint in the day of adversity, when it seems to them that they are victims of chance or victims of unfortunate circumstances; but I would remind them that I am ever the God of circumstances for I have my hand on the hammer.

God also likened his dealings with his prophets to a crucible where the refiner's fire would be put to work.

For is it not declared in my word that that which withstands the fire shall be made to go through the fire? For I know what I am doing, says the Lord. . . . It is I, the Lord, who sits as the refiner and the purifier of the silver. . . . Therefore submit to my dealings and though at times it may seem the flame is hot, I will not permit it to be one degree hotter than is needful, nor keep the metal upon the flame one minute longer than is needful, that they might be the men that I wish them to be—purified and refined, as gold that comes forth from the crucible, reflecting something of my glory and with the imprint of my image upon them.

They all felt it would be important for them to meet together again, and in one of the prophecies God gave them specific instructions about this.

For in your coming together again you shall come together to share what I have continued to minister to you. For I have caused each of your spirits to quicken the other . . . that you will seek even further in the secret place. For three times this year shall you meet and seven shall be your number, and you shall understand why I have ordained this in your coming together.

This specific direction led to some discussion among them. As Lance Lambert had been unable to come, there were only six of them, and yet the prophecy had specified seven. They all felt that Lance was not intended to be the seventh man.

After some prayer and discussion it was agreed that John Noble should be invited to join the group. John had established an unconventional but successful fellowship at Romford which met each Sunday in a private room in 'The Cauliflower', a local public house. The year before he had written a hard-hitting little book called *Forgive us our Denominations* in which he referred to denominationalism as disunity and sin. John was generally perceived as a radical and anti-establishment figure, but they all felt that he would make a very positive contribution to the group.

☆   ☆   ☆

In May 1972 Arthur and Eileen became grandparents when Sylvia gave birth to a baby girl, Katrina Joy. Although the birth was somewhat premature, both mother and baby were fine, and as soon as they could Arthur and Eileen travelled north to view the new addition to the family.

After their marriage the previous year, Jonathan and Sylvia had initially spent several weeks based at The Forge House where they were able to look after Supplyline while Arthur and Eileen were abroad. They too had married before finding themselves a permanent home or job. After a few weeks Jonathan found work in Birmingham and they moved to the Midlands, where they settled in Solihull and played an active part in a newly formed fellowship.

In August 1972 Jonathan, Sylvia and Katrina joined Arthur and Eileen on a week's holiday in South Wales. In the confines of their small holiday cottage Arthur soon learned the meaning of 'Grandpa's privilege': he could cuddle little Katrina while all was sweetness and light, and give her back to Sylvia as soon as she cried or filled her nappy!

☆   ☆   ☆

Arthur's 'mini conference on prophecy' had turned into something far more radical and far-reaching in its impact than he or any of the other men had expected. Whatever their preconceived ideas and expectations,

God had directed them very specifically, and they made plans for further meetings later in 1972.

John Noble was invited to join with them, and the seven of them met again twice that year. In some ways the last of these meetings was the most significant of all, for it was at this gathering that God spoke to them very clearly and unequivocally about authority and commitment, matters which have become the subject of much misunderstanding and controversy since that time.

This meeting took place in December 1972 at Tourners Hall, near Chigwell in Essex, where David Mansell was living. Everyone turned up except Graham Perrins, and none of the others seemed to know what had happened to him. Eventually they discovered that he was taking some meetings not too far away, but had not thought to let them know that he was not coming. The others were somewhat put out by this and decided to ask him to come over.

It transpired that Graham was not happy with the way their gatherings were progressing. He had always had a deep love of the prophetic scriptures, and was disappointed that they had deviated from the original purpose of their gatherings. Instead of telling the other men, he had decided to communicate his displeasure by not turning up.

By talking together face to face, the whole thing was brought into the open, Graham was very apologetic, and relationships were restored. Although this incident was comparatively insignificant in itself, God used it to bring to a head the whole matter of commitment. What is the basis of our commitment to one another, and what does it really mean in practical terms?

There was a good deal of frank and open discussion between them, and as they spent time in prayer, God spoke to them through the prophetic word. He told them to consider the way he dealt with individuals down through the years, men like Abraham, Noah and Job. They were not perfect, but God was prepared to commit himself to them.

Have I not often committed myself to individuals, committed myself in deepest pledge? . . . Consider the ways of your Lord and Master, Jesus. Did he not commit himself to a handful of men? . . . Were they perfect men? Were they perfect with each other? You know this was not the case. But notice the depth of his commitment, their Lord and Master who had insight into their temperaments, into their extravagances, into their follies. But did he not see the potential of the grace of God within their lives? . . . My Son was committed, first to me but also to these men. Were they a body? Were they flowing together? No, not at that time, but he saw what they would become with the enduement of my Spirit upon them. . . .

And the prayer of my Son, my beloved Son will yet be answered. I will yet have ministries that are one even as I am one with Jesus and he is one with me. And you will become one, organically one, for I am doing something in life. I know your different temperaments; I know why I have called you together, as samples; for you are not all, you are not exclusive; I am working among many of my prophets and many of my teachers, and many of my elders and many of my apostles all over the earth. But I am beginning, this is my workshop. I am teaching you things of human nature, I am teaching you things of life. I am committed to you, my sons. Walk before me as imitators of your God. . . . Love one another with a perfect heart and be committed in depth, says the Lord.

This prophetic word not only emphasised the whole question of commitment, but it also gave them an important clue as to the basis of their meeting together. God had drawn them together as 'samples', as 'a workshop'. They were dealing with issues which were foreign to the church of their day; no one else was proclaiming this depth of commitment within the body of Christ.

God was not calling them to form a super new denomination; he was not even making them into an apostolic team. What he was calling them to be was a workshop, a group where the principles he was teaching them could be talked through and thrashed out. Their relationship together was to be an example to follow rather than an end in itself.

They were not a group where these things could ever be completely worked through. That could only come as the principles they were learning together were taken and applied in the church. God's purpose was to work something out among them that they in turn could impart as a foundation into many other situations.

> You shall be committed for this purpose, that as one voice of authority you shall lay the foundations in many fellowships that they might become expressions of my body. ... And you shall not merely be given to them to lay foundations of truth but you shall continue to minister to them to raise the foundations into a structure through which my truth can be expressed. ...
>
> And in this way you shall bring glory to my name in your ministries and you shall find fulfilment ... no longer as isolated ministries, but as corporate ministries, so that multiplicity of ministry will bring the multiplicity of manifestation and demonstration that is needed in your day.

God was not looking for individuals each doing his or her own thing, but for an expression of unity which would be seen as people with differing gifts and ministries learned to work effectively together. This would demand not just commitment, but also submission one to another.

> As you will teach my children by your example of commitment, so too will you teach them of submission, for you will teach them by your submission one to another. For in this, my children, you have very much to learn. ... I have spoken in my word that you should all be subject one to another, and this submission is that which is lacking in my church in every strata, and in this you will come together and you will discipline one another and teach one another. For you have all expressed needs, weaknesses and failings, but that in which you are weak, another brother has as his strength. ... And as you teach one another that in which you excel and learn to be disciples of one another, so you shall be welded

into a rod in my hand . . . a prophetic manifestation of what I am.

In the same way that Jonathan and David were joined together by a covenant of love, God was calling them to be joined and committed to one another.

> Your souls shall be knit together even as I knitted the soul of Jonathan to that of David, so that David and Jonathan loved each other and Jonathan loved David as his own soul. This was a love covenant. Yours shall also be a love covenant. And you shall recall that the outworking of that love covenant was that this young prince stripped himself of the robe that was upon him and gave it to David, even to his sword his bow and his girdle. And there shall be a stripping; this shall be part of the price of commitment, a stripping and a giving.
>
> And you shall know too how there was between these two a loyalty, and you shall recall how Jonathan covered David and stood for him when his father spoke ill of his friend. And so you shall be required to stand one for another before the world and before your brethren, for each of you shall come under attack and there shall be a price in the place of reproach to pay for your committal; but in this you shall know a deepening of the bond and a release of the blessing and a strengthening of your love, for this is my work.

The things that God was saying to them were probably of more significance than any one of them could fully take in or appreciate at the time. Nevertheless much time was spent discussing the practical implications of what this covenant bond of commitment really meant. As well as looking out for one another's spiritual welfare, they felt it also involved such down-to-earth areas as care for the widow if one of them should die.

As the initiator and 'elder statesman', Arthur had found himself the non-elected chairman of a group of strong and single-minded men. They approached things very differently from him, and would often 'fly by the seat of their pants', shooting off convictions and feelings that they had not thought through deeply and prayerfully. Arthur, on the other hand, needed time for careful consideration before he felt able to pronounce judgement. Their ability and mental sharpness often made him feel like the plodder of the group. No one could accuse him of being afraid to confront issues head on, but he was by nature gentle and sensitive, and to be in a position of having to handle a group of young spiritual tigers was at times somewhat overwhelming.

Some of the prophetic words that God had given them stressed the need to reach out and include others, and not to become exclusive. Some took this to mean that the group of seven should be widened to include others. Why should men who shared the same vision as the seven be excluded? After their initial three meetings, therefore, the decision was taken to widen the group in the future.

Bryn Jones was quite opposed to this. He felt that such a move was premature, not because God wanted to keep other men out, but because the seven of them weren't even ready for what God had already given them. He felt that they first needed to work through the things God had already said in a deeper way before widening it out to others. When they did so, it would then be from a much more solid and secure foundation.

The majority view prevailed however, and a further seven men were invited to join them: George Tarleton, Gerald Coates, Barney Coombs, Maurice Smith, Ian McCullogh, John MacLauchlan, and Campbell McAlpine. The seven had suddenly grown to fourteen, and what had been a lively but manageable group doubled in size.

18

A Home of Your Own

With the continued development of Supplyline, The
Forge House was a constant bustle of activity. What had
started in one bedroom was beginning to take over the
rest of the house. A number of regular helpers came to
and fro each day, and Nancy Samson, the acting secretary of Supplyline, was living with Arthur and Eileen.
Ma Wallis, whose condition was steadily deteriorating,
was also in residence for half the year. Not only that, but
the house was the base and meeting place for the
church. There was never a dull moment!

On one visit to Arthur and Eileen, Bryn Jones
described their home as 'Piccadilly Circus in the rush
hour'. He told Arthur that it was time for him and
Eileen to find a home of their own. Arthur replied that
he wanted to find a place for the work of Supplyline and
for the church first; only then would he think about
somewhere for themselves. Bryn urged him to start
looking for a home as well.

For some years Arthur and Eileen had been praying
about property. One idea was to find a large house
which could become a headquarters for Supplyline, a
meeting place for the church, and a home for any
workers involved. They also had visions of a significant
base emerging which could include training and conference facilities and perhaps even a Bible school.
Whenever any large properties in the area came onto

the market they eagerly went to view them. Although they had no money for such a major purchase, they believed that God would provide the finance when the time came.

One such property came up for sale at the little village of Plymtree, not far from Talaton. It would have cost a massive sum of money to buy and equip, but Arthur and Eileen felt it was right to put in an offer. Much prayer went up and they were convinced that God would supply the necessary finance. The Lord seemed to have other plans, however; their offer was not accepted.

Often as they were praying, both together and with others, God would speak through the prophetic word. Many times there would be reference to 'the house of the Lord' and they interpreted this in terms of a literal building. They found it all too easy to apply what God said to their own preconceived ideas and desires. Having taken these prophecies very seriously it was perplexing when many of them apparently remained unfulfilled. Later they began to see that much of what they were interpreting literally was in fact fulfilled spiritually in terms of 'the house of the Lord' as the church.

Another perplexing episode resulted from some scriptures which God gave to Arthur and Eileen concerning a 'field'. 'Finish your outdoor work and get your fields ready; after that, build your house' (Prov 24:27). 'She considers a field and buys it; out of her earnings she plants a vineyard' (Prov 31:16). They interpreted these verses to mean that they would buy a field, on which the work of the church and of Supplyline (the 'vineyard') would be established. Only after they had built suitable accommodation for the work of God would they build a home of their own.

When a field suitable for building came up for sale right in the centre of Talaton they got very excited. They could immediately see the potential for their plans to come to fruition, and became convinced that this was God's provision. On several occasions they walked across the field, praying and claiming the ground they'd walked on. It was a great disappointment when the land was eventually sold to a property developer. Again they could only accept that God must have a different plan.

It was a humbling experience to step out in faith and share their convictions with others, only to find that what they thought to be faith was in fact presumption. Nevertheless, God had been very gracious to them; he had blocked the way before any financial commitments were made. They could so easily have fallen flat on their faces, but their hearts had been in the right place and God had graciously overruled.

Arthur learned much through these experiences. Whenever his prayers seemed unanswered, or things did not work out as planned, he would always seek the Lord to know why, rather than simply accept or write off the situation. Over the question of the property, he could see how they had allowed their preconceived ideas to sway their judgement when interpreting Scripture and prophecy. He knew that God was well able to move supernaturally on their behalf, but they had been over-spiritual in their approach. Where practical common sense did not accord with their expectations they had written it off as unbelief rather than realistically facing the issues and seeing that God could also be speaking through this means.

Gradually Bryn's comments began to gel with Arthur and Eileen. Perhaps God was wanting them to look for a home of their own. It was something they had longed for for many years, but they had always pushed the thought to the back of their minds, believing that 'the work' had to come first. The reality was that they were very much part of the work, and it was becoming important for them to have somewhere to relax and be quiet, away from the day-to-day hubbub of The Forge House.

Developments in the church were slow but encouraging. A number of new people had joined, and some had left. Mike Stevens had been posted to Northern

Ireland in 1970, and so he and Penny had only been in the church for a short while during its early development. After a spell in Londonderry he was posted to Yorkshire where he joined Bryn Jones and the church in Bradford. A thriving ministry centre had developed there under Bryn's leadership.

Operating under the name of 'Harvestime' the Bradford centre had become the focal point of a developing network of churches around the country and was also responsible for the publication of *Restoration* magazine, launched in the mid seventies to express the vision for the restoration of the church. Mike eventually left the army to work full time with the Harvestime team.

One of the couples who became part of the church at Talaton were John and Ruth Ward, who moved into the village a few doors away from Arthur and Eileen. John was the son of Billy Ward, an original participant in the monthly revival prayer meeting and one of Arthur's companions on his evangelistic expeditions in the fifties. Billy had died in 1969, and John had married Arthur's niece Ruth, Peter's eldest daughter. She was a competent secretary, and managed to combine bringing up a young family with doing a lot of typing for Arthur and Supplyline.

Another couple who moved into the area were Robin and Celia Talbot and their family. They had been missionaries in Thailand and came into contact with Arthur and Eileen through Supplyline. Very quickly they got involved with the day-to-day running of the work, and Robin took over the main responsibility for Supplyline on a full-time basis.

By 1974 the church numbered about thirty adults. People were coming from all over the district, and it was becoming clear that the base for the fellowship should be moved into Ottery St Mary, a small nearby town of about 5,000 inhabitants. This was an obvious centre for the church to reach out into the surrounding area with its many small villages. It also seemed the best place to look for a new home.

In 1974, not long after Arthur and Eileen celebrated their silver wedding, Ma Wallis died. During the last few months of her life she had deteriorated physically, and was virtually bedridden. She died peacefully in Peter and Meg's home, and was buried in Bristol alongside her husband.

Ma had spent the last five years of her life living with her two sons, and the final months of constant attention and nursing had not been easy for Peter and Meg or Arthur and Eileen. In the end her death was a great relief to the family, knowing that for her it was a glorious release and a joyful reunion with the husband she had so sorely missed over the years.

For Arthur and Eileen, Ma's death coincided with finding a new home in Ottery St Mary, and they moved in not long after the funeral. With the restriction of caring for Ma now removed, it seemed like a new beginning for them. They were able to purchase a beautiful modern bungalow, situated in a prime position on the edge of the town, which they named 'Shalom'.

It was a spacious property, with glorious views over the surrounding countryside, and a large and well-stocked garden. Part of a small estate of bungalows, theirs was the one that the builder had constructed for himself; it was in the best position and fitted out to the highest standard. Nothing could have been a greater contrast from the old and well-worn surroundings of The Forge House which had been their home for nearly twenty-five years.

On one occasion when they were praying about finding a property for Supplyline and the church, Eileen had received a vision of some pampas grass waving in the wind beneath a sunny blue sky. It had become something of a joke, and whenever they looked over a property they would always look for the pampas grass. They had not given this any thought when choosing their new home, and were somewhat surprised when, just a few days after moving in to 'Shalom', they looked out of the window to see some pampas grass waving in the breeze in the corner of the garden. They had not noticed it when they first looked over the property. It seemed as if God was saying to them, 'Just in case you had any doubts, you really are in the place that I have chosen for you.'

This new phase of their life brought fresh challenges for Arthur and Eileen in the area of finance. They had saved some money towards the property and had also inherited some capital; this gave them enough for a substantial deposit, but they still required a mortgage for the balance of the purchase price. Never having borrowed money in their lives before, it took a while to adjust to the idea of a mortgage. Surely if it was right for them to have this property then God could supply them with the cash to buy it outright?

God had to show Arthur that they needed to learn to live by faith in a different realm, to trust him to provide the mortgage payments each month in the same way as thousands of others. This was quite a challenge, the rent at Talaton had been very low, and now their monthly mortgage payment was going to be more than their total living expenses at The Forge House!

One of the ways in which God supplied their needs was through the regular support of the church. Throughout their early married life it had been considered unspiritual to talk about finance; people in full-time Christian service were expected 'to look to God and not to man' for their needs. This meant not knowing where, when or how much they would receive. In many ways this was an exciting way to live, and Arthur and Eileen had proved the Lord's faithfulness on many occasions. By the mid-seventies however, it was generally recognised that there was nothing unspiritual about the principle of tithing and providing regular support to those in full-time ministry.

Up till this point, Arthur had received no regular financial support from the church. His income came from money he received when preaching away from home. Others in the fellowship could see that there was a wrong principle here and proposed that Arthur and Eileen begin receiving regular support from the church. This was a great help when it came to meeting their regular mortgage commitments.

Under the direction of Robin Talbot, Supplyline continued to operate from The Forge House, which was now devoted exclusively to this work. The church obtained the use of a Roman Catholic Convent School for their meetings, right in the centre of Ottery St Mary.

Arthur and Eileen settled happily into their new home. For a while they found it difficult to adjust to the comparative luxury of the bungalow after the basic simplicity of The Forge House. Arthur enjoyed working in the large garden and growing tomatoes and cucumbers in the greenhouse, reviving skills he had learned as a young man in the nursery at Claverham. The house was built on sloping ground and had extensive foundations, some of which were large enough to walk around in. Arthur made one of these rooms into his study; here he could work in peace, looking directly out over the garden.

As Supplyline developed, there would be a steady flow of missionaries wanting to visit the work and meet those involved. To cater for this in an organised way, small conferences were arranged at regular intervals. These provided a direct opportunity for missionaries to receive spiritual ministry and fellowship while at home from the mission field. At first Shalom was an ideal base for this; the meetings and meals were held there, utilising the large sitting room and adjoining sun-lounge. Arthur and Robin gave ministry, along with some outside speakers, and the local church helped with catering and the provision of sleeping accommodation.

Arthur and Eileen thought about converting some of their basement area into rooms that could be used to provide further accommodation for some of these visiting missionaries. In some ways they were a bit embarrassed to have such a nice home just for themselves; to explain that it was going to be used 'for the work' was one means of overcoming their embarrassment.

Of course many guests did stay in their new home, but Arthur and Eileen came to see that God actually wanted them to enjoy his provision for themselves. It was a love gift from a Father who enjoys giving good gifts to his children. They stopped trying to justify it, and never got round to putting any further rooms in the foundations.

19

Division

As a young man with a burning vision for revival, Arthur envisaged something in the mould of the Welsh or Hebridean revivals that had first inspired him. These revivals were sovereign interventions of God, moves of the Holy Spirit which brought great waves of repentance in their wake, with hundreds and thousands seeking after God's righteousness. Over the years he had come to realise that, however exciting these revivals might have been at the time, there was a missing ingredient. The evidence of history was that they simply did not last.

He was only too well aware that if he were to visit the Hebrides again, he would find little ongoing evidence of the revival which took place just twenty years previously. Similarly the South Wales region which experienced such a mighty move of the Spirit was now an area of spiritual darkness, with many of the chapels born out of the revival having closed. Although these revivals represented significant milestones in the lives of many believers, they had made little lasting impact on the church or world at large.

As Arthur pondered these matters he could reach only one conclusion: the nature and structure of the church had simply been unable to contain the blessing that God was pouring out. Jesus made it quite clear by parable that if you try to contain new wine in old wineskins disaster will result. Arthur felt this was precisely what had happened in the revivals of days gone by. New wine requires new wineskins and this, he could see, had profound implications for church life and structure.

The revelation that God was now imparting about the restoration of church life and structure excited him, not simply as an end in itself, but because he could see it was an essential prerequisite to an end-time revival that would exceed anything that had gone before in power and lasting impact. Arthur was beginning to understand that commitment to revival presupposed commitment to restoration. He remembered the words he had written in the front of his first book *In the Day of Thy Power*: 'If you would do the best with your life, find out what God is doing in your generation and fling yourself into it.'

Arthur was in little doubt that God was in the business of restoring the church in his generation, and he was determined to fling himself into it wholeheartedly, whatever problems, difficulties and opposition he might face. He had always resolved to be radical in his pursuit of God's purposes, and was not afraid of criticism from others who seemed wedded to the status quo.

In committing himself to the group of seven, Arthur was aligning himself with younger men who were on the whole far more radical and 'avant garde' than himself. They had each caught a vision of the new thing that God was doing and were generally quite uncompromising in their pursuit of it. The meetings of the seven were marked by prayer, prophecy, waiting on God, and a clear sense of God's presence. Somehow things changed after the group widened and the emphasis shifted to discussion and dialogue. There was usually a divergence of views and opinions on the many topics that arose, and they were not afraid to voice their differences and openly disagree with one another.

The covenant between the seven was never reproduced among the fourteen. Bryn for one could not commit himself wholeheartedly to the wider grouping, and attended very few of their meetings. Some of the others came to an occasional meeting. Although Arthur felt a love and commitment to all the men, he came to share Bryn's view that to enlarge the group so soon was a mistake. As a group of seven they could have worked through their differences and established a far deeper commitment together than was ever possible in the wider context.

God had called them together as a workshop in which the principles of commitment and relationship could be worked out and then applied in the wider context of the church. There was much of value emerging from their discussions, but Arthur would have liked to have seen a much greater commitment to prayer and waiting on God so that these things could be worked through in depth.

One of the most important areas which did emerge from the workshop was insight into the nature and function of the gifts or ministries mentioned in Ephesians chapter 4, verses 11 and 12:

> It was God who gave some to be apostles, some to be prophets, some to be evangelists, and some to be pastors and teachers, to prepare God's people for works of service, so that the body of Christ may be built up until we all reach unity in the faith and in the knowledge of the Son of God and become mature, attaining to the whole measure of the fulness of Christ.

They were convinced that these ministries were not merely intended for the New Testament era but were foundational gifts on which the church would be built throughout history. When Jesus said, 'On this rock I will build my church' (Mt 16:18) he was referring in the first instance to a man whom he had just named Peter, the rock; in the more general sense he was establishing a principle that the divine revelation on which the church was built was entrusted to men like Peter. The gifts and ministries of Ephesians 4 were foundational to the church which God was building. Such men will not be perfect, Peter even denied his Lord, but they were none the less the instruments that God had chosen to use in building his church.

The early meetings of the seven had concentrated on the ministry of the prophet; they were beginning to see that the role of the apostle was equally important. Earlier in the book of Ephesians, Paul talked about the church being 'built on the foundation of the apostles and prophets'; it was apparent therefore that these ministries should operate side by side and were of particular significance in the building of the church. Prophetic insight on its own was not enough, but the apostle brought the wisdom of a 'master-builder' to ensure that a solid foundation is laid in the church (1 Cor 3:10).

Arthur had for a long time felt that there was no scriptural basis to support the view that apostles somehow finished with the early church. But what about the practical implications? How are those with an apostolic gift to be recognised? What is the basis and extent of their authority? These were difficult questions.

Each of the men was keen to clarify his own function and role in ministry. They were generally agreed that if God has called someone to be an apostle or prophet, he will already in some measure be doing the job of an apostle or prophet and this should be clearly recognisable by others. Some of the fourteen were already functioning in this way, and their gift and calling could be acknowledged and recognised. Arthur was in some ways quite difficult to categorise and never saw himself as an apostle but more as a prophet. He was perhaps most clearly 'a prophet of the pen', one who through his writings would express what God was saying prophetically. As an older man he was also looked on by a number of the others as a father figure. His commitment to righteousness was widely acknowledged and appreciated.

As those with the gift and calling of the apostle were recognised, many independent groups began to align themselves with them and the sphere of their ministry was rapidly expanding. A key issue became the nature of apostolic authority, and how this was worked out in and through the rank and file of the church. Concepts like 'shepherding' and 'discipling', 'covering' and 'submission' began to emerge, and to be widely propagated throughout the 'restoration movement'.

There was little doubt in Arthur's mind that these principles represented important areas of truth that were being restored. For too long the church had been marked by the independence of those determined to 'serve the Lord' by doing their own thing. He could see great value in Christians being prepared to open their lives to one another and to 'submit to one another out of reverence to Christ'.

Before long the whole subject of shepherding and submission was generating a lot of controversy and criticism in Christian circles. Some of it was undoubtedly justified. There is always a danger that a particular truth can be over-emphasised and taken to extremes, and a number of 'horror stories' emerged as these principles were worked out. Some church leaders abused their position and sought to domineer those under their care, a clear sign of insecurity on their part; other Christians became so dependent on their relationship with 'those over them in the Lord' that they lost all sense of hearing personally from God for themselves.

Invariably Arthur would be asked about these things as he travelled around. He was always at pains to stress that the abuse of a principle does not negate the underlying principle. He would point out that Satan never seeks to bring about a distortion or a counterfeit of something that is not real in the first place, and he then endeavoured to bring his listeners back to a balanced understanding of what the Bible really teaches. At the bottom line, the church was built on relationships of love and respect for one another, and deep commitment. In his dealings with leaders, Arthur would emphasise the need for godly character and attitudes:

leaders should be those who serve rather than domineer. He considered that it would be disastrous to introduce principles of shepherding structure without this type of foundation.

When the 'workshop' of fourteen came together, Arthur would have the job of chairing the proceedings. In some ways he was the ideal chairman, tactful, diplomatic and disciplined, and he carried the respect of all the men whatever their viewpoint. When it came to the cut and thrust of debate, however, he sometimes found it difficult to hold things together, and lacked the sharpness required to bring issues to a resolution. Although very good at getting to the heart of things on a personal level, he found it far more difficult in a group context. After a while, therefore, it was agreed that Graham Perrins would act as co-chairman with Arthur. It was hoped that Graham's clarity of thought would add a more purposeful edge to their deliberations.

In September 1974 God instructed them through the prophetic word to meet less as a large group and to concentrate on working out at a local level the principles they had learned together.

> The time has come to be more and more integrated with those men that are in your vicinity and within the sphere of the calling and the place that I have planted you.

They were directed back to the covenant the seven had made with one another and told that 'this that has become your history becomes your future'. These principles of covenant were to be worked out in their own spheres of operation and thereby multiplied through the inclusion of many others. Although God was encouraging them to continue in loving relationship with one another, the fourteen were not destined to become a closely-knit unit.

It was becoming clear that serious differences of opinion and approach were emerging within the group. One of the most prominent areas of division centred on the whole matter of law and grace.

All the men would have agreed that we are no longer under the law, but under grace; none of them would have wished to hold on to legalistic attitudes in matters of external practice. They would have no intrinsic problem with Christians being free to go into a pub and have a drink, or to have a glass of wine with a meal, or to play football on a Sunday, or to turn up at church in a pair of jeans. However, serious differences did emerge over how this freedom was promoted and at what point freedom turned into licence.

These were controversial issues in many of the evangelical churches of the day. Arthur would often find himself listening to the concerns and criticisms of Christians from these churches who approached him in the confidence that he would view these matters from a biblical and godly perspective. It was not always easy for him to know how to answer their questions. On the one hand he was committed to remain loyal to his covenant brothers; on the other hand he shared some of the genuine concerns that were being expressed.

Arthur and Bryn felt that their behaviour in these external matters of conscience should show consideration for the views of others and be adjusted according to the company they were in. Whereas they felt quite free to drink alcohol, for example, and would not evade the issue when asked, they did not feel it was appropriate to promote their freedom aggressively. They would point to scriptures like Romans chapter 14 to justify their approach:

> Accept him whose faith is weak, without passing judgment on disputable matters. . . . The man who [does] must not look down on him who does not, and the man who does not . . . must not condemn the man who does, for God has accepted him. . . . Each one should be fully convinced in his own mind. . . . If your brother is distressed because of what you [do], you are no longer acting in love. Do not because of your [doing] destroy your brother for whom Christ died. . . . Let us therefore make every effort to do what leads to peace

and to mutual edification. . . . So whatever you believe about these things keep between yourself and God.

Others within the group, like John Noble and Gerald Coates, felt that Bryn and Arthur were not being completely honest and open by effectively keeping part of their life under wraps. Their concern was to live open rather than secretive lives and they saw no need to hide their freedom. Neither did they feel they were out to promote it aggressively, even if it appeared that way to others. On the other hand, where it was a question of exposing legalism rather than a mere difference of conscience, they saw justification in taking a more aggressive stance, just as Jesus did with the Pharisees.

One evangelical 'sacred cow' that came under attack from the proponents of freedom was the daily 'quiet time'. Most Christians had been brought up to believe that the only way to start the day was to have a 'quiet time' in which they read the Bible and prayed. For many this had become a dry and legalistic routine, yielding little joy if adhered to and much guilt if missed. This became another focal point of the law and grace debate. Some of the brothers brought a strong emphasis on God's grace, and encouraged people into a place of liberty where they could enjoy God and fellowship with him at any hour of the day, and be free from any sense of guilt if they missed their 'quiet time'.

Arthur had a real problem with this approach. A disciplined approach to life had been instilled into him from childhood, and he felt that there was some value in a regular commitment to spend time with God, even if on occasions it was dry and dull. He saw a real danger that the baby would be thrown out with the bath-water and Christians would end up spending no time with God at all.

Undoubtedly, some of Arthur's misgivings were a result of personal taste and style rather than doctrine. In matters of dress he was at the conventional end of the spectrum; to him a shirt was made to be worn with a tie, and he had never owned a pair of jeans in his life! He found it difficult to square up some of the brothers' flamboyant style with the decorum he expected from Christian leaders.

Despite his misgivings over some of their views, actions or dress, Arthur felt fully committed to each of the other men, and never questioned their integrity. When approached by others he would strongly defend their character, even if he could not fully approve of their actions. The deep covenant that the seven had made to one another was something he took seriously.

As a group they were unafraid to deal with the sort of questions that other Christians skated round or avoided. Topics such as masturbation were the subject of full and frank debate, although Arthur did not find it easy to talk openly and freely about this type of issue.

A further development during this period was the establishment of links with a group of men in the United States who had independently reached similar conclusions regarding the restoration of the church to New Testament principles. This group, known as the 'Fort Lauderdale five', comprised Ern Baxter, Bob Mumford, Don Basham, Derek Prince and Charles Simpson. Their influence within the United Kingdom first came to prominence with the visit of Ern Baxter to the Lakes Bible Week in 1975.

Ern's ministry at the Lakes made a tremendous impact. He was a gifted and effective communicator, and his inspired talks on Saul and David were very well received. He drew an effective comparison between the humanly based 'head and shoulders' leadership of Saul (whose physical stature made him stand out as 'head and shoulders' above anyone else) and the anointed leadership of David, a man after God's own heart. He stressed the need for committed 'covenant' relationships, using Jonathan's covenant with David as a model.

The Fort Lauderdale men felt that the differences

and difficulties that were emerging in the British scene were primarily a result of a lack of effective leadership, or 'headship'. Their counsel was that Arthur should take on the leadership of the group, and that the other men should all submit to him. Although willing to be obedient to God's calling, Arthur was only too well aware of the difficulty of the task and of his own inadequacy.

If this was the will of God, then clearly it was vital that it found general acceptance among the British brothers, but none of them could see it. They felt that the Americans were trying to push Arthur into a role that he was neither suited to nor anointed to fulfil. Their grouping was a workshop, not an apostolic team, and God had not instructed them to establish any formalised leadership structure. Their commitment and covenant to one another was based on mutual respect, but if any one of them chose to do his own thing or to go his own way, there could be no formal basis for bringing discipline or resolve.

The Americans had perceived that there was a need for someone to hold the British men together. However, it was already evident from the increasing tensions between them that this would be very difficult, if not impossible, for anyone to achieve. It only reinforced the view that they had enlarged too quickly and too soon. Although the seven had made a deep covenant with one another, it was now very difficult for them to resolve their differences in the context of the enlarged group.

Things finally came to a head in 1976 at the South and West Bible Week which was held at Monkton Combe near Bath. The main speakers at this week, Ern Baxter and Bob Mumford, were also coming across to the Dales Bible Week, due to be held just before. Peter Lyne, who was the main organiser for the South and West Week, had advertised the Week extensively on the basis of these two well-known speakers. Things did not get off to a good start when he was told at a late stage that Bob Mumford had withdrawn and Ern was to be coming alone.

Ern ministered with great power and authority at the Dales. He was comfortable in his relationship with Bryn and Arthur, who both valued his input. They did not see Ern as having any governmental or 'covering' authority over them, but welcomed his prophetic and inspirational ministry. Whereas he felt accepted and at ease at the Dales, it was a different story when he came down to the South and West.

On arrival at the South and West, Ern's wife, who was travelling with him, was taken ill and had to be admitted to a hospital. This was an understandable pressure on him, but it soon became apparent that he was not happy in other respects. He made no attempt to identify with the praise and worship and was clearly uncomfortable in the meetings. When he stood up to speak, it did not seem to be the same man as at the Dales.

Arthur was also ill at ease in the meetings which were highlighting existing concerns of his in the area of worship and dance. He had always enjoyed worship and entered into it fully, but was troubled at what he saw as an over-emphasis on dance from men like Graham Perrins, who was leading the worship at the Bible Week, and John Noble. A large space had been kept clear at the front of the marquee for use in dance, and Arthur felt this gave it undue prominence. He also felt that people were being pressured into worship in a way that was not helpful.

It was obvious to Peter Lyne and Graham Perrins that Ern was not at ease, but they were unsure what lay behind his discomfort. Realising there were issues to sort out, Peter asked Graham to broach the subject at their next morning get-together. Used to being frank and open among his brothers, Graham challenged Ern to share what was obviously troubling him. 'We're here to learn,' Peter added. 'Do tell us what it is.'

But such an open confrontation made Ern all the more unhappy and he was not prepared to be forthcoming. Instead he wanted to catch the next plane home, but was persuaded to stay. The week continued amid great tension.

Arthur was deeply disturbed by this, and felt very much caught in the middle of things. Ern, their guest and a man whom he held in the greatest respect, was obviously unhappy with the situation. Arthur felt that the way he had been challenged bordered on rudeness. On the other hand, Peter and Graham were clearly bewildered by what was going on and could not understand Ern's refusal to be specific about what was concerning him. Arthur had been hoping that Ern's presence at the Bible Week would help to bring healing to some of their differences. Instead he had proved to be a catalyst.

He decided to ring Bryn, sharing what had taken place and requesting he came down. By the time Bryn arrived, Ern's concerns had clarified in his mind and he shared them with Arthur and Bryn. He had been conscious of a spiritual force opposing him from the moment he took his seat on the platform. Having sought God about this, he was seriously concerned.

Arthur was deeply disturbed in his spirit. Much of what Ern was expressing struck a chord with him and confirmed to him things that he had already been feeling, but he did not feel he could accept Ern's serious judgement of the matter without a clear word from God himself. What was God saying? What did God want him to do? How could these issues be resolved? After the next evening meeting, he stayed up to seek God. Throughout the night he walked and prayed, crying to God for wisdom in the situation. By the end of the night, he felt that God had given him an answer.

The Bible Week ran its course. It was not the time and place for any further confrontation. Instead the cracks were papered over and things kept running as smoothly as possible. For Peter Lyne, who felt personally responsible for the event, the whole week was a living nightmare, and he could not wait for it to end.

After the Bible Week was over, Arthur was keen to arrange a meeting to confront the issues that were threatening to undermine their relationship. However Bryn, who shared his concerns, was by this time in the United States for an extended period, and Arthur did not feel it could await his return. They agreed on the telephone that he would formulate a letter to send to John Noble and Graham Perrins, laying out their mutual concerns. Arthur felt that it was appropriate that he, rather than Bryn, wrote the letter, because much that he wanted to say resulted from the things God had specifically revealed to him at the Bible Week.

It was a strongly worded letter, outlining clearly the matters that had caused tension between them, and identifying what he believed to be the spiritual issues involved. But Arthur was anxious not to appear judgemental and he also sought to express his deep love and concern for his brothers.

> I cannot convey to you the effect that all this had on me. I knew that God had spoken, but the men about whom he had spoken were my brothers who had been drawn together in the first instance at my invitation. I had broken bread with them in solemn covenant, promised to cover them in time of attack, to minister to them in time of need, even to care for their widows and children if they should be prematurely taken. How could I receive this word? I told God that I still loved my brothers, and that there was not a shred of animosity in my heart towards any of them. . . . I can tell you, it just broke me up.

The letter went on to make it quite clear that they could not continue in working relationship together until these things were resolved. Eileen, when she read it, wondered how it might be received but, more than anyone else, she knew how much prayer and heartache had gone into it on Arthur's part and kept her reservations to herself.

In wording the letter as he did, Arthur was trying to

express unequivocally what he felt God was saying, and to stress the seriousness with which he viewed the issues involved. His intention was that it would lead them all to a place where they could sit down together, seek God and find a resolution to the issues. But he underestimated the impact it would have, and events developed very differently.

The letter came as something of a bombshell to John and Graham. They felt as if they had been tried, found guilty and sentenced with no opportunity to speak for themselves or properly talk through the issues. The letter became well-publicised and notorious. Arthur had expected it to be shared with close associates, but it was circulated far more widely which surprised and shocked him. He had intended it as a private letter to the men concerned.

Having to write the letter was a cause of deep pain and heartache to Arthur, but he was convinced it was something God required him to do. He had always sought to maintain the unity of the Spirit, and yet his actions now resulted in deep division. Each of the men found themselves having to make a choice of allegiance, even if, as happened with some, they felt a strong commitment to men on both sides. Arthur was genuinely heart-broken.

He felt the enemy had totally distorted what was a real effort to bring clarity and resolution to serious issues. His motivation was still to see the church established and restored as a glorious expression of the body of Christ, fit to receive and contain a great outpouring of revival. He had endeavoured to put God's kingdom and righteousness above all else, and yet his efforts had resulted in a divided kingdom.

In retrospect he began to see that the matter had not been handled wisely. Although still convinced of the truth of what he had written, to convey it in the form of a letter was a mistake. Despite his efforts to convey his love for his brothers, a letter is cold and formal and open to misinterpretation. Perhaps if they had met face to face, even if their differences were not resolved, they could have shared their hearts with one another and agreed to part on a far more amicable basis.

As things stood, all he could do was to commit the situation to God with many tears and to pray that good would come out of the situation. What could have become a burden that crushed him, he turned into a burden of intercession and determined to begin working towards healing the breach.

20

Moving North

With the developing emphasis on restoration of the church, the nature of Supplyline was changing, moving towards the support of the indigenous church rather than overseas workers from Britain. Eventually the responsibility for running the work was moved up to Middlesborough under the auspices of David Tomlinson. David, together with Philip Mohabir who moved to Britain from Guyana to work with him, had a clear vision for the way the ministry should develop and reach out into the third world.

Robin Talbot's involvement therefore was decreasing, and this left him with much more time to devote to the church at Ottery which was steadily growing. Arthur took the overall leadership responsibility, but there were other men working with him, including Robin, who was now an elder of the church.

John Ward was also developing into a leadership role and became an elder of the church in 1978. John had been Jonathan's best friend for many years and so had a close relationship with Arthur and Eileen. After Billy Ward's death in 1969 Arthur had become a father figure to John, and they used to meet together regularly for fellowship and prayer. Another man who became part of the leadership team at this time was David Dixon. He had been a Baptist minister in East Grinstead before moving to Devon to take up a pastoral role in the Ottery church.

On the wider front Arthur continued to do all he could to restore relationships with the men on the other side of the 1976 divide. Although he could not alter his convictions, he was keen to renew friendships and establish a basis for dialogue. He determined to renew contact with men like John Noble, Gerald Coates, Graham Perrins and Peter Lyne. On various occasions, when in the vicinity of their homes, he would call in unexpectedly. His efforts were warmly received. There were still significant differences of opinion on the issues involved, but a door of communication was opened, and the opportunity taken for face-to-face dialogue and reconciliation.

One of the key issues of the day was the nature and extent of apostolic authority. Arthur and Bryn had come to see the role of the apostle in very clear-cut terms. They felt that if the apostle's ministry was to be effective within a local church, there needed to be clear recognition of his authority by the local leadership. Not everyone could see this. Men like Jack Hardwidge felt that to accept this degree of apostolic input diminished the position of the elders who, in reality, held the ultimate authority for the local church. Jack was now leading a fellowship on the outskirts of Exeter with which Arthur had been closely involved over the years. Much as he loved and respected Arthur, he could not accept all that he was now saying on this issue.

Arthur was never one to pull any punches. He was radical in his beliefs and completely wholehearted in his pursuit of whatever he believed God to be saying. As one of those pioneering a new area of truth, he was undoubtedly too unbending at first. As things progressed, while still holding to the fundamental importance of the role of the apostle, he became somewhat more flexible in his approach, and saw that authority and relationship needed to go hand in hand.

Another area of teaching on which Arthur held particularly strong views was the thorny subject of women's head-covering. From his study of

1 Corinthians chapter 11 he concluded that Paul's 'apostolic injunction' could only be obeyed by women physically covering their heads when praying or prophesying. Many fellow leaders, who had experienced the legalistic stance taken by the Brethren over this issue, could not accept this interpretation. They would say that the important thing was heart attitude, not what a woman wore on her head, and it became an area of tension for some.

Arthur could accept that inner attitude was more important than outward conformity. He was not looking for legalistic obedience, but for a heart attitude of acceptance that, in a similar way to baptism, was reflected in outward actions. It was never his intention to turn head-covering into a major issue, but he did feel it was something that was clearly presented in God's word and could not therefore be ignored.

To some, Arthur's stance appeared legalistic, although this was never his intention. On this, as in other areas, he was uncompromising in his commitment to what he believed to be the teaching of the word of God. It was a subject which aroused deep feelings in many and inevitably got blown out of all proportion.

☆   ☆   ☆

During the mid seventies, Arthur had been approached by CLC about *In the Day of Thy Power* which was now out of print. They felt there was still a demand for the book, and wanted to reissue it in paperback format.

Arthur was not altogether happy about this. He felt that his vision for revival had progressed a long way since the early 1950s when the book was written, and considered that it needed to be brought up to date. He promised CLC that he would work at revising or possibly rewriting it. The more he thought about it, the more he realised that a mere revision would be insufficient. Not only were there new areas in which he felt his vision had expanded, but he also saw the need to prune the original.

The result was a new book entitled *Rain from Heaven* which was published in 1979. Arthur summarised how he felt his vision had changed in the introduction to the book.

This book is old yet new. . . . *In the Day of Thy Power* was a hardback which eventually went into four editions. When the publishers approached me a few years ago about re-issuing it in paperback, I discouraged them from doing so. I felt that it had the characteristic faults of a first book. It was too long and too heavy for the average reader. Even more important, it needed to be brought up to date in the light of all that had transpired since it was first issued, not only in the church but in the author's heart! . . .

Those who possess a copy of the old book will find that among a number of omissions are some of the chapters on prayer. This is not because I now disagree with what I wrote, or feel that prayer is not so important after all. Far from it. But what may be related to revival, and what is strictly relevant to revival are not one and the same, and there was much in the earlier book that was related rather than relevant. This has been cut in order to keep the book within the compass of a normal paperback, particularly as three new chapters were being added.

People have sometimes asked me, 'Have you changed your convictions about revival since you wrote your first book?' The answer is 'No'. Reading through it after a number of years was a salutary exercise. There were things that I had let slip, and that I needed to hear God speak again to my own heart, but nothing that I wish I had not written. However, *Rain from Heaven* is a new book; it is different. This is because I have come to see the importance of revival, not so much in its short-term results for the church, but against the grand back-drop of God's age-long purpose for the church and the world. This has brought a significant change of emphasis . . .

Taking the twenty or more years since my first book was published, I believe the most significant event that has taken place in the church at large has been 'the charismatic movement'. . . . Though I was involved in the movement

from its earliest beginnings, and have never doubted that it
was born of God, I do not believe that it was or is revival.
The following chapters will explain more fully the reason
why. . . .

The message of *Rain from Heaven* is intended to challenge
us all for the greater thing that God is waiting to do, and
especially those whose personal experience of the Holy
Spirit and his gifts tempted them to feel, 'This is it! We are in
revival.' I would say again, 'God has something bigger on his
heart.' He is ready to give us both the vision of it and the
hunger for it. But let us remember that praying for it
pre-supposes a willingness for all that it entails. We must be
ready for change, for moving on with God, to abandon
everything that God shows us is a hindrance, and to embrace
whatever new light he causes to break forth from his holy
word.

Arthur's intention was to retain the essential message
of his original book, but to link this in with all that God
was now doing through the 'charismatic' and 'restoration' movements. His original material was greatly con-
densed, and three new chapters were included.

The first of these was entitled 'Community Style'.
True New Testament 'koinonia' or 'fellowship' involves
the restoration of family relationships, and of the body
of Christ functioning in true unity. Arthur saw this as an
essential mark of revival.

His next new chapter was entitled 'A New Structure'
and was based on Jesus' parable of the wine and the
wineskins. New wine cannot be contained in old
wineskins, and a fresh outpouring of the Spirit cannot
be contained in old forms and structures. This chapter
clearly illustrated how Arthur's vision for revival linked
with his commitment to the restoration of the church.

His final chapter was also new, entitled 'The Revival
of Tomorrow'. In it Arthur maintained that the outpouring of the Spirit in revival is not an end in itself, but
that God's ultimate purpose is that the body of Christ
comes to full maturity as a 'bride' made ready for the
return of Christ, the 'bridegroom'.

What then are we to look for in the revival of tomorrow? Of course we want to see the people of God set on fire. We want to know that overwhelming sense of God's presence which brings the fear of the Lord. We are expecting too that powerful impact on the secular community, resulting in multitudes converted, baptised and filled with the Holy Spirit. We are looking for signs and wonders, miracles and healings performed in the name of Jesus. But we are also expecting that many will begin to share God's heart in relation to his church. That there will be a willingness for reformation and recovery, for man-made structures and ecclesiastical appointments to be replaced by relationships resulting from bone coming to bone in the body and the recognition of the anointing of the Spirit as the only qualification for ministry. . . .

I believe that the greatest chapters of the church's long history have yet to be written, and that it will be said of the generation that brings back the King, 'This was their finest hour.'

When published, however, *Rain from Heaven* did not have anything like the success or impact of the original book. Some readers found the emphasis introduced in the new chapters unacceptably radical. Reviewing the book in *Renewal* magazine, the Reverend Tom Walker made the following comments:

It is disappointing that in pleading for 'true unity and maturity' in Christ's body the author has possibly heightened the tension between leaders in denominational churches and those in 'the new undenominational churches' by imputing suspicion and a feeling of being threatened to the former.

Arthur would have expected some opposition for speaking out against the 'man-made structures and ecclesiastical appointments' found in many of the historic denominations. However, even some of those who were in sympathy with this emphasis found the book mildly disappointing. To add three new chapters, and yet to still end up with a book of less than half the length of the original involved drastic pruning. Many readers who had been challenged by the message of *In the Day of Thy Power* agreed that something important was lost in this process.

In the Day of Thy Power was a classic textbook on revival. It had a quality that was timeless, even if, with the passing of the years, the language and style had become somewhat dated. Perhaps, in his desire to bring the book up to date, Arthur had underestimated the ongoing impact of the original.

☆   ☆   ☆

It was now 1979, and although they had only been in their delightful bungalow at Ottery St Mary for about four years, Arthur and Eileen were seriously considering moving. When they had first gone to Ottery they had offered their home back to God, and vowed that they never wanted it to take over their hearts and rob them of God's best for their lives. They now faced the challenge of giving it up.

Bryn, and a number of the other men to whom Arthur related, felt that he was rather cut off in Devon. They could see that his heart and vision were for something big, but the setting at Ottery was somehow too small for him. Bryn strongly encouraged him to move up to Yorkshire. A further factor was that Arthur was about to become editor of the new *Restoration* magazine, and this would be much easier if he was on the spot.

At first Arthur and Eileen could not see the logic in moving. Devon had been their home for nearly thirty years, and the thought of leaving took some coming to terms with. As they prayed about it, however, they began to see that for Arthur to move away would be a positive thing for the church.

'I feel a bit like a clucking hen at Ottery,' Arthur remarked to John Ward one day. 'If the church is to realise its potential, I need to move aside so that you other men can develop in leadership.'

Arthur and Eileen no longer had any family ties in Devon; Jonathan, Sylvia and their two girls were settled in Solihull in the Midlands. Katrina was now seven years old, and the youngest in the family, Fiona, was three years younger and about to start school. Arthur and Eileen would still see as much of their family if they were based in Yorkshire as they did in Devon.

Selling their bungalow at Ottery proved no problem; it was snapped up privately by the friend of a neighbour even before it was properly on the market. Finding a suitable house in the Bradford area was somewhat more difficult. Having always lived in the country, the streets of Bradford did not give them much joy. What they really wanted was a nice bungalow with a sunny aspect and country views, rather like the one they'd just left! In the end they decided to move to the area and rent a house while they continued to look for the right property to buy.

When they heard of a country bungalow that was for rent, it sounded just what they were looking for. This property was in the small village of Askwith, about halfway between Otley and Ilkley. It was a modern three-bedroomed bungalow that had been built by a farmer for his retirement. Situated about half a mile up a narrow lane that led only to the owner's farm, it faced south with a glorious view of the beautiful Wharfdale valley and the moors rising away to the rear.

It could not have been a more idyllic situation, far more 'country' than their home at Ottery, and yet still only half-an-hour's drive from the centre of Bradford. The minute they saw it, they knew it was God's provision.

'Father must want you to write another book here,' said Eileen as they looked over it for the first time.

21

The Radical Christian

In May 1979, Arthur and Eileen moved up from Devon and quickly settled into the new environment of the Yorkshire Dales. Askwith was a superb setting for anyone who appreciated the outdoor life, and in their spare time they were able to do more walking and bird-watching than ever before.

At this time Bryn Jones was living in the United States, and so Arthur saw no more of him than he had done when living in Devon. Mike and Penny Stevens, on the other hand, were quite nearby and Arthur was able to renew regular contact with Mike. They would often walk and talk together, and regularly played tennis. True to his competitive nature, Arthur usually managed to win their matches, something which Mike, as the younger man, found very frustrating!

Eileen's initial comments about writing a book at Askwith proved to be prophetic. Already ideas were forming in Arthur's mind for what he felt would be his most important book to date. Despite all the blessings of the charismatic renewal, there was still much which passed for Christianity that simply did not stand up in the light of God's word. He could see that most Christians just accepted the status quo, and shied away from facing up to these issues head-on.

In Arthur's opinion the charismatic movement, having flourished in the seventies, was now in decline and he felt that these *laissez faire* and compromising attitudes were to blame. One of the qualities he had inherited from his father was an intense dislike of compromise, humbug and wishy-washy Christianity, and he determined to address this area. It would be his most hard-hitting book yet, and Arthur could see that many Christians would find what he had to say unpalatable, but he was convinced he had a message that needed to be heard and faced up to. The book was to be called *The Radical Christian*.

As Arthur sat down to put pen to paper in the quiet and peaceful surroundings of the bungalow at Askwith, he found it difficult to translate his thoughts into words. It seemed as though his mind would come under attack as soon as he gave himself to the task, and he struggled to make much headway. He felt there was more of a spiritual battle taking place over this book than he had experienced with any of his previous writings. If Satan was so opposed to it, he reasoned that God must be wanting to give the book a particularly significant impact. This only increased his determination to persevere and see his original vision brought to fruition.

On a personal level he had come to terms with the fact that writing such a book might close doors that were otherwise open to him. Was he willing for rejection? He could not allow such thoughts to deter him from conveying all that God had given him to say. The radical message he was bringing was one to which he was wholeheartedly committed, and he was prepared to live with the consequences.

Arthur stuck at his task, and the result was a book which lived up to its title and demanded a radical response from its readers. *The Radical Christian* was finally published by Kingsway in 1981. It addressed 'the absence of biblical radicalism' and its underlying message was a simple one: 'Don't compromise.'

To talk about 'the absence of biblical radicalism' probably leaves most of us untouched because we don't quite know what it means. Let's call this malaise by its true name—compromise. This has been defined as 'the partial surrender of one's position, for the sake of coming to terms' (*Oxford Dictionary*). For the Christian it means that he concedes something that God has given, or sets aside something that God has revealed, for the sake of coming to terms with the situation that he faces. . . . When we are dealing with truth, if there is concession there is compromise. . . .

We never compromise out of ignorance, only out of knowledge. The temptation does not arise until God reveals truth to our hearts. It was obedience to new truth that brought the charismatic movement into being. It was failure to give continuing obedience to further revelation that has brought it to a halt. Men who had taken radical and costly steps of obedience at the beginning began to shilly-shally. They were not sure that they wanted to go where God might be leading. They applied the brakes—and the movement ground to a halt. But God moved on. . . . If it is true that God has moved on, where is he now? If he has a fresh word . . . what is that word? If God is still moving, where is he headed? If we have got left behind, how can we catch up? These are some of the questions that this book seeks to answer.

It has not been an easy word to bring. It will not be an easy word to receive. It will not leave the reader in a comfortable place of neutrality. It will call for a verdict. . . . The response of the reader to whatever God may say to him in this book will determine whether he is a compromiser or a radical.

The message of the book was one that could be summed up very simply in three propositions:

1. The God of the Bible is radical in all his dealings with men.
2. This fact was most clearly and powerfully demonstrated in the life and ministry of his Son, Jesus Christ.
3. The kingdom of God is therefore utterly radical in its demands.

What does it mean therefore to be a radical Christian?

A true radical of the kingdom is a man who stands on clear ground in relation to truth. He cannot compromise his conscience, tamper with his convictions, or bend biblical principles for the sake of status or security. Though he does not court unpopularity for its own sake, he is not afraid of it if it comes. His concern is to obey God, and leave the consequences with him. All forms of unreality or pretence are an anathema to him. In words and actions he is captive to principle rather than expedience. This means that he will not hesitate to speak the truth in love for fear of hurting someone's feelings. Nor is he happy to ignore matters which need to be raised, in order to avoid an unpleasant confrontation. In the kingdom of God radicalism means unswerving righteousness.

In Arthur's view, the effect on the church of the absence of true biblical radicalism had been tragic, and Christianity was 'leavened with unreality, hypocrisy and compromise'. The starting point of his thesis was that God himself is radical, and that this radicalism involves qualities such as anger and intolerance that do not go down well in modern society.

Anger and intolerance is the inevitable reaction of a holy God towards all that contravenes that holiness. In this primary sense, God is radical. . . .

One reason why many of us shrink back from any serious consideration of righteous anger is that nowadays society in general and religious circles in particular have tended to treat tolerance as though it were almost the cardinal virtue before which every other righteous principle must give way. We must not confuse that fruit of the Spirit called patience, or the grace of forbearance, with a weak and sickly tolerance, advocated by those who are lenient towards themselves, and want everyone else to act towards them in the same way. . . .

The kind of religious hotchpotch that goes by the name of the World-Council of Churches, that seems to be based on discovering the lowest common denominator of truth that all those involved can agree upon, is equally an anathema to God. It smacks of an easy-going tolerance and of compromised convictions that are altogether foreign to the character of the God of truth.

Arthur was very careful in his treatment of this subject to stress that human intolerance should not be confused with the righteousness of God. There was no place in God's kingdom for a spirit of harshness or aggressiveness stemming from man's insecurity or pride. The radical Christian would also have a spirit of meekness when it came to dealing with others. 'The radical Christian is strong, but his toughness is mingled with tenderness, and his conviction with compassion.'

Having established that God was radical, Arthur then took a look at the radical aspects of the life and ministry of Jesus.

A people bored to tears with the platitudes of the scribes gasped in astonishment at the revolutionary teaching that fell from the lips of the prophet of Nazareth. But it wasn't simply his teaching; his life style was wholly in keeping with what he taught. In stark contrast with the prevailing religious fashion, he focused on men's inward rather than their outward state. He was primarily concerned with heart condition, with attitude and motive. And like all radicals, he was wholly intolerant of unreality and hypocrisy . . .

Christ's radicalism stands out in sharpest relief when we find him in a confrontation with the religious leaders. At times his words and actions were intentionally provocative, as though he was determined to bring issues to the surface, and he did not hesitate to use the most scathing language to denounce their hypocrisy.

Jesus was utterly radical in his family relationships, in the way he rebuked his disciples, and in his approach to people with problems and needs.

Arthur then turned his attention to a radical appraisal of kingdom life, starting with the 'terms of entry' which were clearly stated by Peter on the day of Pentecost, 'Repent and be baptised, every one of you, in the name of Jesus Christ, so that your sins may be forgiven. And you will receive the gift of the Holy Spirit' (Acts 2:38).

Arthur dealt with each of these three elements, starting with repentance. Too many preachers proclaimed a 'free and easy gospel', avoiding bringing people through 'the narrow gate of repentance'. Repentance was an essential 'foundation stone' without which we are 'building on sand'.

The second entry condition was water baptism. Arthur was totally uncompromising in his treatment of this issue, strongly advocating 'believers' baptism'. He could not tolerate the practice of infant baptism which he saw as 'both erroneous and harmful'. To him it was erroneous because he believed that it had no scriptural justification, and harmful because it created false hope in thousands who, because they had been baptised as infants, believed themselves to be Christians. Infant baptism should therefore be rejected by the radical Christian.

Peter's third entry condition of the kingdom was the baptism (or gift) of the Spirit. As Arthur saw it, baptism always spoke of initiation, and the baptism in the Spirit was a vital part of our initiation into the church. In 1 Corinthians chapter 12, Paul stressed this corporate aspect of the experience when he said, 'We were all baptised by one Spirit into one body' (1 Cor 12:13). Arthur could see that many people within the charismatic renewal had fallen into the trap of over-personalising this experience.

> Commitment to Christ is commitment to 'a body', and baptism in the Spirit is baptism into 'a body'. ... The dynamic of the early church was not in Spirit-filled individualism but in Spirit-filled corporiety. ... Baptism in the Spirit is to make our position in the body of Christ truly functional in the power of the Spirit.

The next area Arthur turned his attention to was 'our attitude to the Bible'.

> Yes, our attitude to the Bible, even how we interpret it and respond to it, will always be determined by our relationship with God ... It is inconceivable that people could have a consuming hunger for God and at the same time be careless and indifferent to his word.

The 'prescribed way' in which God expects us to conduct ourselves in his kingdom was determined, not by our own feelings or tradition, but by his word. 'The Christian who is radical, who trembles at God's word, will not allow tradition, sentiment, personal preference, or anything else to prevent him from conforming to what he knows is God's prescribed way.'

Arthur then came to what would undoubtedly prove to be the most controversial area of his book, an examination of church structures and traditions to see whether or not they conformed to the New Testament. If there was 'dry rot in the structure' then radical treatment was required.

God's family suffers because 'the professionals', the spiritual builders, the men in leadership who are meant to know, have shrunk from applying the radical treatment that decaying church structures require, and have contented themselves with superficial treatment. The interior may look spick and span as a result of 'operation renewal' but this will not save the house in the coming storm if the structures are faulty and flimsy. . . .

A church is not fully renewed if the structures are left untouched. To have within a traditional church a live group composed of those who have received the Spirit and are beginning to move in spiritual gifts; to introduce a freer and livelier spirit into the worship with renewal songs; to permit the clapping and lifting of hands and even the dance; to split the week-night meeting into home groups for purposes of discipling; to replace a 'one-man leadership' with a team of elders—all these measures, good though they are, will only prove to be a patching operation. Individuals will undoubtedly be blessed. There will be an initial quickening of the church. But if it ends there, the long-term results will be detrimental. There will be a quiet struggle going on between the new measures and the old structures, and you may be sure that the old structures will win in the end.

One of Arthur's sections on church structure was titled 'The myth of the mingled church'. He maintained that the only biblical basis for the church was for all members to be believers; they did not have to be mature, but they should be clearly born again and committed.

Each believer could then be in a position to find his or her part to play in the local body.

In his extensive treatment of traditionalism, he demonstrated how down through the years man has allowed God's ways to be replaced by human traditions that find no place in God's word.

> How come the development of a priestly caste wearing special vestments and adopting special titles? How is it that churches are now worshipping in 'consecrated buildings', with fixed forms of service, with rites and ceremonies, and numerous other ecclesiastical innovations? It is certain that none of this came from the New Testament. . . .
>
> Of all these developments none was more detrimental in the long term than the return to the priestly caste of the Old Testament. It brought a great divide between priests and people. It divided the flock of God into clergy and laity. It shackled the bulk of every congregation in ignorance, passivity and non-involvement. All priestly functions were now left to 'the professionals'. 'Weren't they paid to do the job?' . . .
>
> The full potential of the body of Christ will never be fully released until this wretched distinction is wholly removed.

Arthur's message was clear. Ecclesiastical traditions tended to obscure or even nullify the word of God, they brought bondage and legalism, and paralysed the effective ministry of the church. This was a hard-hitting message, particularly for those readers who found themselves in traditional churches. What were the practical implications? Should they leave their churches?

Arthur devoted a chapter entitled 'Denominational Dilemma' to answering these questions. There was no hard-and-fast answer to the question of staying in or coming out, and he stressed the importance of the individual hearing from God and knowing his will. 'Provided a believer is convinced that his membership of a local church is in the will of God he should always be encouraged to be loyal to that local body of believers.' Knowing clearly that God had called you to stay in a denominational church was a very different thing to denominational loyalty. There was nothing sacrosanct about denominations or traditional structures of any description. Our only loyalty should be to God's word and to his church.

In the same way, there was nothing wrong with a breakaway movement, provided it was inspired by the Spirit of God. Throughout church history the restoration of 'new' areas of truth had usually resulted in division as the new thing was rejected by the establishment. Division was not necessarily evil.

> Whenever in the history of the church God has done something new the cry of 'Division!' has come from the diehards. . . . It was a widespread cry in the early days of the charismatic movement. It is heard today whenever mention is made of someone leaving his church. . . .
>
> It is a sad but inescapable fact of spiritual experience that truth divides. The truth of the gospel divides families, husband from wife and parents from children. It divides those who receive from those who reject. . . . We pay too high a price for unity if it costs us the truth.
>
> When people leave their churches because they are following convictions which they believe God has given them, let us not be swift to accuse them of being divisive, not at least until we know all the facts. If we do we may be the ones who are grieving the Holy Spirit.

Arthur offered practical advice to those considering leaving a church and stressed the importance of having a right motivation and attitude particularly towards the leadership. It was never right to leave a church harbouring bitterness and rebellion; better first to put right your attitude and relationships in the place where you are. Arthur always encouraged any Christian who was feeling it was right to leave a church to share the reasons for his decision fully and honestly with the pastor or church leaders.

The final major issue dealt with in the book was legalism. Arthur introduced this with an interesting account of 'where the first church failed'. He showed how legalism and Judaism were allowed to creep into the early church, contributing ultimately to its decline. Legalism was still, he felt, 'a major cause of dedicated and devoted Christians failing to move on with God'. He based his treatment of this issue on Paul's letter to the Galatians.

> When they had first received the gospel, the Galatians had got off to a good start. They had begun in the Spirit. They were running a good race. Then they had veered off course and got entangled with Judaism. They were behaving like a man with a life sentence who had just been pardoned, and who, when scarcely out of prison, behaves in such a way that the authorities are obliged to put him straight back behind bars. 'O foolish Galatians!'
>
> There are many believers today in the same position. They too got off to a good start, knowing full well that they have been saved on the basis of grace. Like the Galatians they have also received the Holy Spirit by faith. But they too have been lured back into the legalistic slavery from which the gospel freed them. O foolish Christians!

Legalism robbed Christians of their inheritance; instead of allowing God's people to receive his promises by faith, it reduced them to the level of self-effort.

> Here are the usual ingredients of legalism: human reasoning without faith; acting in the flesh instead of in the Spirit; trying to accomplish the will of God by natural instead of supernatural means . . .
>
> We are faced with a simple choice. Either we believe God for the supernatural working of his Spirit, or else we settle for legalistic substitutes, and that may mean simply perpetuating the status quo.

In Arthur's view, Christians needed to be utterly radical in their commitment to eradicate legalism from their lives. Only then would they receive their true spiritual inheritance. He touched on areas like Sabbath-keeping, and some of the other external rules and regulations that can so easily put Christians into legalism.

In his final chapter, 'The Land of the Radical', he aimed to sum up what sort of people would be 'a people of inheritance': a people free of legalism, but not self-indulgent or undisciplined, wholehearted in their devotion to the Lord, unmotivated by material prosperity, rich in faith and good works, and ready to embrace the cross of Christ; a people of vision for whom 'the best is yet to come'. They would not be loners, but committed to the body of Christ and able to submit to spiritual authority. Like Caleb and Joshua, they would be ready and willing to enter the land and take their inheritance.

It is an hour of decision and destiny for the church. Growing numbers of God's people are coming to 'the plains of Moab'. Either they will move on with God, cross the Jordan and enter their rest and their inheritance; or they will settle for what they are currently enjoying, and cling to the 'safety' of that which is institutional and traditional, be it ancient or modern.

This is for some of us the moment of truth when we show ourselves to be radicals or compromisers. One thing is certain, God is going over into his rest. The question is, Are we going over into ours?

Arthur had no illusions that he had comprehensively dealt with all the matters over which God requires a radical response from his people. There were other areas that he considered including, but decided to omit, feeling they would only detract from what he had already written.

The Radical Christian created quite a stir when it was published by Kingsway, and later by Fleming Revell in the United States. Much of the comment in the Christian Press was fair-minded and favourable, but there was some antagonism. The reviewer in *Buzz* magazine pronounced that Arthur must be 'suffering from a bad case of the Tony Benn syndrome: he's so obsessed with the organisational structure of the church that its real job is likely to be neglected'.

In *Renewal* magazine the reviewer seemed to miss the point of much of the book. Concluding a rather jaundiced summary of what Arthur had written, he decided to use his review as a platform to express his apprehensions about certain aspects of the 'shepherding' movement, most of which bore no direct relevance to the subject matter of the book.

Most other reviewers, even if not in full agreement, accepted the book as stimulating and thought-provoking. The positive comment did not only come from those already in 'restoration' churches; the Scottish minister who reviewed the book in *Scottish Renewal* was refreshingly positive:

> I have no doubt whatsoever that God's mighty hand has been on the pen of Arthur Wallis as he wrote *The Radical Christian*. This book is a must for all renewed Christians who have resigned themselves to a back pew. . . . Beware! This book could cause a rushing mighty wind that might in one puff send you to the front seat challenged in a way you have never been before.
>
> Have you ever wondered what has happened to the charismatic renewal in Scotland? So have I. Have you ever asked yourself where this genuine renewal in the Spirit is taking us in respect to the mainline denominations? Does it mean staying in or coming out? Then there is that continual problem about division in the church. Can division ever be justified? Have you ever wondered whether your church is an old wineskin or a new one? What about traditionalism or legalism, baptism in the Spirit and baptism in water, clericalism and professionalism? These are some of the great issues of today in this disturbing book . . . You may well ask how any author can pack so much perception and insight into 187 pages when others have taken a book to each of these subjects. That's all the more reason to rush out and buy 40 copies for the housegroup. . . .
>
> Arthur Wallis is certainly crystalising the thoughts of many of us and I have no doubt that his contribution, along with that of men like Howard Snyder and Michael Harper and many others, will be a factor in the changing scene we will see in Scotland. Incidentally if you plug this book it might be the most radical step you have taken for a long time. I dare you to buy one for your minister!

In Arthur's mind, *The Radical Christian* was the most important and significant book he had ever written. It was a message that he passionately believed in and stood for, and its prophetic impact was widely recognised. In the American *Christian Destiny* magazine, the reviewer concluded his positive appraisal of the book with these words: 'Few books have been written about the restoration of the church, so *The Radical Christian* stands out as a prophetic voice concerning God's intention towards this end. It fills a gap; it meets an urgent need. Arthur Wallis has written an important and timely book.'

Tony Morton reviewed the book for *Restoration* magazine and succinctly summarised the reaction of many readers.

> As one reads the developing theme of *The Radical Christian* it becomes apparent that this book is different. Because of its relevance and challenge it is impossible to read it with mere interest, whether you come from a restoration, renewal or evangelical background. Urgency and candour emphasised by the scriptural insights of the author give this book prophetic stature . . .
>
> I found *The Radical Christian* vital, stimulating and compelling reading. It is a book which will be the cause of much heart searching and enquiry, and of blessing too for those radical enough to apply it.

22

On the Move

Although the bungalow at Askwith was a delightful place to live, Arthur and Eileen had not expected to be there for more than a few months before finding a place of their own. Eileen in particular did the continual round of estate agents, looking for the house that would become their home for the next period of their lives.

They expected to be based in Yorkshire for a good few years, and even considered buying a plot of land and building their own property, something they had longed to do ever since they had 'claimed a field' back in their Talaton days. Eventually they did find a very nice plot, bordering the river Wharfe, and their offer for it was accepted. It seemed ideal, but neither of them felt completely at peace about it without really knowing why. Eventually their solicitor discovered that there was a restrictive covenant on the land preventing further building.

Both Arthur and Eileen were slightly puzzled as to why, after nearly two years, they still could not find the right property. It did seem that God wanted *The Radical Christian* completed before they moved from Askwith, and once it was finished they intensified their search. They decided to start looking in the Bingley area, and at last found what seemed to be the right property. It was a four-bedroomed detached house, virtually new, in an attractive estate called Oakwood Park on the outskirts of the town. The house had been built for the son of the builder responsible for the estate, but had come onto the market virtually straightaway due to the break-up of his marriage. Small details like the colour of carpets and curtains all seemed right, and they felt assured that this was God's provision.

At the end of August 1981, Arthur and Eileen moved into 10 Pinedale, Oakwood Park, and named the house 'Shalom' as they had done at Ottery. Some friends in the Bradford church were beginning to wonder whether they had any real intention of staying in the area and were quite relieved they had finally bought a place of their own. Arthur and Eileen had not harboured any thoughts of moving away from Yorkshire, and were quite surprised when Bryn's brother, Keri, commented, 'So you are planning to stay after all.'

If they had been intending to move away from Yorkshire in the near future, it would have made no sense to have bought this property. When they moved in, however, Eileen had a feeling that they were not going to be there very long, although this bit of feminine intuition did not strike much accord with Arthur's masculine logic.

For a number of years Arthur had had a close involvement with The Community Church in Southampton. His links there went back to the Lakes Bible Week in 1975 when he was approached by a group from an evangelical church at West End on the outskirts of Southampton. A number of them had recently experienced the baptism in the Holy Spirit and needed help as to where to go from there. They wanted Arthur to visit Southampton and he agreed, thus beginning a regular involvement with the West End church.

Meanwhile, during the mid seventies another church, based in the centre of Southampton, was developing under the leadership of Tony Morton. It had started off as a group of university students which had been joined by other Spirit-filled Christians from Baptist and Pentecostal backgrounds. They were receiving regular help and input from Ian McCullogh and David Mansell, and about forty were meeting at the Blind School in Southampton.

Close links developed between these two churches, and in 1977 they merged into one, bringing the numbers to around 170 people. Arthur continued to visit regularly and took on the main responsibility for providing the church with apostolic 'covering'. He and Eileen got to know the leaders in Southampton very well, and felt a real 'knitting of hearts' with the church.

For several years Tony Morton had been serving the church in Southampton and the surrounding area in a full-time capacity, and Arthur could see that God had given him a gift and calling that went beyond the confines of the local situation. Through Arthur's involvement and encouragement, Tony became part of Bryn's Harvestime team and regularly travelled up to Bradford for team meetings.

By the early eighties Bryn and Arthur could both see that Tony had a clear apostolic calling, and that the work he was establishing in the South would be best served by a separate team. Bryn was happy to release Tony to develop his own base in Southampton.

In the autumn of 1981, at a meeting of the Harvestime team at Ilkley, Tony's apostolic gift was openly recognised and he was commissioned to establish his own team. At the same time Keri Jones was also recognised as an apostle, but his intention was to continue working closely alongside his brother.

One of the results of this development was that Tony asked Bryn if he would be prepared to release Arthur to work with him in Southampton. Tony felt the need for an older man alongside him and, because of Arthur's close involvement in Southampton, considered he was the ideal person to fulfil this role. Bryn said he had no problem with this provided Arthur was happy about it.

Arthur and Eileen had not considered moving South, and they began to ask God to confirm whether or not this was his will. The more they prayed, the more at peace they felt about the idea. Even Arthur's position as Editor of *Restoration* magazine was coming to an end, and David Matthew, who had been working with him as Assistant Editor, was shortly to take over. They had only been in their new house a few months, but it was looking as if Eileen's 'sixth sense' was correct and that God did not intend them to be there for long.

Before making a final decision, Arthur was keen to spend time talking the whole thing through in detail with Bryn to find out how he really felt about it. Bryn was just about to return to the States, and so Arthur decided to hold the matter before God until he next returned to Britain and they could talk it through.

During this period Jonathan and Sylvia came to spend a weekend with Arthur and Eileen and told them that after nine years in Solihull they were seriously considering moving away from the area. Jonathan had been to some conferences on Christian business, and felt God was calling him to leave his job with a Birmingham-based insurance company and launch out into a new business venture. Both he and Sylvia believed that God was also leading them to move to a new area and church, although they did not know where.

They had been in the Solihull Christian Fellowship virtually from its inception and were part of the leadership team. Despite their many friends in the church, they both felt that God was telling them to move on. Their only condition was that they moved to a church where Arthur had a regular involvement and input, and where there would be others with a vision for Christian business. They asked him what he thought about it.

Arthur had felt for some time that Jonathan and Sylvia should be moving from Solihull. Could it be that God was leading them to Southampton as well? If this was the case, he wanted it to be clearly God's leading; he made no mention therefore of the possibility of his move. Instead he encouraged them to visit one or two churches and ask God to clarify what he was saying to them. There were two churches in particular that seemed to meet their criteria; one was in Cardiff, the other was in Southampton. Arthur and Eileen prayed that they would make the right choice.

Within a few weeks Jonathan and Sylvia arranged to spend a weekend with Tony and Hannah Morton in Southampton. God clearly confirmed to them both that this was where they should be moving; they never did get round to visiting Cardiff. It was not all plain sailing, however. Jonathan shared how he felt God was leading him with the elders in the Solihull church, but none of them were happy about it; their counsel was that Jonathan and Sylvia should stay in Solihull.

Arthur had still not talked to Bryn, and so he made no mention of his own plans, but encouraged Jonathan to trust God that the issue would be resolved amicably with the Solihull leaders. If the move was right then God would open the way for it to happen without Jonathan and Sylvia having to disobey those whom God had placed in spiritual authority over them. He suggested that if they still failed to reach an agreement, the matter should be raised with David Tomlinson, who was the apostle responsible for the Solihull church.

A few weeks later, Arthur finally got the opportunity to talk with Bryn, who knew nothing of these recent developments. One of his first questions was 'How is Jonathan getting on?' Arthur explained that Jonathan and Sylvia were wanting to move from Solihull, and felt particularly drawn to Southampton.

'Arthur, that confirms to me that it is right that you and Eileen move to Southampton also,' replied Bryn. He had for some time felt that Jonathan and Sylvia and their family should be living near to Arthur and Eileen. This clinched the matter for him.

With a sense of excitement Arthur and Eileen at last shared the news with Jonathan and Sylvia, who felt very encouraged. They had made their decision without any inkling that the family would be moving together for the first time since their marriage. It was God's encouragement to continue believing that the impasse with the

Solihull leadership would be resolved. Eventually Jonathan was able to raise the matter with David Tomlinson, who agreed that they should be released to move to Southampton.

With the way now opened up for the family to move, the final test of faith for both Arthur and Eileen and Jonathan and Sylvia involved the selling of their properties. The property market was rather sluggish during 1982 in both Solihull and Bingley.

Jonathan left his job in May 1982, and he and Sylvia moved down to Southampton to set up a new insurance and savings business. Initially they had to live in rented accommodation and didn't manage to sell their house in Solihull until the end of the year.

Arthur and Eileen found what they believed was the right house in Southampton, but still had no buyer for the Bingley property. It was the first time they had been involved in the hassle of fitting together a sale and purchase. After the disappointment of one or two promising looking buyers who failed to clinch matters, Arthur felt God saying that they must win the prayer battle and resist any hold-up in the spiritual realm. They began to pray all the more earnestly, and to declare the victory in the name of Jesus. One evening they decided to march up and down the lounge declaring their faith: God *did* intend them to move; they *had* found the right house to buy; and a buyer *would* speedily emerge for their Bingley home.

The very next day a couple came who were being moved by their firm; they had ready cash and liked the house. They offered the asking price, the deal was struck, no chain and no problems! God had answered prayer, and in September 1982 Arthur and Eileen moved into their new home in Bassett Close, Southampton. It was an older property, a four-bedroomed detached house in a good district and the nicest home they had owned. God gave them a particular promise for this move: 'He led them by a straight way to a city where they could *settle*' (Ps 107:7).

This was soon to become a reality, and Arthur and Eileen quickly settled in the Southampton church. They had developed a close relationship with the leaders over the years, and felt very much part of things from the word go.

It was a great joy for Arthur and Eileen to have their two grand-children close at hand. The Southampton church had a clear vision for Christian education, and both girls started at 'The King's School' at its inception in September 1982.

Katrina was now ten, and was the quieter of the two. She had always shown an unusual spiritual sensitivity and would think things through very deeply for a girl of her age. Although she was sad to be leaving her friends in Solihull, she could accept that God had told the family to move and was sure that he would give her many new friends in Southampton. She was not brilliant academically, but applied herself diligently to her schoolwork and was gifted artistically. Her main love was dance, and she soon got involved in a local dance school in Southampton.

Fiona was quite different in temperament to her sister, a bright and breezy seven-year-old, always eager to please. Whenever she spent time with Arthur and Eileen she was always full of 'whys' and 'wherefores'. Whereas Katrina would quietly take things in, Fiona would invariably give an instant reaction, usually before she had fully heard what was being said. To her, life was very black and white; people were either 'goodies' or 'baddies' and she found it difficult to understand that there might be shades in between. She soon earned the nickname 'The Nanny' because of her love for babies and younger children; they seemed to gravitate towards her, even as a seven-year-old. Fiona was also keen on dance and went to the same dance school as Katrina.

Arthur and Eileen could appreciate the very different qualities of each of their grand-children and enjoyed the time they could now spend with them. Katrina and Fiona were able to visit them regularly, and they felt they were beginning to get to know them in a way that had not been possible before.

This meant some adjustment for Arthur at times. He would often get engrossed in a deep spiritual conversation at the meal table, only to be brought back down to earth with a bump as Katrina or Fiona attempted to join in. Having always been very cautious about the place of dance in worship, he was also having to come to terms with two grand-daughters and a daughter-in-law who were dance mad!

Some people, when they heard that Arthur had moved from Bradford down to Southampton, assumed that behind this lay some disagreement between him and Bryn. This was not the case. Both men continued to have the deepest love and respect for one another. There were aspects of the work at Bradford that Arthur was not happy about, and he was always very open and straight with Bryn about such issues. His diligence in expressing his areas of concern only served to deepen their relationship. Bryn knew that Arthur loved him and would only express any misgivings out of a fatherly concern for his welfare and a deep desire to see the work of God prosper.

One of the many things they discussed together was the concept of an 'apostolic team'. Whereas Arthur was very clear about the need for apostolic ministry, he was never fully convinced about the scriptural authority for 'teams'. He could see the need for men to work in relationship together, and inevitably an apostle would draw a 'team' around him. But he could see no justification for an inflexible team structure that could so easily become something rigid and exclusive.

Arthur believed that the New Testament advocated only one permanent structure, the church. The apostles and prophets were servants of the church, and the idea of a team was merely a practical way of functioning which should be flexible enough to meet the needs of the moment and of the situation being served.

He realised the danger that a team can become a

'political' thing, with any expression of misgiving being interpreted as disloyalty. Arthur was only too well aware of these dangers and was not interested in toeing anybody's party line; his only commitment was to kingdom principles, righteousness and integrity. As a result he was sometimes called in to judge a situation where a dispute had arisen. On occasions, where Bryn was also involved, Arthur would disagree with his judgement of the matter; nothing, including the deep love he had for his friend, would sway him from holding to what he believed to be the righteous course. This was undoubtedly frustrating for Bryn, but their differences of opinion never resulted in a division of spirit.

In many ways Arthur had learned much from the 1976 division. The situation then had been very black and white, and whereas he never changed his judgement, he realised that you cannot simply 'cut off' brothers who clearly desire the Lord and the glory of his kingdom. Arthur would never compromise what he believed to be the truth, but this did not prevent him from remaining open-hearted towards those who saw things differently. He learned to 'build bridges' with those of different 'streams' and would frequently encourage Bryn to do the same.

Bryn, on the other hand, was so taken up with what God had called him to do that he tended to look on bridge-building as a diversion. Others viewed this single-mindedness as exclusive, whereas Arthur knew that this was not Bryn's intention and would often find himself defending his friend to others.

At times, when called in as a trouble-shooter, there would be enormous pressure on Arthur to come down on one side or the other, whereas in reality this was not always possible. He would never back individual men, but would always look for a solution which promoted love and unity. He would never be pressured into making a pragmatic decision for the sake of clarity. Instead he simply spent time waiting on God and limited his judgement to whatever God gave him, even if it brought no resolve to the problem. For this reason he was sometimes seen as impractical, but what he was really advocating was to approach issues with less haste and more prayer until God's real solution became apparent.

What Arthur longed to see in men was a willingness to seek God in humility and the patience to wait for his will and purpose to be revealed. He expected others to approach issues with a simple and prayerful open-heartedness that placed their own ambitions and position to one side in a desire to see God's kingdom glorified. It saddened him when this spirit was missing.

☆　　☆　　☆

As Arthur visited many new churches and fellowships around the country, he found a widespread need for foundational teaching. It was all too easy for new Christians to come into a church and receive a 'charismatic' spiritual diet of worship, exhortation and encouragement which left them without any real understanding of basic Bible doctrines. Most older Christians took these foundational truths for granted and failed to realise that new converts could all too easily miss out on them.

The Southampton church would always try and ensure that a new Christian had someone older in the faith to give personal help and encouragement and so Arthur decided to put together a discipling course that could be used in this context. He called it *Living God's Way* and much of the material was tried and tested in the church before the book finally went into print in 1984.

It comprised a total of twenty studies in three main sections: 'Coming into Christ', 'Getting Along Together' and 'Growing in God'. Each chapter had a brief introduction, concise study material, a memory verse, and a 'home task' to help establish the practical outworking of the principles being taught. The subjects covered included repentance, new birth, baptism in water, baptism in the Spirit, church relationships, the covenant meal, leadership, finance, the conscience, prayer, the Bible, temptation, the second coming of Christ and even a down-to-earth chapter on sex.

Arthur was keen to see *Living God's Way* used among young people as well as adults, and he encouraged Sylvia to do the course with Katrina, who by now was twelve. She found it very helpful, the main criticism being that there were rather a lot of big words she didn't understand! Generally the book found wide acceptance as a useful and practical aid to the discipling of new believers.

23

China Miracle

One day towards the end of 1983, Arthur was relaxing in his lounge reading *Open Doors* magazine. Brother Andrew had written about the tremendous revival that was taking place in the house churches in China. 'One day,' he wrote, 'perhaps quite soon, someone will write about this revival, and we shall advertise the book.' As Arthur read those words, a voice within said, 'You do it.' He was taken completely by surprise; such a commission was totally unexpected. Could it really be God?

Arthur had heard of the growth of the church in China, of the millions of converts, and of the suffering and persecution that they were experiencing. He had been stirred, and felt that God had something prophetic to say through these things to the western church. He felt totally inadequate to write such a book. He only knew what he had read from the pen of others, and had never even visited the country. God did not seem to take too much notice of his misgivings, the conviction grew, and within two months he was in China.

He was travelling out to Hong Kong in January 1984, and so he made plans to meet other Christians who were already making regular trips into China. He was hoping for a travelling companion, preferably Chinese, who was fluent in Mandarin and could take him into the country and provide the openings. His over-riding desire was to meet some house-church leaders and see for himself the local church in action.

Arrangements were made for Arthur to travel by train to Canton and from there to fly to Shanghai, where he was to meet up with his guides, an American Christian and a group of Chinese Christians from Hong Kong. Things did not go to plan. The others travelled overland and were late getting to the arranged meeting point. Arthur arrived at the hotel where he was staying, having failed to make contact, and dined in solitary grandeur. The authorities were, at that time, careful to ensure that foreign visitors had as little contact as possible with the Chinese.

Having failed to meet up with his contacts, he decided to have a look round the centre of Shanghai. He took a taxi to a department store in the heart of the city. It was a few days before Chinese New Year and the streets were packed. As Arthur got out of his taxi into the thronging crowd he found himself literally propelled into the store by the shoving multitude! It was just like being outside Wembley Stadium after the cup final. He had never seen such crowds.

He managed to buy one or two items to take home for Katrina and Fiona and made his way outside again. In vain he searched for a taxi. No one had told him that you cannot just hail one on the streets, but have to go to special pick-up points. He found himself, a solitary stranger, jostled along amid a sea of inscrutable Chinese faces. Despite the crowds around him, he suddenly felt most dreadfully alone, and for nearly an hour he traipsed the streets of Shanghai.

> I was cold. An injured ankle began to ache. I did not know where to go. I could not communicate. I looked in vain for a western face. During that hour a thousand pairs of Chinese eyes must have surveyed me with curiosity. Surely some of these people must be Christians, I thought. I had been told there were one million in Shanghai. A great longing swept over me just to grip one believer's hand, just to exchange a smile of greeting, just to say that word that every Christian

knows, whatever his language—'Hallelujah'. But there was no way we could find each other. I had never experienced such a feeling of utter helplessness and desolation. Had I come all the way to China for this?

Eventually he managed to find someone who understood enough to direct him to a taxi, and he was able to get back to his hotel. As he sat alone in his room, reliving this experience, God spoke to him:

I have given you today for a few minutes a tiny taste of what thousands of my children continually experience in China. They know what it is to feel cut off, even from their fellow Chinese. When it comes to fellowship, they speak another language, belong to another culture. They are 'aliens and strangers' to the world, and likewise the world to them. Some of them are in prison for the sake of my name. Others are in labour camps, hundreds of miles from home, loved ones and Christian fellowship. I gave you this experience that you might begin to identify with them, pray for them and encourage others to pray.

Arthur eventually met up with his guides and was able to visit some Christians in their home. Being winter it was cold. The house had no heating and so they sat around in overcoats. The uncomfortable reality of their living conditions was a stark contrast to the warmth and love with which he was received.

The next day he flew from Shanghai to Peking, where he met some other western Christians but did not fulfil his desire to see a house church in action. Despite this disappointment, the experience of being in China began to give him a feel for the country, an essential starting point if he was to write effectively.

Of course, much of the information that he would include in the book had to be learned from those who had lived and worked in China for most of their lives. He needed his facts to be clear and accurate, but he did not feel that his major purpose was to give a full and authoritative account of the revival. Rather, his aim was to apply some of the lessons that can be learned from

China to the church in the West—a 'now' prophetic word rather than a text book.

Later that year, Arthur took the opportunity to meet Doctor Paul Kauffman in Hong Kong. An American who had spent much of his life out there, he had written a book called *China, the Emerging Challenge* which provided Arthur with much essential information and inspiration as he began his research. Paul had a tremendous vision for China, and when they met was full of encouragement for Arthur in the project that he had undertaken. Others that Arthur contacted questioned the wisdom of someone writing about China who had never been directly involved in working in the country, but he remained convinced that God had called him to undertake this task.

Someone else who provided great encouragement for Arthur was Ross Paterson. Ross, who had spent a number of years as a missionary in Taiwan, was now pastoring a church in York and working closely with a number of organisations who were involved with China including the Overseas Missionary Fellowship (OMF), formerly the China Inland Mission. He had heard that Arthur was writing a book on China and wrote, offering his help to check Arthur's manuscript for any inaccuracies.

He too had considered writing a book along similar lines, but pressure of time and other commitments had forced him to abandon the project. They were able to meet up, and Ross generously put much of his material at Arthur's disposal and gave him further valuable contacts.

☆   ☆   ☆

During the past few years Arthur had developed strong links with a church in the Mid-west of the United States at Columbia, Missouri. The contact started early in 1981 while he was still living in Yorkshire. Arthur and Eileen had gone to tea with Bryn and Edna Jones one day and met a young American who was visiting them. His name was Joe Tosini, the pastor of the Christian Fellowship of Columbia. As Arthur sat by Joe over tea, he started asking him questions, eager to find out about the church. As Joe began to share some of the things God had taught them about prayer and commitment, Arthur was deeply moved. Tears came to his eyes and he immediately sensed that this was a church that he would like to visit.

Joe was eager for him to come, and in June 1981 Arthur made his first trip to the small university town of Columbia. What he found there surprised and excited him. Here was a church where people gave themselves to prayer, where there was a real spirit of servanthood and a refreshing absence of ambition. He found a deep sense of community and relationship together, a commitment to excellence and a deep spirit of worship in the meetings.

For Arthur it was love at first sight; he had no illusions that he had found the perfect church, and yet what he was seeing was exactly the expression of church life that he always looked for. He recognised that God had done something special among this group, and was immediately filled with a fatherly concern to see that they kept on track and were not diverted from the vision God had given them.

The feeling of instant love was mutual, the people immediately took to him, and the elders openly received him as a father. They were humble enough to recognise their need for help and guidance, and saw Arthur as someone who could give it. He made regular visits to Columbia over the next few years.

In January 1985 Joe visited Arthur and Eileen in Southampton and told them he was planning to go into China with a Chinese pastor he had got to know in the United States. While there he was hoping to visit a house church.

Arthur's heart leaped at this news. His burning

ambition was still to visit such a church and he was due to be in Hong Kong at the same time as Joe.

☆　　☆　　☆

In February 1985, Arthur met up with Joe Tosini in Hong Kong. Travelling into China with them were Phil Schaeffer, another elder from the church in Columbia, and Joe's brother, John. The plan was that they would go by train to Canton, where they would meet the Chinese pastor who was to be their guide.

As they settled down to the long train journey, Joe and Arthur were soon deep in conversation, talking about the church and all that was happening at Columbia. The conversation got onto publishing, a subject about which Joe had strong views. He was concerned that most of the 'Christian' publishing houses in the States were owned by large secular corporations. Although the editorial control was still generally in the hands of Christians, the basic motivation was to make money rather than to publish material that would be used to build the church. Christian publishing was big business.

Joe's conviction was that God was calling the church in Columbia to launch a publishing house. He had discussed this before with Arthur, who poured cold water on the idea. 'No, Joe,' he said, 'I don't think that publishing is something that the local church could do. You need a lot of finance, and expertise in so many different areas. I just don't think it's realistic.'

But Joe would not give up on the idea. Each time he raised the subject, Arthur would let him have his say and then ask a string of difficult questions. How would you develop the marketing expertise? What if one of your colleagues writes a book? Would you feel obliged to publish? What if you had to turn it down? Arthur never shut the door on the idea, but he clearly thought it a bit of a pipe-dream.

The Radical Christian had been published by Fleming Revell in the United States and Arthur was expecting that they would also take *China Miracle*. 'Well Arthur,' said Joe, 'whatever you say about the difficulties of publishing, I still believe that we can do it. I'm going to pray that Fleming Revell turn down *China Miracle*. It can be our first book!'

Arthur smiled to himself. He could see that Joe had got hold of something that he would not lightly let go. In some ways Arthur was surprised that Fleming Revell had published *The Radical Christian* because its message was not one for which they, as a house, had much sympathy. Nothing would delight him more than to work with a publisher who was motivated by similar spiritual objectives. Maybe God was in this publishing idea. But if he wasn't, it could be a very expensive disaster.

Their conversation was interrupted by a Chinese girl who was coming along the train selling refreshments. She asked them if they would like something to drink.

'What do you have?' asked Arthur.

'We have beer, coke, lemonade, orange,' she replied.

'Oh, I'll try a Chinese beer,' said Arthur.

Joe and Phil looked at one another in amazement. Christians in their circle didn't drink, and here was Arthur Wallis, a spiritual father that they looked up to and respected, ordering a beer! Joe's brother, John, was also looking on with interest. He was not a Christian and his clear perspective was that Christians didn't drink. Suddenly he began to see Arthur in a new light. Here was a man who was spiritual, yet could enjoy a beer!

John and Arthur both had a Chinese lager, which was not the best they had ever tasted; Phil and Joe stuck to Coke! During the next few days, Arthur got to know John quite well and spent a lot of time chatting to him. At the end of the trip John told Joe that Arthur had made a big impression on him; he had decided he really did want to follow God.

They met the Chinese pastor at the train station at Canton and he travelled with them to their hotel. They couldn't talk freely until they were in their hotel room, where their friend explained that he was hoping to take them to a house-church meeting. He would know the next afternoon whether the leaders of the church were happy for them to come. Arthur was tremendously excited at the prospect and would have been bitterly disappointed if the answer had been 'no'.

The next day they received the go-ahead and that evening travelled by taxi to within walking distance of where the church met. Arthur was to recount in his book his vivid recollections of that occasion.

We dismissed the taxi and made our way down a very long narrow street, almost like an alleyway. Thankfully there was no street lighting. The terraced shops and apartments provided enough light just to pick our way until we came to an unmarked doorway. A narrow flight of wooden stairs brought us to the first floor of the building, housing the overflow of the meeting which was in progress. Here were Chinese Christians, Bibles in hand and notebooks at the ready, listening to a voice coming over the loudspeaker. Up another flight of stairs, to a floor jammed with people of all classes. There were professional people and students mingling with working-class people in their overalls, all sitting on simple wooden benches.

We were conducted to the only empty seats we could see. They had probably been reserved for us, as the leaders knew we were coming. We found ourselves within a few feet of the preacher, whose address was being relayed throughout the house. I had read of house churches in China with 200 or more people and had often questioned how you could fit that number into a private home. Here I was, right in one. I counted over 150 people on that floor alone and even then I could not see those tucked away in little rooms and cubbyholes.

This house church had four regular meetings each week, one for worship, one for prayer, one for sharing, and this was the mid-week Bible study. The house church leader who was speaking when we arrived, apart from a smile of welcome, seemed totally unaffected by our presence. The people too seemed far more preoccupied with the message than the presence of their foreign visitors. There was a pause in the preaching, a song was announced and the people began to sing to music relayed over the PA system. Then the Bible teaching continued.

This house church leader, who I would guess was about fifty, spoke the word with verve and authority. His face shone as he ministered, but it was not until afterwards that I understood why. Our Chinese friend explained that he was a very courageous man of God who had spent many years in prison for his faith. He was highly respected by the other house church leaders in the area. On inquiry, we discovered that there were about 500 other house churches in this great city.

Because of the risk—not to foreign visitors, but to their hosts, we stayed only for an hour, and then slipped away into the dark of the street. I felt that I had just for those few minutes stepped into the pages of the New Testament.

As they made their way back to the nearest taxi-point, Arthur was deeply moved. There were tears in his eyes, and he could not stop thanking God for the privilege of that short visit. He found himself quoting some words from Scripture: 'They wandered in deserts and mountains, and in caves and holes in the ground. . . . The world was not worthy of them' (Heb 11:37–38).

Joe was a little concerned. They were supposed to be keeping quiet as they rode back in the taxi, but Arthur could not stop praising the Lord!

Within three months of this trip, Arthur submitted his completed manuscript to Kingsway who published it under the title *China Miracle—A Voice to the Church in the West*. It was a book which provided many Christians with a new insight into what was happening in China and a concern for their brothers and sisters in that land. Arthur's focus was not 'What can we do for the church in China?' but 'What has the church in China to teach us?'

Throughout the history of this great nation, men and women have given their lives for the gospel. For some it meant martyrdom, for all it involved embracing the cross of Christ. Some like Hudson Taylor came from without, others like Watchman Nee from within; a handful were well known, thousands more were unsung heroes. 'The soil of China has been made rich by the blood of its martyrs.'

Arthur could see that the tremendous wave of revival now seen sweeping the land was something for which many had given their lives. The harvest never came during their lifetimes, but it was no less the fruit of what they had sown. Out of their sacrifice a generation had been born who were prepared to embrace the cross and stand firm in the face of persecution. A church had emerged that was thriving in the midst of suffering. Here were Christians with an intense hunger for God and for his word, and a dynamic prayer life. To them the supernatural was natural and healings were a part of their everyday Christian life. There were even a number of accounts of angelic intervention.

Arthur's call to the church in the West was to learn the lessons, to embrace the cross, and to develop the same hunger for God as could be seen in the church in China.

> Here then is the message from our brothers and sisters in China: 'Embrace the cross and be a conqueror.'
> Some Chinese Christians, now in the West, are finding that it is in some ways harder to do it here than it was in China. But Scripture assures us that a generation of overcomers will arise who—
> by the blood of the lamb, and
> by the word of their testimony, and
> by loving not their lives even unto death—
> will finally hurl down Satan from the heavens, and draw forth the triumphant cry, 'Now has come the kingdom.'

The British edition of *China Miracle* was published by Kingsway in time for Christmas 1985. Joe Tosini's prayers were answered, and in the United States Fleming

Revell turned it down. Soon afterwards Arthur went out to Columbia to see how Joe's vision for a publishing house was progressing.

When he arrived, Joe gathered together everyone in the church who shared an interest in the publishing project. There were about fifty people at that meeting, some were skilled in journalism, others in graphic design; in fact most of the skills necessary for publishing were covered. It was as though God had been preparing them to move into this field. Columbia University specialised in journalism and publishing, and many members of the church had joined while at university and stayed on after graduation.

As Arthur registered something of their enthusiasm and commitment, he was deeply moved. He immediately sensed that what they were planning was of God. After a while they turned to prayer, and the Spirit of God came on him powerfully. He prophesied that their newly formed publishing company would emerge as a leader in the nation, and that God would give them a million-seller.

In Joe's mind, that was the day that Cityhill Publishing was launched. Arthur gave them the American rights to *China Miracle* and promised them his other books as and when he could arrange for the rights to be released. Having his support, as an established author, gave them the platform they needed to launch the business. *China Miracle* was their first title, and they went on to publish *Living God's Way*. Later Fleming Revell agreed to release the rights for *The Radical Christian* and this too was published by Cityhill.

24

Heart and Bone

Following Arthur's move to Southampton in 1982, he expected to develop an increasing role towards the churches in the South of England linked with Tony Morton and the Southampton-based 'Cornerstone' team. To an extent this happened, but God began opening doors for him across a much wider sphere. A new phase in his ministry was beginning, and he found himself invited to many churches, both in the United Kingdom and overseas, which were not connected in any way with Tony's work, and had no direct association with 'restoration' circles.

These invitations would often come as a result of church leaders reading *The Radical Christian* and responding to its challenge. One such opportunity arose early in 1983, just a few months after Arthur and Eileen had settled into their new home. The telephone rang at 7.30 one morning. Arthur was away from home and Eileen answered. A man with a South African accent asked to speak to him. It was Pastor Ivan Vorster from Hatfield Baptist Church, a large church in Pretoria with over twenty pastors. He had read *The Radical Christian* and wanted Arthur to speak at their Easter convention in two months' time. Would he be able to fit this in at such short notice? A fairly intense week of meetings had been planned and Arthur would be required to speak seventeen times. Eileen too was invited, and after the convention the church planned to take them both for a few days' holiday to Kruger National Park, before fitting in visits to churches in Durban, Johannesburg and Pietermaritzburg.

For some reason the prospect did not fill Eileen with much enthusiasm, but she promised to convey the message to Arthur. Ivan said he would ring back a day or two later. When Arthur returned home, he immediately warmed to this opportunity and shared it with Tony who was also enthusiastic. Within a few days the arrangements were confirmed and their tickets booked for South Africa.

Not long before they were due to leave, Arthur was up in Yorkshire speaking to the students at Riddlesdon College, Bryn's leadership training school. Just before leaving to return to Southampton, some of the students suggested that they prayed for Arthur and Eileen. During this prayer time God spoke through a prophetic word, indicating that this trip was going to be a significant one for them. Some would receive Arthur's ministry and others would reject it, but God would lead them to key people with whom lasting relationships would be formed.

This proved to be exactly what happened. Arthur coped well with the intense programme of meetings, and he and Eileen began to form a close relationship with Ivan and Lynne Vorster and Tim and Sally Salmon from Pietermaritzburg.

Arthur found a hunger among many of the South African church leaders to learn all about 'restoration'. They were eager for him to speak about church structure, authority and submission, relationships, apostolic ministry and teams, all of which were hot topics of discussion among them. They had many questions, but responded positively as Arthur carefully expounded the biblical principles involved. He majored on the fact that the church is primarily about relationships and stressed the need for God's people, particularly leaders, to come together 'bone to bone' and truly relate together and submit to one another. He spent time expounding Ephesians chapter 4, explaining that the gifts and ministries listed in that chapter were essential if the church was to come to full stature and maturity.

This visit to South Africa became typical of many such trips, both at home and overseas, during the next few years. It was as if leaders in other churches and streams viewed Arthur as an ambassador of the restoration movement and a father figure whose opinions and views they could trust. He had no particular axe to grind, no empire to further, and no 'team' of his own to promote. His sole concern was God's will and God's purposes. His detailed and methodical biblical teaching was not motivated by some desire to promote 'restoration' as a movement, but by his burning desire to see the church established and prepared for a great outpouring of God's Spirit in revival.

People Arthur met had invariably heard about the division among the English brothers and he would often be asked about this. He would outline the history of restoration in the United Kingdom, openly talking about the mistakes as well as the successes. He made it his practice not to go into detail about personalities or specific issues but to concentrate on the lessons learned in the area of relationships. He was excellent at handling the many questions that would be fired at him, always trying to bring his answers back to biblical principles. In many of the places he went to, Arthur was a forerunner. His visits paved the way for other apostles and prophets to come and give ongoing help and encouragement.

Arthur and Eileen also made regular trips to the United States as well as visiting Hong Kong, Australia and New Zealand. Wherever they went they looked for the same thing, the opportunity to establish close relationships with key people. Whenever possible they preferred to stay in homes rather than in hotels, because it was only in the home that they really began to get to know people. It was by establishing such relationships that Arthur and Eileen believed they would make the

greatest impact. Meetings, however good, were soon
forgotten; but relationships were of lasting value.

☆   ☆   ☆

During 1984, Arthur and Eileen returned to South
Africa for a six-week trip. This time they had been
invited by Tim Salmon, who led a large church in
Pietermaritzburg. As well as various meetings within his
own church, Tim arranged for Arthur to visit a number
of other churches in the Natal district for which he was
responsible.

During this time Tim and his wife Sally arranged to
have a few days' break by the sea together with one or
two others from the church. They stayed in a friend's
bungalow on the 'Wild Coast' in the Transkei. Tim
would let off steam by riding an old motorbike over the
grass and dirt tracks around the bungalow. Much to his
surprise and apprehension, Arthur asked if he could
have a go. He had not ridden a motorbike since his army
days but managed to stay upright and avoided hitting
anything, much to Tim's relief.

It was a remote spot and the beach was deserted.
There were strong under-currents in the sea and so it
was only safe to swim well within your own depth. When
Arthur and Eileen went swimming, they were accompanied by one of the pastors in Tim's church, a tall
young man named Garth. Not fully appreciating the
danger, Arthur suddenly found himself drawn out of
his depth by a strong current and unable to get back.
The large waves were beating against him and he found
himself tiring rapidly and gripped by a fear of
drowning.

At first his pride would not allow him to admit defeat
and call for help, but Garth spotted him and asked if he
needed help. 'Yes,' Arthur cried, and Garth
immediately came to his rescue. Being young, strong
and well over six feet tall, Garth managed to reach

Arthur and pull him to safety. Arthur was very relieved
to feel the sand beneath his feet again and lay down on
the beach, quite exhausted from his lesson on humility.

In the Spring of 1986, Arthur received an invitation to
be the main speaker at a leadership conference in New
Zealand, arranged by Hudson Salisbury of Upper Hutt,
near Wellington. Arthur had felt for some time that he
would return to New Zealand but had turned down a
number of previous invitations, feeling somehow that
the timing was not right. Apart from a brief trip in the
early seventies he had not been back to the country since
his extended visit over twenty years previously.

Now the timing seemed right, and the invitation
coincided conveniently with a request from Andre Van
de Linden to visit Melbourne, Australia. Arthur
accepted both invitations, and on 1st March 1986 he and
Eileen flew out to Australia.

'Wouldn't it be marvellous to travel first class if we
ever do a long trip like this again!' remarked Eileen, as
they arrived tired after a forty-hour journey. Her wish
was to be fulfilled sooner than anticipated.

After two fruitful weeks of ministry in Melbourne,
they flew on to Auckland where they were met by
Blyth and Jan Harper with whom they were to be
staying initially. A full itinerary awaited them and a
few days later they flew down to Christchurch in the
South Island for a series of meetings. Wherever
Arthur went he was greeted by people who remembered his first visit.

Back on the North Island they stayed with Hudson
and Joan Salisbury at Upper Hutt. Hudson had
arranged a busy itinerary for Arthur, visiting many of
the churches that he was in touch with and spending
time with elders and church leaders. Arthur and Eileen
then travelled right up to the northern end of the island

for further meetings in the Dargaville area before ending up back at Auckland with Blyth and Jan Harper.

At Auckland, Arthur was to be speaking at a weekend camp at a site called Carey's Park. This was arranged by the Valley Road Church which Blyth and Jan attended, and most of the church were camping on site. Various meetings were arranged over the weekend, with ample recreation time. Arthur and Eileen stayed with Blyth and Jan, and came onto the site each day. At the Saturday morning session Arthur spoke on relationships in the church, dealing with the importance of being 'knitted together' and committed to the local body. One of his illustrations was of a bone breaking; in order to heal properly the pieces have to be aligned, reset and then given time to knit together.

After lunch Arthur was loaned somebody's room to have a rest, and Eileen went out to enjoy the fresh air. Many of the campers were sitting round in the grounds relaxing, others were playing volleyball. Various activities had been arranged for the children, including a 'flying fox'. This comprised a cable fixed at a gradient between two trees to which was attached a pulley with a metal crossbar. The kids would climb on at the higher end, sit on the crossbar, and have an exciting ride down the cable.

After a while Arthur emerged from his rest, made his way over to the volleyball game, and stood watching the action. Eileen walked over to join him. Neither of them noticed that the cable of the 'flying fox', which was not being used at the time, passed right over where they were standing.

Before anyone could appreciate the danger, a young lad got onto the 'flying fox' and came shooting down the wire. To make his ride more exciting he was sitting backwards on the crossbar, and so could not even see what was about to happen. Arthur was standing there, totally engrossed in the volleyball and blissfully unaware of anything else. The apparatus narrowly missed Eileen, but caught Arthur full force on the head. Knocked instantly unconscious, he fell at Eileen's feet, blood gushing from his forehead.

Eileen looked down at him, transfixed by a feeling of shock and horror. Her first thought was that he had been killed. Immediately others rushed over to help; a lady doctor and a trained nurse were on the site and they took charge of the situation. Someone stemmed the blood from his wound, while others went for a mattress.

After a few minutes Arthur came round a little and tried to move, but they restrained him. He was lifted onto the mattress and taken to Auckland General Hospital in a large estate car. Eileen, the doctor and the nurse went with him. On the way there he recovered his senses and asked what had happened.

'You were hit by a flying fox,' said the doctor.

'I didn't know they flew,' said Arthur in a puzzled voice. He then complained that his right leg was hurting.

It was Saturday afternoon, and the casualty department was like a battlefield! There were patients everywhere: rugby injuries, road accident victims, and an assortment of minor injuries. The staff were all run off their feet. A hospital doctor took Arthur's blood pressure and examined his head wound and eyes, checking for any obvious signs of brain damage. He was then left in a cubicle to wait while they dealt with those more seriously injured. Eileen of course stayed with him, and every now and then a doctor or nurse would come by to check that everything was OK. Arthur was as comfortable as could be expected, but constantly referred to the pain in his right leg, which seemed to be troubling him more than his head.

It was eight hours before a doctor became available to examine him fully. The X-rays revealed that there was no fracture to his skull, but a tibia plateau fracture in his right leg. In the early hours of Sunday morning his head wound was stitched up by a young doctor. No nurses were available to assist him, so Eileen had to revive her nursing career! Arrangements were then made for

Arthur to be transferred to the orthopaedic wing at Middlemoor Hospital where he was finally admitted at 5.30 am.

Blyth and Jan, who had stayed at the hospital all night with Eileen, eventually took her home for breakfast. On Sunday afternoon, twenty-four hours after the accident, Arthur was taken to the operating theatre. Some bone from his hip was grafted onto the broken leg and a metal plate screwed into place. He emerged with the prospect of a good few weeks' recuperation.

Eileen was allowed to visit the hospital as often and for as long as she liked, and for the next few days Blyth dropped her off each morning and picked her up again at tea time. Arthur had many other visitors, but would tire very quickly.

He was still determined to make it to the leadership conference and envisaged getting up to speak on crutches! After all, this conference was the climax of his visit, the main reason why he had come to New Zealand. He found it hard to accept that he might not be able to fulfil this commitment.

The reality of the situation was that, short of a miracle, just going to the conference was quite out of the question. It was not just his immobility, but the blow to his head and the resulting shock to his system had affected his ability to think and concentrate for more than a short period. Eventually he had to come to terms with reality. For some reason he could not comprehend, it appeared that God was not allowing him to speak. He could only accept it and leave the reasoning to the Almighty.

David and Dale Garratt of 'Scripture in Song' fame, kindly offered Arthur and Eileen the use of their home when Arthur was discharged from hospital. He would have been somewhat uncomfortable on Blyth and Jan's single beds, whereas at the Garratts' he could sleep on a king-size bed providing ample accommodation for his restlessness! One problem remained, however. He was going to be on crutches, unable to bend his leg or put his foot to the ground for at least six weeks. How was he going to fly home? There was no way that he would be able to cope with normal economy class accommodation.

It was at this point that Eileen remembered the insurance cover they had taken out when their air-tickets were booked. Arthur had been rather annoyed about it at the time. He never paid for insurance if it was not absolutely essential, preferring to trust God rather than the insurance company, but on this occasion a friend had booked the tickets for him. By the time he realised that insurance was included in the deal, it was too late to do anything about it.

As a British passport holder, Arthur did not need to pay for the medical attention he received in New Zealand, but the insurance also covered other things including the cost of changing any travel arrangements. Eileen's immediate thought was that the problem could be overcome if they were able to travel first class where Arthur would have the room to stretch out his leg in comfort. Blyth offered to telephone Jonathan in England and get him to liaise with the insurance company to see what could be arranged.

The medical officer from the insurer got in touch with the doctor at Middlemoor to discuss what arrangements would be necessary from a medical point of view. They decided that Arthur would be fit enough to travel sixteen days after his operation, and that he would need to be able to lie horizontally on the flight. Much to Eileen's frustration they came to the conclusion that the best arrangement would be to have three economy seats side by side rather than one first-class seat. Eileen did her best to dissuade them from what she thought was a crazy idea, but without success. The insurers were paying the bill and so things had to be done their way. She dutifully booked four economy seats between the two of them.

When the day for their departure arrived, Blyth and Jan drove them to the airport and said their farewells. A few minutes after they had checked in Eileen was called back out of the departure lounge to the check-in desk.

'Mrs Wallis,' said the lady at the desk, 'we think we can make your husband much more comfortable in first class. We can exchange your four economy seats for two in first class, and it won't cost you any more. Would that be all right?'

'Yes, please. That would be fine,' said Eileen, absolutely delighted that God had worked things out for them at the last minute. They travelled first class, and Arthur was able to lie fully reclined in complete comfort. Not only that, but he was treated to continual fuss and VIP treatment from the air-hostesses!

It took him a long time to recover from his encounter with the 'flying fox'. It had obviously caused a considerable shock to his system, and he took no meetings for three months. His concentration continued to be affected for some time, and God had to teach him fresh lessons. The book of Job took on a new significance for him and he began to appreciate the ways of God even through accident and seeming mishap.

Many Christians concluded that this accident was a victory for the devil, preventing Arthur from fulfilling the purpose for which he had gone to New Zealand. But Arthur strongly refuted this suggestion. God's ways were very different to those that men would choose, so who was he to presume that God's purposes had been thwarted? He could see the guiding hand of providence, even in the accident. He could easily have been killed if the blow had been in a slightly different place, and God had even over-ruled in practical details like the insurance. Any part that Satan had played in the incident had only been by God's permission.

25

God Picks a Rose

At the beginning of August 1986, just a few weeks after
Arthur finally discarded his crutches, Tony Morton and
his Southampton-based Cornerstone team held a Bible
Week at the Royal Bath and West Showground at
Shepton Mallett in Somerset. They had organised such
an event for a number of years, ever since Tony
established his own team in the early eighties.

Turning an agricultural showground into a Bible
week venue was a major undertaking which provided
opportunity for many in Southampton and the other
local churches to serve in all manner of ways. There
were seminars in the morning, and main meetings each
evening, as well as children's and teenagers' meetings to
arrange, and practical areas of involvement like
catering, security and cleaning the loos. Bible Week was
an exhilarating and fulfilling time, but for those involved
in the organisation it was certainly not a holiday.

Arthur took a couple of morning seminars on
'Enjoying God', and then in the latter half of the week he
and Eileen were involved in some further seminars
specifically for the over forties. Jonathan, Sylvia and
family were also camping on site, and taking part in the
musical ministry of the week. Katrina was greatly
enjoying the teenage meetings, and Fiona the activities
for the younger age group. Both of them were particularly taken with Friends First, a multi-racial group from

South Africa who visited for a couple of days and captivated everyone with their infectious brand of African music.

Katrina had made great progress with her gift of dance. In the Southampton dance festival a few months previously she had shown a stage presence that had caught the eye of the judges and won her several cups. She was now beginning to use her gift in the church, and even her non-Christian dance teacher remarked that there was a 'spiritual quality' in her dancing. At the Bible Week, together with a friend, she choreographed a dance to a Steve Camp song which expressed something of how God felt about a dying world, and they were able to perform this in one of the morning seminars.

A week or so after Bible Week, Arthur and Eileen were due to travel to the United States. It was Arthur's first ministry trip since his accident, and they were flying to Chicago for a few days, and then on to Portland, Oregon for a conference in Dick Iverson's church. They were also scheduled to visit the church in Columbia before returning home. The day before they left, there was a meeting of the Southampton church and Katrina was part of a group who were dancing in the service. At the end of the meeting she came running up to Arthur and Eileen to kiss them goodbye and to wish them a good trip to America. Little did they imagine that this was the last time they would see her.

Ern Baxter was the other speaker at the summer conference at Portland. Arthur had kept in touch with Ern by letter, but had not seen him face to face for a number of years and was looking forward to this opportunity to renew personal contact.

The conference lasted for a week. Ern was taking the evening sessions, and Arthur was speaking in the morning. He and Eileen would make breakfast in their room and eat out during the day. It proved an enjoyable and fulfilling time, and as the end of the week approached, Arthur received a clear sense from God of the message he should bring on the last day, Friday 29th August.

He and Eileen were sitting eating breakfast in their room that morning when the telephone rang. Arthur answered. To his surprise it was Jonathan phoning from England.

'Dad, I'm afraid I've got some bad news for you,' he said. 'It's Katrina. She died this morning.'

Arthur could not believe his ears. Only a fortnight before he had seen his grand-daughter alive and well and dancing in the meeting. How could she possibly be dead?

☆   ☆   ☆

Jonathan and Sylvia were on a week's holiday at Exmouth in Devon, staying in Sylvia's parents' home while they were away in Yorkshire. Katrina had not been well, experiencing worsening stomach pains. She had been having very painful periods for some time and this appeared to be the main cause of her discomfort. Jonathan and Sylvia did not imagine that it was anything more serious.

On the Wednesday evening, Jonathan decided to go for a walk on the beach to pray for Katrina. He was concerned that she seemed to be getting worse rather than better. As he prayed, God spoke very clearly, confirming that his hand was on her, and that he was going to meet with her in a very special way. Jonathan had little idea what this really meant.

By Thursday she was still not improving and they were getting concerned. They planned to visit John and Ruth Ward and family at Ottery St Mary that afternoon, and Katrina was eager to come. She made an effort to get up, have a bath and dress nicely for the occasion. Although she coped well with this outing, she was clearly in pain.

John and Ruth's daughter, Helen, was keen for Fiona to stay overnight in Ottery, and so Jonathan and Sylvia left Fiona with John and Ruth and took Katrina back to

Exmouth that evening. They decided they would find a doctor to see her first thing in the morning.

They both spent time sitting chatting to her that evening.

'I must go and get some sleep now, darling,' said Sylvia late that night. 'If I don't get my sleep I'll be too tired to look after you in the morning. We'll get a doctor to see you then. You try and get some sleep now. I do love you.'

'I know you do. I love you too Mummy,' replied Katrina, as Sylvia kissed her goodnight.

Those were the last words she heard Katrina say. In the early hours of the morning Jonathan and Sylvia were suddenly awakened by a crash in the bathroom. They rushed in to find that Katrina had got up to go to the toilet and collapsed into the bath. They immediately telephoned for an ambulance but it was too late. She never regained consciousness.

In their state of numb shock, they found it hard to believe that this was actually happening. It seemed like a bad nightmare. As the reality hit them, and while the ambulance men were still doing their utmost to revive her, they prayed as they had never prayed before, resisting the devil, rebuking the spirit of death, and claiming God's victory in the situation. It was to no avail. Amid their tears, the truth gradually dawned. God had taken her, and there was nothing they could do to bring her back.

The first people they told were John and Ruth, asking them to bring Fiona across so that they could break the news to her. She was devastated. Katrina had become her closest friend and confidante. They put their arms around one another and all cried together.

Katrina had actually been suffering from peritonitis. It would appear that her appendix had been gradually seeping for some time, infecting the rest of her body. It must suddenly have swollen and burst very quickly just before she died.

☆   ☆   ☆

Arthur listened in shocked amazement as Jonathan recounted what had happened, and relayed the information to Eileen. Katrina always had a very special place in his heart, his first grandchild and a beautiful girl in every way. He was particularly badly hit by the news.

After he had put the phone down, he sat with his arms round Eileen and they wept together. He then went to tell Ern and Ruth Baxter who were staying in the same motel. They immediately came to the room, and Ern got in touch with Dick Iverson. Dick immediately released Arthur from any obligation to speak at the meeting that morning and promised to arrange a flight home for them as soon as possible.

The earliest available plane was not until late that afternoon, and so Arthur decided to speak at the morning session and to continue with a scheduled radio interview. Fulfilling these commitments would at least take his mind off the situation.

The morning meeting was quite an experience for Arthur and Eileen. After Arthur had spoken, a number of the leaders gathered round to pray for them and many members of the church queued up to say goodbye. They felt completely submerged in the love of the body of Christ as Christians they had never met before surrounded them with hugs, tears and words of comfort and prophecy.

Within twenty-four hours they were back in England with Jonathan, Sylvia and Fiona. There was deep grief in the family and in the church, but in the midst of the tears God's comfort was very real.

'Ever since it happened,' Jonathan told Arthur, 'we've felt the presence of God so close. It's been something tangible, as if we could reach out and touch him.'

The reality of God's presence was a very precious thing to each member of the family, as was the appreciation of belonging to the body of Christ. Messages of love and sympathy, assurances of prayer support, and flowers and cards came pouring in, many from people they had never met but who were part of the larger family of God. The sense of belonging to such a world-wide body of loving, caring people was a great source of strength and comfort in itself.

Coming to terms with Katrina's death was a struggle, and they each had to prove that God's grace was sufficient. For Fiona, it was a question of facing up to the loss of a sister who was a very close friend and companion; at the age of eleven she was suddenly an only child. For Jonathan and Sylvia, it was a battle of 'whys' and 'wherefores'.

'Why didn't we realise?'

'What if we'd called a doctor earlier?'

'Was it our fault?'

The devil was very quick to bring condemnation, and they each had to accept the fact of God's sovereignty. He was in control, and even if they had been at fault, they knew he would not have allowed Katrina to suffer because of their mistakes.

For Arthur and Eileen there was a very real sense of personal loss, but there were also wider issues. There had been several deaths in the church over the preceding months. Two fathers had been killed in accidents, and a number of babies had died in cot-deaths. What was God saying? Was this an attack of the evil one? Had Satan won a victory by snatching a young girl's life? These were questions that the leaders of the church could not ignore.

Arthur could never accept that Katrina's death was a victory for Satan. Just as with his accident earlier in the year, he felt assured that God was in control. Katrina had entrusted her life to God. There was no way that Satan could snatch that life; it belonged to God.

'I see it a bit like a rose-garden,' said Arthur. 'Most of the roses the gardener will leave to bloom and die in the natural course of time. But occasionally he will choose a beautiful young rose, not yet fully in bloom, and he will pick it for the vase on his mantelpiece. God has looked around his garden and picked a young rose.'

To Arthur, it was no problem to accept God's sovereignty in this way. Psalm 139 says that 'all the days
ordained for me were written in your book before one
of them came to be.' Surely this was a trustworthy
statement. To believe otherwise would be to accept that
Katrina had missed God's plan for her life, that
somehow she had received less than God's best. The
reality was that she was now in a far greater place of joy
and blessing than she could ever know on earth. She was
enjoying the presence of God.

Jonathan and Sylvia could see that God had been in
control of the situation, preparing Katrina for what was
to come. They discovered things that she had been
doing that they knew nothing about: times when she
had witnessed to people on the bus, friends to whom she
had ministered God's love and grace, letters she had
written sharing her faith with pen friends. It seemed
that God had already used her in a way that went
beyond her years. She had been ready.

God's grace and love were very real to them. Simple
things spoke of this, like the fact that Fiona was
unexpectedly staying with John and Ruth the night
Katrina died. God was sovereign, and Jonathan and
Sylvia found that worshipping him was their greatest
source of strength. It was a two-way process in which
they entered God's presence and brought their lives into
line with his purposes, and in which he drew near to
them, imparting his comfort, healing and strength.

It was Fiona, in fact, who first encouraged a spirit of
worship in the family when they were travelling back to
Southampton on the day Katrina died. 'I think we've
had enough crying for a while,' she said. 'Katrina would
want us to put on some happy music!'

They started playing the Dales Bible Week Children's
Praise tape as they drove along. It didn't stop the tears,
but it seemed to bring the presence of God into the car,
and as they worshipped they began to experience a deep
joy and peace that was beyond their understanding. It
was to be this joy of the Lord, released through their

worship, that became their greatest strength as they came to terms with their grief.

Of course, Satan tried to tell them that it was not appropriate to worship God under these circumstances. The reality was that it was the only appropriate thing to do. Katrina was in God's presence, worshipping him in glorious freedom; when Jonathan, Sylvia and Fiona were worshipping they not only felt close to God, they also felt close to her.

The biggest problem was simply adjusting to the great hole that her loss had created in their hearts and lives. There were many tears and much heartache but, by God's grace, no bitterness and no sense that God had let them down.

Katrina's life had already been fruitful, but Mike Stevens encouraged Jonathan and Sylvia to see that the fruit from her life need not cease with her death. A few years previously, Mike's youngest daughter had been killed in a boating accident, and this was something he had learned. It was a great encouragement to see that they could continue to bear fruit for Katrina. To allow bitterness and resentment to come in would have resulted in a victory for Satan. To allow God's grace and love to fill their hearts turned their experience into something positive which would continue to bear fruit for God's kingdom for many years to come.

A poem sent by a friend in the church was to prove a great comfort, and they included it on a card they sent out as a family in appreciation of all the love they had received.

Gift of a Child

I'll lend you for a little time
A child of mine he said
For you to love the while she lives
And mourn for when she's dead.

It may be six or seven years
Or twenty two or three,

But will you, till I call her back,
Take care of her for me?

She'll bring her charm to gladden you
And should her stay be brief
You'll have her lovely memories
As solace for your grief.

I cannot promise she will stay,
Since all from earth return,
But there are lessons learned down there
I want this child to learn.

I've looked this wide world over
In search of teachers true
And from the throngs that crowd life's lane
I have decided upon you.

Now will you give her all your love
Nor think the labour vain
And hate me when I come to call
To take her back again?

I fancy that I hear them say
'Dear Lord, your will be done,
For all the joy this child will bring
The risk of grief we'll run.

'We'll shelter her with tenderness,
We'll love her while we may,
And for the happiness we've known
For ever grateful stay.

'And should the angels call for her
Much sooner than we planned,
We'll brave the bitter grief that came
And try to understand.'

        English poem—writer unknown

Katrina's funeral took place at the Southampton
crematorium. Arthur took a short service for the
immediate family. In the afternoon a memorial service

was held in the hall of the King's School. It was packed with friends from all over the country as well as from Southampton. Many who knew Katrina through her dance school were also there.

There was a very clear sense of God's presence throughout the service which was marked by a deep spirit of worship. Jonathan, Ken Courtney (Sylvia's father) and Arthur each spoke, and Sylvia joined with the worship group in singing 'Let me feel your heartbeat'. As a family, they were determined to give God the glory, and to ensure that Katrina's life would continue to bear fruit, even after her death.

26

Well Done, Arthur, You've Won!

Arthur's vision for revival had never altered over the years. What had changed and developed was his understanding of the role of the church in the fulfilment of this vision. All that he now believed about the principles of New Testament church life was not a departure from his original vision, but an integral part of it. He saw that God's purpose was not just to bring revival but to sustain it, and to see the church established as a glorious expression of God's kingdom. All he was teaching about the government of the church and the ordering of life within God's community was essential to the outworking of this vision.

Also central to Arthur's vision was his desire to see true unity among God's people. He continued to keep in regular touch with the leaders of different groups and 'streams' within the restoration movement. These men, despite their busy and successful ministries, looked to him not only as a friend but as a father. Bryn Jones continued to value his close personal relationship with Arthur. Terry Virgo, who led a thriving apostolic team based in Brighton, also met up with him regularly to talk on a personal level.

He continued to do all he could to establish contact and rebuild friendship and trust with the men who had been alienated in the 1976 split. As the 1980s progressed, many of the former divisions were being broken down, and men within the different streams were beginning to share fellowship together and establish a mutual respect and recognition of each other's ministries. Arthur was a key figure in working to this end through the personal contacts he nurtured.

Although he kept in touch with many people, he was not interested in a cosmetic unity, he was looking for something deeper. He did not expect men to agree totally with one another or suddenly to abandon their differences and work together. He was not looking for compromise, but for humility of spirit and a willingness to acknowledge and honour one another. More than anything, he longed for Christians to give priority to prayer and seeking God instead of coming together merely to discuss their own ideas and plans.

He could see that there was a tendency for Christian leaders to get so caught up in the busyness of their own ministries and programmes that they missed out on the furtherance of God's wider purposes. He knew that revival would never come unless leaders were prepared to forget their differences in order to seek God together.

Arthur had always been a man of prayer; he would much prefer to spend time praying about an issue than discussing it. When faced with any decision his reaction was first to pray, then to wait for God to speak, ready to hear and obey whatever he might say. Once God had spoken, discussion became of less importance, the practical outworking was usually apparent and God invariably provided the right key to unlock the situation.

He regularly rose between 6.00 and 6.30 am to start the day in prayer. If something was particularly concerning him he would often rise earlier. When it came to the preparation of a message he was to give, he put personal preparation in prayer before detailed study of his sermon material. He consistently applied this principle in every area of his life and never made any important decision without first bringing it to God. In addition to his own devotions he generally spent some time each day praying with Eileen. Sometimes they would combine this with a walk across Southampton Common, praying as they went.

Prayer was so much a part of Arthur's life that he found it difficult to understand when others appeared to give it less importance.

☆   ☆   ☆

With an increasing number of invitations coming from overseas, it would not have been difficult for Arthur to have spent a high proportion of his time abroad. After the accident in New Zealand, Tony said that he felt Arthur should restrict his overseas visits to take up no more than three months in each year. He was keen that both Arthur and Eileen were completely fulfilled in the church, even when Arthur was not preaching. Tony also felt that Arthur, who was now sixty-four years old, should be looking to reduce his work load.

At first Arthur found this hard to receive. He had never countenanced any thoughts of retiring, always thinking he would 'die with his boots on'. Nevertheless he accepted Tony's advice, and began to limit his overseas engagements.

He had, from the time they moved to Southampton, got involved in the discipling and training of up-and-coming leaders in the church. Each group would run for about six months, meeting every week for prayer, Bible study and discussion. He was very much in his element in this context and called these his 'Timothy groups'.

Originally Arthur had regularly attended the Southampton elders' meetings but he would get frustrated by the plethora of practical matters that needed discussing. As this became apparent, Tony suggested that he was sent a copy of the minutes to read each week, but that he only came along when he felt there was something he particularly wanted to share. He would go through these minutes in detail, and would often write to Tony with a long list of comments and suggestions. It was important to him to feel fully part of all that was going on in the local church.

There were many occasions when Arthur would express misgivings about what was happening or about the direction things were taking. His unease would often relate to what he saw as a lack of depth in the prayer life, or to some other expression of spiritual superficiality. Now that he was spending more time at home he did all that he could to encourage the prayer life of the church.

Arthur and Eileen were not only at home among the leaders, but helped to initiate a group called 'Harvesters', specifically geared to the over forties. They were aware that it was all too easy for the growing number of older people in the church to feel that, because most of the leaders were younger, there was little part for them to play. Harvesters was formed to provide a channel for the wisdom and talents of this age group.

Not long after Katrina's death, Arthur finished his next book *On to Maturity*, a follow-up to *Living God's Way*, published by Kingsway in 1987. As the name implies, it was a study course designed to help Christians grow in character and develop in spiritual maturity. *Living God's Way* had been geared to use in the local church setting where a new Christian is being personally discipled by an older believer. *On to Maturity* was far more suitable for personal study.

Arthur included a total of eighteen studies in the book, each finishing with a Scripture verse to learn, a 'home task' to work at, and other questions under the title 'For further study'. The book was based in three broad sections. 'The New Person' dealt with the practical implications of being 'a new creation' with separate studies on areas like the mind, the emotions and a sound judgement. 'Growing Strong' covered different aspects of building up our faith and resisting the evil one. The final section, 'Living in the World', dealt with the pressures of the world on the Christian life.

Arthur had tried and tested many of these studies on

his 'Timothy group' and proved their practical worth and value. He envisaged this as the first of a series of study books, and hoped to produce further material on subjects like church life and the prophetic scriptures.

☆   ☆   ☆

Arthur had always lived a healthy life, enjoyed plenty of exercise, and eaten the right things, but none the less his health was beginning to give him cause for concern. He had from time to time suffered from stomach problems which affected his sleeping pattern, and these were getting worse. Only rarely would he feel really refreshed by his sleep.

Not only this, but during 1986 he began to experience regular bouts of nausea and breathlessness if he did anything involving more than usual exertion. These bouts would come on quite unexpectedly and last for a few minutes at a time. Arthur consulted his doctor who found that he had high blood pressure and a slightly enlarged heart. He was put on a course of medication which lowered his blood pressure but did not eliminate the bouts of nausea.

Arthur was naturally concerned about his health and this led to much prayer. Whenever he had encountered problems over the years, the first question he would invariably ask was, 'What are you saying, Lord?' As he sought God about his health he began to see that there were spiritual principles affecting his physical condition. He had not always been functioning out of the true rest that God promises his children, but had been striving to achieve and to accomplish things for God. An element of self-effort had replaced the flow of the Holy Spirit.

Over the months that followed, as he spent time praying and waiting on God, Arthur believed that God was changing his attitudes and spirit and fully expected his physical condition to improve gradually. He could see that his healing would not be an isolated event, unrelated to God's dealings with his spirit, but he continued to believe God for a miracle and would often ask his fellow Christians for prayer.

If it had been left to him, Arthur would have been content simply to trust God for a divine solution to the problem. Eileen, on the other hand, was concerned to ensure that his medical condition was properly diagnosed and she encouraged him, as only a wife can, to continue taking medical advice. He was referred to chest and heart specialists, and diagnosed as having atypical angina. The doctors assured him that, provided he was sensible about how much he did and what he ate, there was no reason for undue concern.

☆   ☆   ☆

On Monday 16th November 1987, Arthur was sixty-five. It was a special birthday in more ways than one. He and Eileen were due to be in Newcastle-upon-Tyne the weekend before, and would be travelling back through Yorkshire that day. They usually tried to call in on Bryn and Edna Jones when in the area, and so Arthur rang Bryn a week or two before to see if he would be around on that day. Bryn was planning to be at home that afternoon, although Edna would be away, and so they made plans to meet.

'That happens to be the day I get my degree!' said Arthur, just before putting the phone down. There was an element of teasing in this remark; Bryn was studying for an external Master's degree!

'Degree? Whatever do you mean, Arthur?' said Bryn, puzzled.

'My graduation certificate,' said Arthur. 'It's the day I become an old-age pensioner!'

Arthur gave this light-hearted conversation no more thought, and on the afternoon of his sixty-fifth birthday, he and Eileen turned up at Bryn's home in Keighley.

With Edna away, they were not surprised when Bryn suggested that they ate out that evening.

They arrived at a nice looking restaurant situated between Keighley and Halifax and went in to the lounge area where they were served pre-dinner drinks and ordered their meal. After a while they were asked to go upstairs to their table. To their complete surprise, they found themselves entering a private dining room to be greeted by the whole of Bryn's team, together with their wives, singing, 'Happy Birthday to you'!

Arthur was quite speechless!

After a superb meal, a huge birthday cake was wheeled in, various speeches were made, and he was presented with a beautiful Bonsai miniature tree. The evening finished with a time of prayer and prophecy in which God said that he was not calling Arthur to retirement as an old-age pensioner, but he was going to strengthen him for active future ministry. He was not on the shelf and the best days were yet to come.

This was a great encouragement. 'The best is yet to come' had long been one of Arthur's favourite mottos. He was still expecting to see revival in Britain during his lifetime. Despite the problems with his health, God was in control and he could believe that there were fruitful days of ministry ahead.

Arthur and Eileen were very happy in their home in Bassett Close, but God began prompting them to consider moving house. On a couple of occasions when they were away, the house had been broken into. They had no possessions of particular interest to a thief and nothing of any significance had been taken, but as they prayed about this God seemed to be indicating that it was time to move. They also felt that, as they got older, it would be good to find a smaller home.

They considered various possibilities and decided to

look for a house in the Shirley area, close to where Jonathan, Sylvia and Fiona were living. They put their own house on the market and very soon had a buyer who offered the price they were asking. The problem was finding a suitable house to buy. They made offers on one or two places, but nothing came to fruition.

House prices were booming during the early part of 1988, and as time went on, the price they had accepted for their home in Bassett Close was no longer realistic. The prices of the properties they were looking at were going up rapidly. Arthur was concerned to act righteously in the situation and prayed carefully about this. The fact was that he simply could not afford to continue with the deal.

He contacted the buyers to explain the situation, and suggested that if they still wished to go ahead he would give them first refusal, but at a higher price. Otherwise he would have to withdraw and put the house on the market again. They did not take kindly to this, accusing him of gazumping, but he knew he had acted honourably. These buyers withdrew and the house was quickly sold at a much higher price. Meanwhile, Arthur and Eileen found just the right three-bedroomed house in Shirley, a short walk away from Jonathan and Sylvia. Contracts were exchanged for completion at the end of August 1988.

Earlier in August, Arthur planned to visit Ireland with his brother, Peter. They still had friends there from their boyhood days, and Peter had suggested that they took a week's holiday to go back there together. When it turned out that this was just before their house move Arthur considered cancelling, but Eileen encouraged him to go.

They had already worked hard over the previous month to sort through the loft, and Arthur had dealt with one of the biggest and most important areas of the move, his books! He had spent a lot of time going through them, classifying them and packing them into tea chests. The study at the new house would not be as large and he had to decide which books to keep and which to give away. The effort of this had left him very tired, and Eileen thought a complete break would do him good.

Peter and Arthur planned to drive together over to Fishguard in South Wales, and catch the ferry to Ros-slare in County Wexford. From there they would do a round trip, heading off west through Waterford to County Cork, north-east through central Ireland to Dublin, and then back south again to catch the ferry home. They had arranged to visit various old friends, including one or two who had been pupils with them at Winterdyne School. They even planned to take a tent with them, so that they could camp on the way where necessary. When they tried to put it up, however, they found that the moths had been having a feast—it was sprinkled with holes! Meg and Eileen were quite relieved when the tent was discarded and they decided to find bed-and-breakfast accommodation instead!

The trip was a great success. They saw friends they had not seen for years, delighted in the beautiful Irish countryside, went to see some of the houses where they had lived as boys, and more than anything, just enjoyed being together as brothers. Arthur was not a great one for reminiscing, but he arrived back relaxed and refreshed to join Eileen in making the final preparations for their move.

They moved into their new house at 18, Kineton Road, Shirley on Friday 26th August 1988, just before the bank holiday weekend. It was less than half a mile from Jonathan and Sylvia's home, and over the weekend Sylvia and Fiona helped Eileen organise the house, while Jonathan undertook the important task of putting up Arthur's book shelves.

Fiona was now able to pop round to see Arthur and Eileen on her bike, and she would often arrive puffing and panting, looking at her watch to see if she had beaten her 'record' of 1 minute 35 seconds! The house was detached, with three bedrooms, two reception rooms and a kitchen. It had a square garden that was big enough to enjoy without being too big. They immediately felt at home there.

On the bank holiday Monday, having worked hard over the weekend to get the house ship-shape, the whole family felt in need of some fresh air and relaxation and went out to the edge of the New Forest for a walk. They had not gone far when Arthur had to stop. He had been overcome again by one of his bouts of nausea and lay down in the sunshine to rest while the others walked on for a little way.

Although these bouts were a regular occurrence, Arthur did not allow himself to become unduly worried by them. The specialist had told him not to be alarmed, but just to rest and then carry on. More than that, Arthur was convinced that God was going to heal him. He did not believe that his work on earth was done, and neither he nor Eileen were overly concerned by these symptoms or fully realised their significance.

Over the next few days, Arthur and Eileen spent quite a bit of time together choosing various items that they needed for the house. These included carpets, curtains, and a new three-piece suite for the lounge. The following Sunday they went to the East-side congregation of the church. Tony was speaking, and Arthur brought a word of prophecy.

After the service, Arthur and Eileen went off together to visit the grave of Lord Radstock. Arthur had begun to put together a compendium of 'Great Saints'. He had often read accounts of Christians, not necessarily well known, who had played a vital role in the history of the church through their devotion to God and their sacrificial service. He wanted to compile a reference work called *Great Saints* which would include brief biographical details of each of these, together with an assessment of their impact on the church. Having spent a few days at the Evangelical Library in London researching this project, he had already compiled a list of about 500 names.

One of these was Lord Radstock, a nineteenth-century Christian who was totally devoted to God and who felt particularly called to share the gospel among the aristocracy. He had lived near Southampton, and as they looked at his impressive memorial Arthur turned to Eileen.

'You know, dear,' he said, 'I don't want any sort of memorial like this when I die. I'm quite happy for my body to be cremated. The only memorial I want is the impact of what I've done to be reflected in the church and in the lives of believers.'

It was something they had never really discussed together, and Arthur had no idea that he had unwittingly prepared Eileen for a decision she would have to take just a few days later.

The next day, Arthur continued to sort out his study and do some preparation for a seminar he was taking the coming weekend, and on the Tuesday he spent the day with Tony and the Cornerstone team. He was due to leave early on Wednesday morning to travel up to Sheffield and join Bryn and his team at a prayer retreat at the Whirlow Grange Conference Centre.

Early on Wednesday 7th September, Eileen dropped Arthur off at Southampton station to catch the seven o'clock train to London. On arrival at Waterloo station, he had to make his way across the underground to King's Cross in order to catch the Sheffield train. There are several different routes between these stations, each involving one change of line. Arthur decided to go via Bank, a mistake in the rush hour. By the time he had fought his way through the crush, he missed his train at King's Cross. He telephoned Eileen, asking her to contact the conference centre in Sheffield and let them know he would be on a later train. It was the last time she spoke to him.

The thought of arriving late was a frustration to Arthur. Partly, it was an affront to his military background. Back in the days when the seven or fourteen met together, if a session started late he had been known to remark, 'Brothers, the Lord was here five minutes ago as planned, and we don't want to keep him waiting!'

More important than this ingrained sense of punctuality was his eager anticipation of this time with Bryn and the other men. They held these prayer retreats at regular intervals, coming together to seek God and hear what he had to say through the prophetic word. There was always a strong prayer burden for revival. As Arthur arrived, they were praying for Scotland and the prophets were prophesying about things God would do in that land.

During the afternoon, Arthur shared some things God had been saying to him from the book of Ephesians about the centrality of Christ in all that they were believing for. Throughout the day their earnestness in prayer and seeking God was matched by a sense of enjoyment as they relaxed together, completely at home in the Father's presence.

After the end of the afternoon session, Bryn came up to Arthur to explain that an urgent matter had cropped up which necessitated him going home that evening. 'I'll see you in the morning, Arthur,' he said before he left.

It was a warm September evening and after their meal, they sat outside drinking their coffee and chatting together, looking out over the croquet lawn. Standing in the border at the edge of the lawn was a large wooden cross, about ten feet tall, almost camouflaged amid the trees and bushes.

Arthur was talking with Keri Jones when someone suggested that they had a game of croquet before it got too dark. Keri had never played the game before, but as an ex-physical education teacher he didn't consider it much of a sport! Arthur, on the other hand, was something of an expert.

'Come on my young brother, I'll teach you,' he said, delighted at the opportunity. This was one game where his age and health were no disadvantage.

They played in pairs, and Arthur partnered Ivor

Hopkins. As Keri found his ball frequently and ruthlessly dispatched to the other end of the lawn, he began to wonder whether Arthur was giving him an object lesson in humility rather than teaching him to play the game! It soon became apparent who was going to win.

'Well done, Arthur, you've won,' exclaimed Keri, as Arthur hit the final peg with his ball. 'Three cheers for Arthur!'

Arthur smiled with the satisfaction of a born competitor. 'I haven't finished yet,' he replied. 'I must go and help my partner.'

He strode purposefully back across the lawn towards Ivor. As he approached the wooden cross, he faltered and suddenly fell face forward onto the grass. The others ran to his aid, but all efforts to revive him were of no avail. He had died instantly of a massive heart attack.

Keri couldn't help wondering whether the first words he heard in heaven corresponded with the last words he had heard on earth: 'Well done, Arthur, you've won.'

☆   ☆   ☆

One of Keri's first tasks was to contact the leadership of the Southampton church. Tony was taking a meeting in Portsmouth, but Martyn Dunsford and Phil Clarke immediately came round to break the news to Jonathan and Sylvia; Jonathan then went with them to tell Eileen. She was stunned.

'But we were believing that we would see revival,' she said through her tears, as the reality began to sink in.

It seemed so hard to understand at first. Arthur had been convinced that he would see revival. He believed that there were many years of fruitful ministry ahead of him and had received prophetic words which seemed to confirm this.

Arthur was not expecting to die, but as Eileen thought about the last few months of his life she could so clearly see that God had been preparing him. So many details fitted into place: his affairs were all in perfect order; the house that was to be her home they had chosen together; and he had even given her instructions about the cremation of his body. Not only that, but he had made all his goodbyes: the holiday in Ireland with Peter, his day with Tony and the Southampton men, and his final hours with Bryn and his team. He may not have been expecting to die, but he was certainly ready.

Arthur's desires for unity within the body of Christ were also finding fulfilment. Just a day or two after his death, a large conference called 'Together for the Kingdom', which incorporated leaders from many of the different 'streams', took place in Sheffield. He had been delighted when this event was convened, and was scheduled to lead one of the seminars.

Arthur's funeral service took place at the Southampton Crematorium. It was a short service, led by Tony Morton, with numbers restricted to family and close friends. Some had flown in specially from the United States; even Blyth and Jan Harper from New Zealand were there. They were visiting England and were due to stay with Arthur and Eileen that very week.

The next day a service of thanksgiving was held at Above Bar Church in Southampton. A mixture of friends, relatives, local people and church leaders from all around the country were there. Many had taken time out from busy schedules to attend and it was an emotional and moving occasion.

Ivor Hopkins and Sylvia led the congregation in song, and Ivor sang 'Fairest Lord Jesus', one of Arthur's favourite songs. As his beautiful tenor voice rang forth there was scarcely a dry eye in the building. There were touching personal tributes from Mike Stevens, Oscar Penhearow, Joe Tosini, Bryn Jones and Tony Morton. Mike asked all the men who looked on Arthur as a spiritual father to stand, and many across the hall rose to their feet. Then Jonathan and David Adcock led the congregation in a time of praise and worship.

There was a real sense of God's presence, and the

climax of the service was a united call for God to send
revival in the words of Graham Kendrick's stirring song:

> Shine, Jesus, shine
> Fill this land with the Father's glory;
> Blaze, Spirit, blaze,
> Set our hearts on fire.
> Flow, river, flow,
> Flood the nations with grace and mercy;
> Send forth your word,
> Lord, and let there be light.

This was the vision of revival to which Arthur was
radically committed. During his lifetime he saw many
indications of God's blessing, but he only ever saw this
ultimate goal through the eyes of faith. The words of
Hebrews 11 applied as much to him as to many others
who have died in faith without seeing all they were
believing for.

> All these people were still living by faith when they died.
> They did not receive the things promised; they only saw
> them and welcomed them from a distance. And they
> admitted that they were aliens and strangers on earth.
> People who say such things show that they are looking for a
> country of their own. If they had been thinking of the
> country they had left, they would have had opportunity to
> return. Instead, they were longing for a better country—a
> heavenly one. Therefore God is not ashamed to be called
> their God, for he has prepared a city for them.

Arthur lived his life in constant unwavering hope. For
him, the best was yet to come: he was expecting revival,
looking for the triumph of God's kingdom, 'longing for
a better country'. He was prepared to be radical in his
commitment to this heavenly vision.

Judging by the evidence of his thanksgiving service,

there were many others who would take up his mantle. They too would be radical in their obedience to God. For them also, the best was yet to come.

☆   ☆   ☆

Lukewarm Christians will never change the world; they are resigned to compromise and content to accept the status quo. Such Christians have no vision and no hope and God's response to them is well documented: 'So, because you are lukewarm—neither hot nor cold—I am about to spit you out of my mouth' (Rev 3:16).

God is looking for men and women who will change the world, radical Christians who do not merely say, 'Thy kingdom come, thy will be done on earth as it is in heaven,' but commit their lives to see it happen. They are the people of hope, their eyes are on a better country; they are the people of whom God is not ashamed; for them the best is yet to come.

Arthur was such a man, but he has now found that better country; for him, the best has come.

The Law of the Kingdom

by

Arthur Wallis

This is the law of My kingdom, marked by the print of My feet,
Stained by the blood of My sufferings, proved in the furnace of
  heat;
Writ with the pen of My Spirit, and shrined in My holy love,
But also in hearts I have conquered, men who are grit to the core;
Swift as the roe on the mountains, bold as the lion in fight,
Fired with the zeal of the martyr, ready to die for the right;
Hating their lives as I told them, casting them gladly away;
Yet deep in their hearts expecting to find them again one day;
Men who dare to be different, men who dare to be true,
Choosing, instead of the broad way, the narrow path with the few;
Not drifting down with the flotsom, but pressing upstream 'gainst
  the tide;
Disdaining the force of convention with a will that is tougher than
  hide;
Who sign a cheque in My favour, leave Me to fill in the sum,
Prepared with joyous abandon to face whatever may come;
Men who will rise by the lamplight and wait at the posts of My
  doors,
Watch for a glimpse of their Master as they eagerly study His laws;
Women of deep intercession, whose cries awaken the dawn,
Hannahs who travail with sorrow till prophets of God be born;
Christians who will to be holy, nor care if the road be hard,
With souls athirst, their aim is first a burning passion for God—
Them will I call My disciples, them will I gladly own.
They shall inherit My kingdom and sit with Me on My throne.

But as for the weak and tepid, I would they were hot or cold,
I would they were overcomers, I would they were strong and bold;
I'm sick and tired of the spineless who bear no light that I ken;
One by one I will spew them out, for all that I seek are men.
These are the lovers of comfort, who love the undisciplined life,
With flesh that is pampered and patted, that shrinks at the touch of
the knife.
Too long has the cause been hindered by salt that has lost its tang,
Fit to be thrown on the roadway and trod under foot of man.
Yet even now for the fruitless the axe is laid to the root,
For all I require in this solemn hour is the tree that brings forth
fruit.

This is the law of My kingdom that only the pure shall thrive,
That in the heat of temptation, only the true will survive.
Such as are poor and needy are heirs to My wealth untold.
The weak, who cast themselves on Me, they are the strong and bold.

Two thousand years I have waited, My work of redemption done;
High on My throne I have waited a day that is yet to come,
When I shall arise in splendour, My glittering sword unsheathe,
And come with the shout of the victor and wearing the victor's
wreath,
To oust the wicked usurper and 'stablish the rule of God.
I grasp with the hand once pierced, the orb and the sceptre's rod.
Two thousand years I have waited the hour when I claim My bride,
Purged and refined and resplendent, and throned at her
Bridegroom's side—
Awaited a generation who will pray, 'Thy Kingdom Come.'
They bind themselves to the altar to see that the thing is done;
Men who fired with a vision will stir My church with their cry—
'Evangelise to the finish! Bring back the King from the sky!'
Storming the ramparts of heaven, they seize the kingdom by force,
Not thinking My gifts and treasures would come as a matter of
course.
With instinct of wrestling Jacob, they plead for the Spirit's power,
Praying and fasting and waiting, till clothed with the tongues of fire.
They speak a word to the mountain, they cast it into the sea,
They tell the slaves of Satan, 'In the name of Christ be free!'
Willing for no reputation, their names men drag in the dirt.
They pray for those who revile them, and leap for joy at the hurt.
Feared by the powers of darkness, they fear only God above,
While hating nothing but evil, they answer hatred with love.
Though men may think them extremists, call them fanatics and
fools,
I will acclaim them My servants, shape them and make them My
tools,

Send them with flaming evangel to reach the uttermost parts,
Till they blazen My name and establish My fame in a million
  heathen hearts.
In the day of My vindication, they shall shine as the noonday sun,
Robed with eternal splendour, and wreathed with the crowns they
  won.
In glory that beggars description, beholding that face once marred,
They shall share in the joy of their Saviour, clasped to the heart of
  God.

But what of the one who failed Me, when he stands at My
  judgement seat,
When the deeds that he thought would commend him are ashes
  beneath his feet?
What will he say when he gazes on the One who died in his stead?

This is the law of My kingdom—that only the pure shall remain.
Surely the day shall declare it, eternity make it plain.

The Radical Christian

by Arthur Wallis

God's Holy Spirit is at work to change us into the likeness of Christ. Do we realize what a radical change this means?

This book challenges us to re-examine some of our cherished customs and beliefs. It shows how Scripture can guide us over such issues as church unity, water and Spirit baptism, and denominational loyalty.

The author confesses that this has not been an easy book to write. Nor will it be easy for us to receive. It calls for a verdict on God's truth—and so for a verdict on ourselves. Each one of us must decide: am I a compromiser, or a radical?

The axe is laid to the root of the tree.

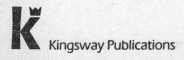

Kingsway Publications

Living God's Way
A Course for Discipling New Christians

by Arthur Wallis

We live in a day of exciting growth, when churches are experiencing a new outpouring of the Holy Spirit and new believers are being gathered in.

The challenge is clear. Christians need to be firmly grounded in the truths of Scripture, so that they are equipped to give teaching and pastoral help to new believers.

This course has been specially designed for use in the local church setting, and is ideal for one-to-one discipling. With a clear and straightforward approach it covers the Bible's basic teaching so that the new Christian can gain a thorough understanding of Christian commitment and how it affects every area of life.

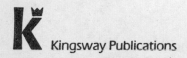

Kingsway Publications

Pray in the Spirit

by Arthur Wallis

In this book Arthur Wallis concentrates on the ministry of the Holy Spirit in relation to prayer, and investigates the full meaning of the apostle's injunction to 'pray in the Spirit'.

He analyses the spiritual and practical difficulties we encounter, and shows how the Holy Spirit helps us in our weakness and makes up for all our deficiencies. We are encouraged to yield ourselves completely to Him, allowing Him to pray through us.

As we enter into the 'deep things of God' unfolded here we shall discover a new power and effectiveness in our Christian lives.

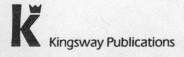

Kingsway Publications

God's Chosen Fast

by Arthur Wallis

Having proved over many years the great value and blessing of fasting, Arthur Wallis has written this book to share with us what the Bible says about this important and neglected subject. His aim is to deal not only with all the main passages in Scripture that touch on the matter, but also with the practical issues involved.

This is a balanced study which seeks to give to the subject the weight that Scripture gives it and to avoid exaggeration and over-emphasis. The book includes a biblical index, and an appendix dealing with the textual problems surrounding four references to fasting in the New Testament.

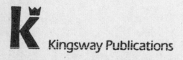

Kingsway Publications